Vocational Education in the Nordic Countries

Vocational Education in the Nordic Countries: Learning from Diversity is the second of two books that disseminates new and systematic knowledge on the strengths and weaknesses of the different models of vocational education and training (VET) in four Nordic countries. Vocational education in Europe has resisted standardisation to a higher degree than other fields of education, and during the last decade, there has been a growth in international, comparative VET research. While the Nordic countries provide an ideal case for comparative education studies, the literature in English on the Nordic VET systems is at present very limited.

This book provides thorough examinations of VET in Sweden, Denmark, Norway and Finland. Each section examines the current challenges for VET, compares how these challenges are managed, and explores recent reforms and institutional innovations. Contributors also analyse institutions and policies at the national level and include comparative studies of two occupations at the micro-level in the four countries. The book explores what can be learned from the diversity of the VET systems in the Nordic countries, which otherwise have many similarities and share a common heritage in education policy.

This volume will help strengthen the knowledge base required for transnational policy learning, and for developing vocational education internationally for the future. As a result, the book will be of interest to researchers, academics and postgraduate students involved in the study of vocational education, educational studies and educational policy, as well as policy makers.

Christian Helms Jørgensen is Professor MSO at Roskilde University in Denmark and leader of the Nord-VET project.

Ole Johnny Olsen is Professor at Department of Sociology, University of Bergen, Norway.

Daniel Persson Thunqvist is an Associate Professor in Sociology at Linköping University, Department for Behavioural Science and Learning, Linköping, Sweden.

Routledge Research in International and Comparative Education

This is a series that offers a global platform to engage scholars in continuous academic debate on key challenges and the latest thinking on issues in the fast-growing field of International and Comparative Education.

Titles in the series include:

Educational Choices, Aspirations and Transitions in Europe
Systemic, Institutional and Subjective Constraints
Edited by Aina Tarabini and Nicola Ingram

Cooperative Education in Asia
History, Present and Future Issues
Edited by Yasushi Tanaka

Testing and Inclusive Schooling
International Challenges and Opportunities
Edited by Bjørn Hamre, Anne Morin and Christian Ydesen

Vocational Education in the Nordic Countries
The Historical Evolution
Edited by Svein Michelsen and Marja-Leena Stenström

Vocational Education in the Nordic Countries
Learning from Diversity
Edited by Christian Helms Jørgensen, Ole Johnny Olsen and Daniel Persson Thunqvist

Higher Education and China's Global Rise
A Neo-tributary Perspective
Su-Yan Pan and Joe Tin-Yau Lo

For more information about this series, please visit: www.routledge.com/Rout ledge-Research-in-International-and-Comparative-Education/book-series/ RRICE

Vocational Education in the Nordic Countries

Learning from Diversity

Edited by Christian Helms Jørgensen,
Ole Johnny Olsen and
Daniel Persson Thunqvist

LONDON AND NEW YORK

First published 2018
by Routledge
2 Park Square, Milton Park, Abingdon, Oxon OX14 4RN

and by Routledge
711 Third Avenue, New York, NY 10017

Routledge is an imprint of the Taylor & Francis Group, an informa business

© 2018 selection and editorial matter, Christian Helms Jørgensen, Ole Johnny Olsen and Daniel Persson Thunqvist; individual chapters, the contributors

The right of the editors to be identified as the authors of the editorial material, and of the authors for their individual chapters, has been asserted in accordance with sections 77 and 78 of the Copyright, Designs and Patents Act 1988.

All rights reserved. No part of this book may be reprinted or reproduced or utilised in any form or by any electronic, mechanical, or other means, now known or hereafter invented, including photocopying and recording, or in any information storage or retrieval system, without permission in writing from the publishers.

Trademark notice: Product or corporate names may be trademarks or registered trademarks, and are used only for identification and explanation without intent to infringe.

British Library Cataloguing-in-Publication Data
A catalogue record for this book is available from the British Library

Library of Congress Cataloging-in-Publication Data
A catalog record for this book has been requested

ISBN: 978-1-138-21980-9 (hbk)
ISBN: 978-1-315-41449-2 (ebk)

Typeset in Bembo
by Apex CoVantage, LLC

Contents

List of tables	vii
List of contributors	viii
Preface	x
Acknowledgements	xii

1 Vocational education and training in the Nordic countries: different systems and common challenges 1

CHRISTIAN HELMS JØRGENSEN

2 Transitions from vocational education to employment in the Nordic countries 29

CHRISTIAN HELMS JØRGENSEN AND ANNA HAGEN TØNDER

3 Progression to higher education from VET in Nordic countries: mixed policies and pathways 51

MAARIT VIROLAINEN AND ANNA HAGEN TØNDER

4 Balancing the esteem of vocational education and social inclusion in four Nordic countries 74

LENE LARSEN AND DANIEL PERSSON THUNQVIST

5 Reforms and innovations in Nordic vocational education: improving transitions to employment and to higher education 95

CHRISTIAN HELMS JØRGENSEN

6 Vocational education for health care workers in the Nordic countries compared 118

HÅKON HØST AND LENE LARSEN

vi   *Contents*

**7   Building and construction: a critical case
for the future of vocational education**   136
OLE JOHNNY OLSEN, DANIEL PERSSON THUNQVIST
AND ANDERS HALLQVIST

**8   Learning from vocational education and
training in the Nordic countries**   156
CHRISTIAN HELMS JØRGENSEN

Index   183

Tables

2.1	Indicators of school-to-work transitions of youth	30
3.1	Transitions from VET to higher education in the four Nordic countries by field of education	64
3.2	Adults who have attained tertiary education, by type of programme and age group	65
A4.1	Indicators of social inclusion of youth	90
5.1	Two fields of innovation in VET: institutions and pedagogical practices	98
6.1	Health care workers in four Nordic countries compared	131
8.1	Increase in non-completion rate in the VET programmes after the reform in 1991	160
8.2	Drop-out rate from VET basic course in Denmark	164
8.3	Trade-offs in the policy architecture for VET	167

Contributors

Anders Hallqvist received his PhD in Education from Linköping University, Sweden. His current position is Senior Lecturer at the Department of Behavioural Sciences and Learning at Linköping University. His research interests include vocational education, popular education and biographical approaches to adult education.

Håkon Høst is Research Professor, Nordic Institute for Studies in Innovation, Research and Education, Oslo, Norway. His research interests are vocational education and training, educational systems, skill formation systems, and the relations between the educational system and the labour market and the labour market actors.

Christian Helms Jørgensen is Professor MSO at Roskilde University in Denmark and leader of the Nord-VET project. His research covers adult education, comparative vocational education, school-to-work transitions, learning in worklife, gender and education and students' drop-out from schools.

Lene Larsen is an Associate Professor at Roskilde University in Denmark. Her research interest is young people's educational transitions and choices, biographies, learning and motivation, and vulnerable youth and in- and exclusion processes.

Ole Johnny Olsen is Professor at Department of Sociology, University of Bergen, Norway. His research interests include sociology of work, labour movements, vocational education and training, occupational socialisation and development of skill formation systems.

Daniel Persson Thunqvist is an Associate Professor in Sociology at Linköping University, Department for Behavioural Science and Learning, Linköping, Sweden. His research interests include vocational education and training, workplace learning and social interaction.

Anna Hagen Tønder is a Researcher and Research Coordinator at Fafo, Institute for Labour and Social Research, Oslo, Norway. Her research interests include vocational education and training, school-to-work transitions and the development of skill formation systems.

Maarit Virolainen, PhD, has been a researcher at the Finnish Institute for Educational Research (FIER), University of Jyväskylä, Finland, since 1996. Her research interests have focused on vocational and professional education, work-based and work-related learning, internships, educational careers, and transitions within education systems and from education to the world of work.

Preface

This book is the second of a two-volume series on initial vocational education and training (VET) in the Nordic countries. The first volume explores the historical development of the national systems of VET in four Nordic countries: Sweden, Finland, Norway and Denmark. The second volume examines the current situation for VET in these countries, comparing how the four VET systems have responded to a number of common challenges.

The Nordic countries often attract international interest due to their ability to combine high levels of social welfare and equality with high economic growth. They are often treated as a coherent group with a shared history and culture, and also due to their similarities regarding the universal welfare states, the consensual and well-organised labour markets and the egalitarian systems of education. The focus of these two books is not on the similarities, however, but on the differences between these countries. While they all transformed the 9/10-year, compulsory education into comprehensive school systems with mixed ability classes, their systems of upper secondary education differ considerably. Their VET systems represent very diverging models, with Sweden and Denmark as the most different systems: a statist and school-based model of comprehensive schooling (Sweden) and a dual system of collective skill formation (Denmark).

These differences make the Nordic countries a fruitful living experiment, where diverging forms of VET can be explored in quite similar societies. These two books investigate why the Nordic VET systems historically developed along diverging lines, and the implications of these differences for the current systems. The first volume includes eight chapters on the historical development of the four VET systems divided into two periods, before and after 1945. In addition, it includes two comparative chapters with a historical perspective. The second book examines the strengths and weaknesses of the four VET systems in relation to four common and interrelated challenges for VET: to simultaneously provide access to the labour market and to higher education, and to combine the inclusion of disadvantaged youth in VET with high esteem of VET among young people and employers. In addition to the comparisons of the four VET systems, the second volume includes comparisons of two multilevel case studies.

The two books are the result of a research project, Nord-VET (www.Nord-VET.dk), comprising researchers from seven research institutions from the four countries. The initial group consisted of Per-Erik Ellström, Linköping University in Sweden, Marja-Leena Stenström, University of Jyväskylä in Finland, Ole Johnny Olsen, University of Bergen in Norway and Christian Helms Jørgensen, Roskilde University in Denmark as project leader. In addition, the project has included the following researchers: from Finland Maarit Virolainen, University of Jyväskylä; from Sweden Daniel Persson Thunqvist and Anders Hallqvist, Linköping University, and Jonas Olofsson, Malmö University; from Denmark Lene Larsen and Gudmund Bøndergaard, Roskilde University; from Norway Svein Michelsen, University of Bergen, Håkon Høst, the Nordic Institute for Studies in Innovation, NIFU, and Anna Hagen Tønder, the Institute for Labour and Social Research, Fafo.

The formation of the research group grew out of previous Nordic collaboration on VET, school-to-work transitions, students' drop-out and learning in working life. This explains why the fifth Nordic country, Iceland, is not included in the project. The group is grateful for the funding obtained from NordForsk for the period 2013–17 as part of the research programme Education for Tomorrow. Since very little comparative research in the Nordic VET systems had been done previously, the Nord-VET project spent the first two years producing 12 country reports, four for each VET system, based on the examination of common research questions. The reports focussed on (1) the historical evolution of the VET systems, (2) the current situation for these systems, (3) recent reforms and innovations in VET and (4) multilevel case studies in the health sector and the construction sector. These reports have been very valuable for the subsequent comparison across the countries. Our reports and these two books draw extensively on existing national research on VET. This has presented challenges to making systematic comparisons, since the existing research has proved to be very diverse and uneven. In addition, the project covers a very broad field of research and represents the first attempt to compare the Nordic VET systems. Therefore, our research has an explorative character to some degree, and some questions are only given preliminary answers. The broad scope of the project has invited an interdisciplinary approach, which has matched well with the broad disciplinary background of the members of the research group, covering sociology, political science, history, youth studies and education studies. Consequently, the research has been driven more by an empirical and problem-oriented approach, than by a specific conceptual framework.

Inspired by the fruitful collaboration in the group, the ambitions of the project expanded and the project plan was extended, even beyond the initial funding. It is only thanks to the strong engagement of the participants in the project and the support of their research institutions that we have succeeded in completing these two volumes. I want to thank all the participating researchers and their institutions for their great contribution to the project.

Christian Helms Jørgensen
Roskilde, January 2018

Acknowledgements

This book is the result of a research project, Nord-VET, covering Sweden, Finland, Norway and Denmark funded by the NordForsk research programme Education for Tomorrow. NordForsk is an organisation under the Nordic Council of Ministers that provides funding for and facilitates Nordic cooperation on research. We want to thank NordForsk for the financial support and for facilitating fruitful collaboration with other projects in the programme.

We also want to thank the members of the international advisory group to the project, Professor Alison Fuller, University College London, and Dr. Lorenz Lassnigg, Institute for Higher Studies in Vienna, for feedback and support for the project. In addition, we are grateful for productive discussions with European colleagues at international conferences, where we have presented preliminary results of the project.

1 Vocational education and training in the Nordic countries

Different systems and common challenges

Christian Helms Jørgensen

In recent decades, there has been increasing international interest in comparative research in vocational education and training (VET) at upper secondary level (Greinert, 1999; Thelen, 2004; Busemeyer and Trampusch, 2012; Gonon, 2016). While a few earlier comparative studies have included individual Nordic countries, no systematic attempts have been made to compare the Nordic VET systems. It is the aim of this book to fill this gap. First, this chapter introduces the wider Nordic context for four countries: Sweden, Finland, Norway and Denmark. In addition, the chapter explains the research approach of the book. The book explores how the Nordic VET systems have managed four key challenges for VET: to offer access to skilled employment and to higher education, to provide social inclusion for very diverse groups of students, and to maintain high esteem among young people and companies. The book takes a special interest in exploring the role of VET in relation to the egalitarian and inclusive aims of the Nordic welfare states. A strong VET system is important for promoting social equality in a period of growing social inequalities and a dualisation of labour markets (Busemeyer, 2015; Thelen, 2014). A VET system that provides high-quality intermediary skills can counteract the polarising effects of, on the one hand, the rapidly expanding system of higher education and, on the other hand, the precarisation of low-skilled labour. In addition, a strong VET system is important for the development of high-quality systems of work and production in the Nordic countries (Dølvik, 2013).

During the last fifty years, the Nordic systems of higher education have expanded tenfold, and they have been transformed from elite systems to systems of mass education (Börjesson et al., 2014). This development has generally been considered an advantage for the shift from an industrial to a knowledge society. However, vocational skills at intermediary level are still vital for welfare in the Nordic countries (Kristensen et al., 2015). In addition, concerns have been raised concerning both the 'over-education' of higher education graduates and also the educational opportunities for young people who do not opt for higher education. A few decades ago, a large proportion of young people went directly from compulsory school into the labour market. Today, globalisation, technological change and the offshoring of production put strong pressure on low-skilled labour. The opening of the European labour market has increased

2 Christian Helms Jørgensen

competition for the jobs that were previously available for early school leavers. This development has raised political alarm regarding young people who are not in employment, education or training. The concern relates to the potential long-term social and financial consequences of youth unemployment. In addition, because of demographic changes, the proportion of skilled workers in the labour force is declining, and this is expected to create a shortage of skilled labour in key industries in the Nordic countries (BCG, 2015). VET has a key role in educating and training youths who do not opt for higher education, and in providing key intermediary skills for all sectors of the labour market.

In addition to these basic objectives, the political aims for VET have multiplied over recent decades. VET is expected not only to prepare youths for employment in a specific occupation, but also to prepare them for life-long learning and mobility in the labour market. VET has become an integral part of a coherent upper secondary school system and is as such expected to promote active citizenship, social integration and personal development. Following the strong growth in higher education enrolment, VET is increasingly also required to prepare the students for further studies at the tertiary level of education. While the political priority of these diverse objectives is shifting, the objectives do not replace one another, but seem to be accumulating. Moreover, policy-makers formulate supplementary aims for VET with shifting emphasis, such as preparing for entrepreneurship, internationalisation, sustainability, multi-culturalism, etc.

Besides these explicit political objectives, the VET systems fulfil various implicit social functions. Similar to other forms of Nordic education, VET shapes and disciplines the upcoming generations into the existing social order and contributes to reproducing the existing gender order and the social division of labour (academic/vocational) (Kivinen and Rinne, 1998). VET also provides 'storage' for young people in periods with high unemployment, and supports the personal development and maturation of young people, before they can enter the labour market. Because of its practical, bodily and manual qualities, VET is also required to take responsibility for the rehabilitation of disadvantaged youth and 'weak learners'.

These diverse tasks and challenges for VET are not only competing, but to some degree conflicting. The same applies to the stakeholders and interest groups around VET who are protagonists of the diverse aims. The state is involved in VET as a dominant stakeholder with contradictory objectives of education policy, employment policy, social policy and industrial policy. Shifting governments have given priority to one or more of these objectives, in accordance with their overall strategies and their social and electoral base. Studies in the theoretical tradition of historical institutionalism has elucidated the development of coalitions of actors around collective interests in skill formation (Thelen, 2004; Busemeyer and Trampusch, 2012). The formation and institutionalisation of such coalitions in the field of VET have developed along different trajectories in the Nordic countries. VET is located at the intersection between the education system, the labour market and the employment system, and it involves multiple stakeholders from these systems. Therefore, the formation of strong interest coalitions across these systems is decisive for the development of VET and for the development of different forms of governance.

Two different political traditions for governance have shaped the Nordic VET systems: the strong state and corporatism. For the Nordic Social Democratic parties, a strong centralised state was the main device to reduce the influence of the traditional social elite and to extend the universal welfare state in all fields of society (Esping-Andersen, 1990; Rothstein, 1996). An important aim of this state was the establishment of the public, comprehensive school system in order to break down the class-based society (Wiborg, 2009). This process implied the marginalisation of employers' influence and the reduction of work-based learning in VET, especially in Finland and Sweden. The other tradition of governance to shape the Nordic VET systems is institutionalised corporatism (Elvander, 2002; Dølvik, 2013). The close collaboration of the labour market organisations and the state facilitated the successful implementation of long-term macroeconomic policy measures of Social Democratic governments in the post-war decades. Thus, the average wage increase was tied to increases in productivity. Another feature was the centralised bargaining and the solidaristic wage policy that resulted in low levels of wage dispersion and high levels of minimum wages. This arrangement accelerated the industrial modernisation process and strengthened the competitive edge of the export industry. In this way, corporatist governance contributed to the prosperous, export-led growth and near full employment in the post-war period until the 1970s (Rothstein, 1996; Brandal et al., 2013). While this corporatism became institutionalised for the regulation of all the Nordic labour markets, it did not develop in the same way in the field of VET. While corporatist governance came to dominate VET in Denmark, the state acquired the leading role in the Swedish and Finnish VET systems, with Norway representing a mixed case. The Nordic VET systems thus represent different outcomes of the rivalry between the state and the labour market organisations over the regulation of VET.

Comparing how challenges for VET are managed

The first volume of this book series (Michelsen and Stenstrøm, 2018) examines the historical evolution of VET in the four Nordic countries, Denmark, Finland, Norway and Sweden, from the middle of the 19th century until today. This volume studies developments over the last two decades and the current situation for the Nordic VET systems. Both volumes are the result of the Nord-VET research project (www.Nord-VET.dk), which explores the key challenges that are defined by the main stakeholders of VET. Carol Bacchi (2009) points out that political problems are not defined directly by changes in the external conditions for VET. Challenges are formulated by collective actors based on their political interests and the desired outcomes of initiatives to manage these challenges. The project has identified the most important challenges that are common to the four VET systems. They concern the contested position of

4   Christian Helms Jørgensen

VET between compulsory schooling and higher education and between the state-led education system, the labour market and young peoples' educational aspirations. These challenges have been identified through analyses of policy reforms and of institutional changes in the Nordic countries (Michelsen and Stenstrøm, 2018).

While these challenges are articulated in specific ways in the Nordic context, they seem to be common to most modern VET systems (Bosch and Charest, 2008; Dumas et al., 2013). The main aim of this book is to explore how these challenges have been managed through processes of struggle and negotiations over reforms of VET. The current challenges have been chosen as the focus for comparison of Nordic VET systems for various reasons. One reason is that a problem-based approach is fruitful for exploring institutional changes in VET. Earlier comparative research has shown how VET is embedded in a complex configuration of complementary institutions. Maurice et al. (1986) demonstrated the institutional complementarities and path dependencies of different national VET regimes. VET regimes develop and function in interaction with the employment system, the industrial relations system and the production system. This involves political struggles, compromises and alliances that become institutionalised over time and evolve along particular development paths. This approach emphasises how different configurations of institutions acquire stability and continuity, once they have been established. A variety of conceptual models has been proposed to explain and classify these diverse configurations (Greinert, 1999; Busemeyer and Trampusch, 2012; Gonon, 2016). Conceptual models of VET systems can be useful tools to highlight similarities and divergence between these systems. However, the categorisation and classification involve the risk of representing VET as separate and static systems that develop according to path dependencies and established historical patterns. The mutual interdependence between the different elements of institutional regimes causes inertia.

This raises the question of how to compare VET systems when, from a synchronic perspective, they are conceived as discrete entities that each have their own particular inner logic. The answer from Lutz (1991), which has inspired this book, is to shift to a diachronic perspective and compare how different VET systems develop as they manage common challenges. Attention is thereby focused on the capacities of VET systems to manage internal and external changes, and on the interests and strategies of the main stakeholders in VET. This approach determines the structure of this volume. Studying the four different Nordic VET systems in relation to common challenges does not imply a functionalist approach, which regards this as adaptations to shifts in external conditions. In this book, VET is seen as a field of struggles between contending political actors. The concept of 'VET system' can therefore be misleading by suggesting a high degree of inner coherence. The historical studies in the first volume (Michelsen and Stenström, 2018) demonstrate that the Nordic VET systems display considerable heterogeneity and combine qualities from different conceptual models. In Norway, for example, VET combines qualities of the comprehensive school with an apprenticeship system, and the former strongly statist Swedish VET system has been reformed to become more market-based (Lundahl et al., 2013). In a review of typologies of VET systems, Gonon (2016) argues that the concepts of national systems of VET tend to ignore the large internal differences within each VET system, which can be more significant than the differences between systems. In addition, the conceptual construction of VET systems as ideal types involves the risk of ignoring everything that does not fit into or falls between the ideal types (Levels et al., 2014; Raffe, 2014). While typologies are useful as heuristics, they have limited value in empirical studies of the Nordic VET systems, which combine characteristics from different ideal types.

An argument for conceiving of VET as pertaining to specific models is that of beneficial institutional complementarities. It is assumed that countries perform better if their institutions fit together so that the functioning of one institution enhances the functioning of other institutions. Moreover, some combinations of institutions are more effective than others, and consequently, countries tend to incline towards one of these combinations or models. However, based on the Danish case, Campbell and Pedersen (2007) question this assumption and argue that hybridity and institutional heterogeneity can provide advantages. This is in line with our approach that mixed systems might be better able to balance the multiple competing requirements mentioned above. In our studies of VET in two different sectors, health and construction, we have found large differences in each country between these two sectors (Chapters 6 and 7). This suggests that despite the standardisation of VET programmes in each national VET system, considerable inner diversity persists. In Sweden, for example, we find large differences between occupations regarding the links between VET and higher education. Only 2% of the students from the VET programmes for the construction sector and car mechanics have taken up higher education three years after completing VET. The corresponding figure for students from the childcare and eldercare programmes is over 20% (SCB, 2012). We therefore use the term 'VET system' with the reservation that systems can be quite heterogeneous.

This book compares how the Nordic VET systems manage a variety of common challenges for VET. This represents a problem-based approach to comparisons, which can elucidate the strengths and weaknesses of these systems in relation to key policy objectives. While it is not an aspiration of this book to provide policy recommendations for managing the challenges, it is intended as a source of knowledge for policy learning. The chapters aim to clarify the nature of the diverse challenges and their interrelatedness. This is important, since reforms tend to focus on one challenge at a time and ignore the trade-offs in relation to other challenges. As a consequence, reforms can have unintended consequences that affect the opportunities for managing other challenges. The concluding chapter summarises the trade-offs in the policy architecture for VET in order to encourage a more holistic approach to policy making, which recognises the policy dilemmas. An additional aim of the book is to examine

6 *Christian Helms Jørgensen*

some recent experiences from reforms intended to manage challenges and provide examples of innovations that seek to overcome the trade-offs. These include hybridizations of existing programmes and the invention of new practices and institutions (see Chapter 5).

As this book takes a case-based approach to comparison, it only to a limited extent involves comparisons of single statistical indicators. One reason for not including more statistics is the limited value of the available statistics for comparisons, especially reliable time series. Nordic studies of, for example, youth unemployment (Albæk et al., 2015) and students' dropout from education (Markussen, 2010), have demonstrated the problems involved in comparisons based on official statistics. Another reason is that the definition of upper secondary VET has shifted considerably over time with regard to what educations and sectors are included in VET, and concerning the delimitation to what became defined as higher vocational education. The VET systems differ considerably regarding how and when they expanded into new service sectors, like retail, office work and public services in health, childcare and eldercare. Moreover, the boundaries between initial VET and continuing and adult VET differ in the four countries. Sweden has an upper age limit of 20 years in upper secondary school, and in 2014 Denmark introduced an age limit of 25 years in all ordinary vocational programmes and introduced separate programmes for adults. Taking a case-based approach implies that we define VET in accordance with the national structures and legal definitions.

Four common challenges for VET

The historical studies (Michelsen and Stenström, 2018) have shown that a main challenge for the stakeholders in the post-war period was to ensure that VET could meet the shifting skill requirements in the labour market. Another key interest was that of the state in forming the upcoming generations into democratic and responsible citizens, and in mobilising the 'intelligence reserve' for the national economy. With the rise of the Social Democratic state (Rothstein, 1996), this was extended to include the abolition of class structure in society by building a public school for everyone. When universal compulsory education had been realised, the demand for a wider social recruitment to higher education came onto the agenda in the 1960s. The aim was to dismantle the elite nature of the state bureaucracy by widening access to the exclusive professions. Providing access to higher education became a challenge for the Nordic VET systems which, at the time, had weak connections to the universities. While VET in Sweden and Finland was reorganised in the 1970s and 1990s to improve the opportunities for students' transitions to higher education, the Norwegian and Danish VET systems maintained apprenticeship systems. While apprenticeships in the two countries had different forms, neither of them provided direct access to higher education.

The political agenda shifted in the 1980s and 1990s, when the increasing rates of youth unemployment became a major concern. VET was increasingly seen as a measure to include and integrate early school leavers and disadvantaged youth. Moreover, the neo-liberal turn in politics and the gradual shift from welfare towards workfare changed the focus of education from citizenship to employability (Kananen, 2016; Blossing et al., 2014). It became a major challenge for VET to improve the links between VET and the labour market and to promote the transition of students into employment. The priority given to these different challenges has shifted over time, but not so that one challenge has replaced another. New political expectations and challenges for VET have been added to the existing challenges and have accumulated over time. While the timing and the priorities have been different in the four Nordic countries, they all face some common basic challenges, which this volume has set out to examine.

The first challenge is how the VET systems have responded to the requirement that VET should provide high and up-to-date competencies for a changing labour market and support the students' transition to employment. In the ideal of a Nordic model of education, general qualifications and citizenship have the highest priority, and in the school-based VET systems of Sweden and Finland, the acquisition of specific vocational skills has not been regarded as important. This assumption has been questioned over the last two decades, and policy-makers in all four countries have taken a keen interest in the modernisation or reintroduction of apprenticeship programmes. Following the turn towards employability, a crucial question, which is examined in Chapter 2, is how to provide work-based learning of high quality and with a sufficient number of training placements for the students (Jørgensen, 2015).

The second challenge for VET is to qualify the students for progression in the education system to higher education, which is examined in Chapter 3. As around half of a youth cohort in all four countries enrols in higher education, it appears increasingly as a weakness of the apprenticeship systems of Norway and Denmark that they do not provide general eligibility for higher education. Similarly, the Swedish experience with apprenticeships has drawn attention to the risk of these programmes becoming 'dead ends' in the educational system. Other countries with VET systems based on the apprenticeship model have addressed the challenge of double qualifications or hybrid qualifications that combine a journeyman's certificate with the exam for admission to higher education (Powell and Solga, 2010). Chapter 5 examines hybrid programmes that provide access to higher education, as well as direct access to skilled employment.

The third challenge examined is how the VET systems cope with the problem of low esteem in comparison to the general upper secondary programmes. Compared to the general programmes, VET enrols a higher proportion of disadvantaged youth, and VET has higher dropout rates of students than the general programmes (Bäckman et al., 2011). Participation in VET in the Nordic countries has historically been high, but it has been decreasing in Sweden and Denmark over the last decade. While enrolment is increasing in Finland, a significant share of students in the Norwegian VET system drop out or switch

8 *Christian Helms Jørgensen*

to the general programmes after the second year. Chapter 4 examines the challenges of esteem and social inclusion in the Nordic VET systems.

The fourth challenge, social inclusion, is related to the targets set by governments to increase the enrolment and completion rates in upper secondary education. Labour markets of the future are expected to have little to offer youths who only have compulsory education. VET programmes that include work-based learning can be particularly attractive for early school leavers, who are tired of the 'bookish' school, and apprenticeships are known to provide easy transition to employment (Wolbers, 2007). Chapter 2 examines the attempts to revitalise apprenticeships in the Nordic countries.

These four challenges are not specific for VET in the Nordic countries, and the Nordic experiences can be valuable internationally. The Nordic countries provide favourable conditions for comparison of VET systems, because they share welfare state models and political cultures, but exhibit significant differences in their models of VET. The Nordic VET systems differ with respect to their integration with general education and the balance between work-based learning and school-based learning. They also have different governance structures, especially concerning the involvement of the labour market partners, and the balance between local-central governance and the degree of standardisation of the programmes. This situation makes the Nordic countries a fruitful experiment with diverging forms of VET that can be compared in similar societal contexts. In addition, the weakening of the welfare state provisions and the increased competition in the labour market has especially hit young people. The marginalisation of groups of young people and the increasing dualisation of labour markets after the financial crisis in 2008 has led to increased public concern over the growing level of social inequalities (Busemeyer, 2015). Despite two decades of neo-liberal reforms, the Nordic countries stand out as societies with high levels of social equality and welfare. Therefore, these countries are interesting cases to explore as representatives of the egalitarian Nordic model. However, the 'Nordic model' is not a clear-cut concept, and the following sections therefore explore different conceptualisations of the Nordic model.

The Nordic countries – what do they have in common?

The Nordic countries stand out as a separate group in many diverse fields of comparative studies. Some of the special qualities that are emphasised for these countries are prosperous economies, social equality, and strong universal welfare states (Bergh, 2014; Brandal et al., 2013). The Nordic countries shifted from positions as peripheral, poor, agricultural economies in the middle of the 19th century, to become among the wealthiest in the world by the end of the 20th century (Buchardt et al., 2013). Senghaas (1985) identifies a special Scandinavian development path of export-led growth based on industrialisation in the processing of agricultural products, wood, iron, etc. Due to low levels of social inequality, the gains from the exports promoted broadly based growth of industries for import substitution.

The development of the universal welfare states and the egalitarian education systems have roots in the class structures of the pre-capitalist Nordic societies. Before the advent of capitalism, social inequality was moderate, and the nobility had a weak position (Wiborg, 2009). In Norway, no class of large landlords developed, and in Sweden the independent farmers were recognised early as an independent Fourth Estate (Knudsen and Rothstein, 1994). In Denmark, absolutism weakened the position of the nobility, and the land reforms in 1789 divided the large estates and created a strong class of peasant freeholders. Here, the processing of agricultural produce was in the hands of the peasants' cooperative movement, which prevented the development of independent agro-industrial capital. The late and slow industrialisation resulted in weak bourgeoisies and strong classes of free peasants in the Nordic countries. Consequently, the liberal parties were based on the rural and urban middle classes and embraced a Nordic form of social liberalism (Nilsson, 1997).

The new class of freeholding peasants was associated with freedom and equality. Since it was based on market-oriented agricultural production, it tended to favour free trade, while also opposing the dominance of large capital. In addition, it became the initiator of a popular enlightenment movement from below, inspired by, among others, the ideas of the clergyman Grundtvig in Denmark. After the turn of the century, this was paralleled in the workers' enlightenment movement and the building of strong labour organisations. Modernisation took place from below through social movements, concurrently with nation-building from above, not least through the early establishment of a universal, state education system (Wiborg, 2009; Archer, 1979). The absence of a strong capitalist class provided room for manoeuvre for the states' nation-building projects. Finland and Norway only gained national sovereignty in the early 20th century, and Denmark suffered severe defeats in the 19th century, with the loss of large territories. Against this background, a national liberalism developed that could form alliances with the Social Democratic Party's national strategies for social reform and social equality. The liberals and the Social Democrats allied in the successful struggle for parliamentary democracy, and the liberals played a significant role in the introduction of the universal welfare provisions in the late 19th century (Baldwin, 1990).

The extension of universal social security to all stages of life became a key objective for the Social Democratic parties that became the dominant parties and entered the Nordic governments during the inter-war years. 'Red-green' political alliances between the Social Democratic parties and the liberal parties agreed on crisis management in the 1930s and provided financial support for small farmers and unemployed workers. This alliance strengthened the welfare state alliance and helped contain the radicalisations that took place elsewhere in Europe (Esping-Andersen, 1990). The exception was Finland, where a civil war took place after the end of the First World War, resulting in the suppression of the left wing of the labour movement. Here, broad-based governments were formed after 1945, mainly based on a coalition between the Social Democrats and the Centre Party. In all four countries, a Nordic form of Keynesian policy

10 *Christian Helms Jørgensen*

developed under governments led by Social Democratic parties that managed to keep unemployment low until the 1970s. During this period, the provisions of the welfare states were extended into the fields of education, health, child-care and eldercare, which allowed women to enter the labour market in great numbers, often as employees in the new welfare state institutions. The risks of unemployment and poverty were reduced as the state guaranteed all citizens a minimum income, independent of their position in the labour market, through old-age pensions, free health services, sickness benefits, etc. The concept of a Nordic model is most commonly associated with this universal welfare state. It provides financial grants for young people during study and unemployment, counselling, support for housing and a range of special needs. These rights are not means tested and generally apply for everyone from the age of 18 years, independently of the socio-economic conditions of their family. Emphasis has previously focused on general social and financial benefits to reduce the risks of the transition process and avoid marginalisation of young people. This has given rise to the concept of a universal transition regime in the Nordic countries (Walther, 2006). Since the 1990s, the focus has shifted from welfare to workfare, and labour market participation has become increasingly important for the entitlement to benefits (Kvist and Greve, 2011). The emphasis in public welfare has shifted from guaranteeing everyone a decent standard of living, to support-ing everyone to become employable and self-reliant. As a consequence, there is a greater focus on the activation of young people through employment, educa-tion and training (Kananen, 2016). The financial benefits and the periods of eligibility have been reduced, and there is more emphasis on individual choices and responsibilities during the transition process. In addition to the Nordic welfare state model, other versions of a 'Nordic model' are related to the com-prehensive school (Antikainen 2006; Wiborg, 2009) and to the Nordic model of labour market and work organisation (Gustavsen, 2011; Dølvik, 2013). Both have relevance for the study of VET.

VET and the Nordic model of education

During the inter-war period, schisms inside the Swedish and Danish Social Democratic Parties prevented unanimous support for the proposal for a com-prehensive school (Wiborg, 2009). After the war, it became a clear aim of these parties to build public, unified school systems with easy passage between the levels and no dead ends. In addition, extending education to everyone was regarded as a means to develop democratic and responsible citizens and pre-vent them becoming attracted to authoritarian movements. The intention was that comprehensive schools would be realised by breaking down the selective, divided structure of the former education system, and by integrating the differ-ent school types, tracks and streams. These schools would be equally accessible across the country and include girls, as well as children from disadvantaged families. It was assumed that this would break down social divisions and ine-qualities based on social class, gender and spatial disparities (Wiborg, 2009).

In addition to the egalitarian aims, the education reforms had the objective of mobilising the full potential labour force of the population to sustain the growth of the small, open economies. This included the female workforce and the 'intelligence reserve' of the lower classes. What became known as the Nordic model of education thus has a double perspective. One aim was to build 'a school for all' characterised by egalitarian values, inclusion and a universalistic coverage (Blossing et al., 2014; Telhaug et al., 2006). Another was to build nation states and open national economies that could remain competitive in the world market. The project of combining these two objectives has generally succeeded very well in the Nordic countries, despite the liberalist assumption of a trade-off between efficiency and equality (Brandal, 2013; Esping-Andersen, 1990; Bergh, 2014).

The nation states were key drivers in the formation of strong, coherent public education systems in the Nordic countries. After 1945, governments led by the Social Democratic party, in collaboration with left wing and liberal parties, took initiatives to abolish the segmented and selective systems of compulsory schooling. In the mid-1960s, this project even involved ideas of creating a common comprehensive Nordic school model for all Nordic countries (Telhaug et al., 2006). Initially, the comprehensive school project did not involve VET for the labour market, which took place after the completion of seven or nine years of elementary schooling. Especially in Finland and Norway, nation-building was more important than training an industrial workforce. In Denmark and Sweden, VET was mainly considered an issue for the labour market organisations.

Before 1945, training for occupational work in all the Nordic countries was mostly organised as an integral part of working life, often in some form of apprenticeship. In addition, practical work schools were organised by municipalities for young people, who after leaving compulsory school were not prepared for employment or who could not find employment. Among these were the Norwegian practical continuation school (*Framhaldskolen*), the Danish Youth School (*Ungdomsskolen*), the Finnish Preparatory vocational schools, and the Swedish workshop schools (*Verkstadsskolan*), all established during the interwar period. The relations between the full-time, school-based VET and the work-based apprenticeship systems differed across the Nordic countries, and VET involved a fragmented variety of different programmes.

In the post-war period, processes of system formation, rationalisation and integration of VET took place (Archer, 1979). The course and outcome of these processes differed considerably between the four countries, but some common patterns can be discerned. Following the formation of coherent VET systems, VET became differentiated from the employment systems. Initially, standardisation was weak and the links to local and sectoral interests were strong, and VET had weak connections to academic education. The political responsibility for specific VET programmes was often distributed across different authorities and ministries (marine, commerce, industry, health, etc.). In the 1960s, after two decades of growth, this was considered inadequate for meeting the changing requirements in a dynamic labour market. The Social

12 Christian Helms Jørgensen

Democratic governments were critical of the employers' control of work-based training and sought to integrate VET under a coherent system of state planning. One aim was to implement a rational, long-term development of the public education system to promote economic growth and full employment. Another aim was to provide educational opportunities for all young people after comprehensive school, and thereby reduce social inequalities. Expanding the opportunities for education for everyone became a key vehicle for the redistributive goals of the Nordic welfare states. Yet another aim was to prepare all citizens for active democratic participation and advance the democratic state control of the economy (Brandal et al., 2013). As a result of successive reforms, the fragmented VET programmes were standardised, formalised and merged into coherent VET systems from the 1960s onwards. According to Jónasson (2003), this involved a steady academic drift and a shift from a strong vocational dominance to a strong position for general academic education in the secondary schools. In this process, the involvement of the labour market organisations declined, and school-based forms of VET expanded at the expense of work-based training, though to different extents in the four countries.

In the 1970s, it became a central aim to reduce social inequality by offering access to higher education for all upper secondary students. Consequently, the academic curriculum in VET expanded and the links between VET and the labour market weakened. However, this process developed differently in the Nordic countries. One explanation for this divergence is the variance of the political interests and coalitions behind the VET systems, especially the position of the labour market organisations and the strength of the Social Democratic governments (Dobbins and Busemeyer, 2014). Readers are referred to the first volume in this series (Michelsen and Stenström, 2018), which presents extensive analyses of the historical evolution of the four Nordic VET systems. Based on the first volume, short introductions to the development of VET in the four countries are presented below.

Sweden

In Sweden, apprenticeships played a major role in the early 20th century, but several attempts to impose binding regulations on the quality of workplace training failed. Part-time vocational training was offered by separate municipal schools as a way to meet the growing demand for skills and the concern for the social integration of the urban youth. Unregulated apprenticeships co-existed with workshop schools in the inter-war period, when high youth unemployment spurred the growth of municipal vocational schools. In 1938, the dominant labour market organisations of the employers and employees agreed to regulate vocational training by voluntary collective agreements within each industry, without any Apprenticeship Act, such as those passed in Norway and Denmark. The employers' organisation opposed state regulation and the employees' organisation feared that apprenticeships regulated by the state would be used to put downward pressure on wages. Lacking a binding common regulation, the quality of apprenticeships was gradually eroded (Olofsson and Persson Thunqvist, 2018). During the inter-war period, the Social Democratic governments in the four countries did not consider VET to be part of the ordinary educational system, and VET was not included in their proposals for the unified public school system. The main educational efforts of the Social Democratic governments in this period was to abolish the middle school and extend the unified elementary school, which only partially succeeded. After the war, the Social Democratic party agreed on a proposal to integrate all school types up to grade 9 into a non-selective school. After a period of experiments, this was realised for all schools, though with a separate vocational stream in grade 9 ('9y'). This vocational stream was not a success, and in 1968 it was replaced with mixed-ability classes at all levels (Wiborg, 2009). Bergh (2014) refers to studies that provide evidence that the introduction of the comprehensive school had a positive effect on equality in the distribution of both education and income, especially benefitting gifted children whose fathers had a low level of education.

Post-compulsory vocational schools expanded strongly in the post-war period in connection with rapid industrial growth. The organisation and practices of these schools were quite diverse and fragmented, and the government took initiatives to integrate them into a comprehensive upper secondary school system. A reform in 1971 established a unified gymnasium that included vocational education, and it became an icon of the Nordic model of upper secondary school. The curricula of the two-year vocational programmes in this school were more general than the former vocational schools, and had a broad, preparatory character. The specific vocational qualifications were to be acquired through work-based training after completion of the programmes. A further step to reduce the divide between the general and the vocational programmes came with the reform of 1991. This extended the duration of the vocational programmes from two to three years and offered eligibility for higher education in all programmes. After this reform, the youth cohorts attained higher levels of post-compulsory education, but also higher rates of non-completion of upper secondary education (Hall, 2012) – see Chapter 8.

The long-term direction of policy towards integration and parity of esteem of vocational and general education was reversed by the reform of 2011, which emphasised the difference between the two types of programmes. The vocational content was strengthened, a new apprenticeship programme was introduced and eligibility for higher education was given lower priority. In addition, a far-reaching decentralisation and marketization of the school system was initiated in the 1990s, and a more differentiated system with larger inequality between schools has emerged (Lundahl et al., 2013).

Norway

In Norway, industrialization was slow and was dominated by small firms, and consequently the capacity for coordination among firms was low. Industry and the crafts could not agree on a common regulation of training, and the state

14   *Christian Helms Jørgensen*

regulation in the field was weak. A law passed in 1894 required that apprentices must pass a journeyman's test to acquire a craftsman's certificate, but applied only for the crafts. In the inter-war period, various proposals for regulation of apprenticeships and vocational schools were rejected in parliament (Michelsen et al., 2014). Besides the evening schools for apprentices, municipal continuation schools were introduced. These were targeted at the urban working-class youth. Vocationally oriented schools developed along two different trajectories, either as full-time vocational schools or as apprentice schools. In addition, schools for commerce and schools for handicrafts developed separately. As state regulation was weak, the vocational schools developed in many different directions, often with strong connections to local trade organisations. A seven-year, comprehensive elementary school system was already introduced before the Second World War. After the war, the strong Social Democratic governments sought to extend this school to nine years. It succeeded in 1959 with the introduction of the compulsory two-year youth school, which was divided into general and vocational streams. The nine-year comprehensive school with mixed ability classes and no streaming was finally established in 1969 (Wiborg, 2009).

In the post-war period, industrial growth and large youth cohorts made the strengthening of post-compulsory VET a high priority for governments. State intervention and educational planning increased, and the formation of a coherent VET system started to take shape, but independently of general education. School-based VET for industry, for commerce, for handicraft and apprenticeships were all regulated separately, and the law on apprenticeships only applied to the urban areas. This heterogeneous system appeared increasingly inadequate, as the demand for education beyond the comprehensive school increased strongly in the 1960s. The educational authorities proposed a unified system with vertical permeability from the lower to the higher levels and without any dead ends (Michelsen et al., 2014). A reform in 1975 integrated school-based VET with general education in a more comprehensive upper-secondary education system. Apprenticeships were kept outside and regulated by a separate law that was extended to cover both urban and rural areas. An increasing level of enrolment of adults in apprenticeships and high youth unemployment created capacity problems in VET and prolonged youth transitions in the 1980s. In a reform in 1994, all young people aged 16–19 obtained a statutory right to three years of upper secondary education, which thus became an age-specific school for youth. General and vocational education, including apprenticeships, were included in the new upper secondary school. In this system, which is still in place, the standard model for the VET programmes was two years of school-based education, followed by two years of apprenticeship training in a workplace. This system came to include new service industries such as health, retail and office work. Generous state subsidies were available to make the supply of apprenticeships match the demand of the students. Students who were unable to find an apprenticeship could complete VET in a school-based third year that provided a final exam of equal value. The first two years' courses included more theoretical subjects, and they were broadened to postpone the choice of

Vocational education and training 15

a specific occupation. Moreover, after completing two years of school-based VET, the students could shift to a third year that prepared them for higher education. The ordinary four-year VET programmes did not provide eligibility for higher education. The reform in 2006 adjusted this basic 2+2 model in order to ease the transition from the first school-based part to the second work-based part of the education.

Denmark

The strong tradition for apprenticeships in Denmark was challenged by the transition to free trade, but an Apprenticeship Act in 1889 and reforms in the inter-war period reinstated a strong regulation of apprenticeship training. While the divergent interests of the artisans and industry in the other countries prevented universal regulation of apprenticeships across sectors, such regulation was established in Denmark. This was due to the dominant position of small- and medium-sized craft-based producers, the weakness of large industrialists and the strength of the cooperatives in the processing of agricultural products. An alliance of artisans, industrialists and skilled workers' unions supported a uniform legal regulation of apprentices' training across sectors, including the commercial sector. This legal framework delegated the authority of supervising the apprentices' training to the joint trade committees, which were composed of the labour market organisations (Jørgensen, 2018). In addition, the strong class of independent farmers represented by the Liberal Party opposed the centralisation of state power. Because of the weakness of the state and the strong coalition behind the apprenticeship system, VET was not drawn into the governments' nation-building project along with the general school system. The strong position of apprenticeships limited the opportunities of the municipalities to establish vocational schools in order to reduce youth unemployment in the inter-war period, as happened in other Nordic countries. Vocational education did not become part of the Social Democratic governments' policy for a comprehensive school system, and was placed in the hands of the labour market organisations at a very early stage.

In the inter-war period, the Social Democratic Party in Denmark was divided on the question of the abolishment of the selective compulsory school. The party initiated a reform in 1937, which introduced a new practically oriented middle school, parallel to the academically oriented middle school. The practical middle school followed five years of elementary school and was intended as an option for pupils who would pursue an apprenticeship afterwards, or who would transfer directly into working life after completing comprehensive school. Due to criticism of the early selection of children at the age of 11, the middle school was abolished by a reform in 1958, which also abolished the separate regulation for schools in rural and urban areas. However, the schools continued the separation of pupils in a practical and a bookish stream in grade 7 until a reform 1975, which also extended the comprehensive school from seven to nine years (Wiborg, 2009).

A reform of apprenticeships in 1956 introduced periods of mandatory day-school for all apprentices. In the mid-1960s, more than half of a male youth cohort went into an apprenticeship. In the early 1970s, the left wing of the Social Democratic Party brought proposals to establish a comprehensive upper secondary school similar to Sweden. However, a swing to the right in parliament and a cross-class alliance of employers and craft unions, which dominated the confederation of trade unions in Denmark, managed to keep the apprenticeship system under the control of the labour market organisations (Jørgensen, 2018). With a reform in 1991, the new standard VET programme started with 6 or 12 months of school-based training to qualify the students' choice of a specific occupation. This was followed by three years of apprenticeship, interrupted by shorter periods of school-based training (typically 10 weeks per year). This model still prevails, though in a modified format after a reform in 2014. In Denmark, the comprehensive school was realised later for the compulsory level than in the neighbouring Nordic countries, and it was never accomplished for the upper secondary level. This development indicates a strong element of path-dependency in the Danish apprenticeship system due to, inter alia, an enduring cross-class alliance of employers and craft unions. Influenced by the commitment of the craft unions to apprenticeships, the Social Democratic Party renounced the demand for abolishment of apprenticeships at an early stage. Denmark has maintained a strong division between the two tracks of upper secondary education, with early selection and little vertical permeability between the tracks. The VET system only offers general eligibility for higher education in a small hybrid programme from 2011.

Finland

In Finland, industrialisation came late and developed slowly, and nation-building was a dominant motive for the initiators of a national education system (Kettunen, 2013). Finland gained independence from Russia in 1917, and compared to the other Nordic countries, the introduction of compulsory elementary schools took place later and progressed more slowly, especially in the rural areas. In addition to compulsory schools, continuation classes were offered that came to include preparatory subjects for crafts and handicrafts. In the inter-war period, the government took initiatives to develop the continuation school into practically oriented vocational education. In a parallel process, traditional apprenticeship training was supplemented by evening schools that developed into craft schools. The emerging large industrial companies had little connection to the former guilds and started to establish private, vocational schools operating under the guidelines of the ministry. From the 1920s, school-based preparatory vocational schools aimed at the 14–16-year-olds, started to develop into the most significant form of VET for crafts and industry (Stenström and Virolainen, 2018). School-based VET developed separately from the apprenticeship system, and the aim of the vocational schools was to provide basic vocational skills before one to two years of apprenticeship training. Besides vocational skills, teaching in these schools included general subjects like language, maths, physics and citizenship education. The municipal continuation schools developed in parallel to the vocational schools until the end of the 1950s.

The fragmented growth of VET increasingly appeared as inadequate as industrialisation proceeded, and by the end of the 1920s, the government established a department to systematise and rationalise VET. A motive behind this was to strengthen VET as an alternative for students from working class origin and women, in order to maintain general upper secondary education as a stronghold for the social elite. Another motive behind the political initiatives to develop vocational education was a concern for the social inclusion of youth from the lower classes in connection with modernisation and urbanisation. In the vocational schools, youths could be controlled and socialised under the supervision of the state authorities (Stenström and Virolainen, 2018). After the war, vocational schools were established in the rural regions in order to reduce migration of youths to the larger cities. The employee organisations preferred school-based vocational training to apprenticeships, which they considered as providing narrow vocational skills and cheap labour for the employers. During the process of industrialisation, apprenticeships declined, as employers generally did not find investment in apprenticeships beneficial. This can partly be explained by the strong position of mass production and processing of forestry products, which did not rely on crafts-based skills. Agriculture and forestry dominated in the national economy (Senghaas, 1985). The adverse industrial relations in the inter-war period, when the employer organisations refused to negotiate collective agreements with unions, were not conducive for the development of a system of collective skill formation.

In the post-war decades, education policy in Finland was strongly inspired by Sweden, which was regarded as the ideal model of a modern, Nordic welfare state. In the 1970s, a Social Democratic government in Finland established a unified, nine-year compulsory school system, emphasising the aim of social equality similar to the other Nordic countries. However, ability-based streaming continued until 1983. Subsequently, upper secondary education was reformed to provide opportunities for post-compulsory education for all young people leaving the comprehensive schools. This included a school-based VET system like in Sweden, but unlike Sweden, the vocational and academic tracks were not unified into a comprehensive upper secondary school system. Apprenticeships had a marginal position aimed at adults and early school leavers. In the 1980s, a new reform integrated VET systematically into the state education system, and established a direct progression route from VET to higher education. The number of specialisations were reduced significantly, and a modular structure was introduced in VET in 1995. In order to reduce the high rates of youth unemployment in Finland, the links between VET and the labour market were improved after the turn of the century. All programmes must include at least 6 months of work-based learning in internships. In addition, assessment is organised in collaboration with companies in 'skills demonstrations'. The

18   *Christian Helms Jørgensen*

Finnish VET system has emerged as a mainly school-based, statist system, but unlike the Swedish system, it is a binary system with separate institutions for academic and vocational education.

Four different VET systems

To summarise the development in the four countries, vocational education had a peripheral position in Social Democratic education policy until the 1960s. The priority was to create a universal, comprehensive compulsory school for all children. This project was realised in stages in all four countries in the period from 1960 to the 1990s for the nine-year compulsory school. It was achieved by first ending the selection of pupils into different schools, tracks and classes of different worth, levels and lengths. Next, by ending streaming of the pupils and keeping them together in mixed-ability classes in the transition through the school system (Wiborg, 2009). In international comparisons, the Nordic countries are consistently identified as among the most equal in the world (Bergh, 2014), and the non-selective, comprehensive school system in these countries contributes to this position (Parker et al., 2016; Pfeffer, 2008).

In the 1970s, the next step for the comprehensive school project was to extend it to the upper secondary level of schooling. An important objective for this policy was to reduce the strong social selection of students in higher education, by offering all students at upper secondary level the opportunity to acquire eligibility for higher education. While the compulsory schools developed along similar lines in the four countries, upper secondary education developed along different trajectories. The unified school was realised most consistently at this level in Sweden, due to, among other things, the strength of the Social Democratic Party, the long tradition of school-based VET and the decline of apprenticeships (Olofsson and Persson Thunqvist, 2018). The Swedish gymnasium offered eligibility for higher education in the general as well as in the vocational programmes, even though this quality is conditional after the latest reform in 2011. Finland followed the Swedish path, but maintained a binary system of upper secondary education. Lasonen and Young (1998) characterise the Finnish VET system as a case of mutual enrichment and Sweden as a case of unification of the different strategies to achieve parity of esteem between vocational and general education. In a sequential model, the Norwegian upper secondary school combines the qualities of the comprehensive school with the advantages of the apprenticeship model. Denmark represents the most significant 'exception' to the Nordic school model, because of the early tracking by the start of upper secondary education and the strong separation between the apprenticeship system and the gymnasiums that prepare for higher education. While the Nordic VET systems differ with regard to tracking and selection, they are all categorised as strong systems that contribute to social equality, because they offer a valuable alternative for students who do not take the academic route (Busemeyer, 2015).

VET and the Nordic labour market model

In addition to the Nordic model of education examined above, a Nordic labour market model has been identified. The implications of this model for VET are explored in the following. The Nordic labour market model is characterised by centralised bargaining, consensual industrial relations and strong labour protection (Elvander, 2002; Dølvik, 2013). This is supported by strong employer and worker organisations, unitary, non-confessional unions and a strong system of corporatist collaboration and mediation. The historical timing of the institutionalisation of centralised bargaining and corporatism differ somewhat across the four countries. We also find differences in labour organisation, as Sweden established industrial unions early and Denmark maintained craft-based unions (Dobbins and Busemeyer, 2014). In all four countries, the high union density and high coverage of the collective agreements have limited the emergence of a separate youth labour market with precarious employment. The tradition for centralised wage setting and the solidaristic wage policy has produced compressed wage structures, which results in relatively high minimum wages, even for young and unskilled workers. The high wage levels give employers incentives to invest in labour-saving technology and employ labour with high levels of skills (Busemeyer, 2015). It also encourages employers to pursue a high skills production strategy that takes advantage of the low costs for high skills. The Nordic countries have strong VET systems, which provide high-quality intermediary skills and constrain the dualisation of labour markets between the rapidly growing group of higher education graduates and a group of low-skilled workers (Busemeyer, 2015). In addition, strong employment protection in the Nordic countries (except for Denmark) gives employers incentives to employ highly skilled labour and to engage in the training of low-skilled workers (Kristensen et al., 2015). While the low skill differentials in pay might give employees little economic incentive to upgrade their skills, the Nordic countries have high levels of public spending on education and further training with no or low fees. In addition, an extensive active labour market policy has given high priority to reducing the risks of unemployment and to getting the unemployed back into employment through retraining, mobility support, etc. (Kananen, 2016).

All the Nordic countries developed strong institutions for multi-level cooperation on wages, working conditions, labour protection and codetermination after 1945. However, it was only in Denmark and partly in Norway that a similar system of centralised cooperation was established around collective skill formation. While the labour market organisations in all countries were strongly involved in the early stages of the modernisation of vocational training, they tended to be marginalised, as VET was integrated into a coherent system of upper secondary education. In general, the stronger VET becomes vertically and horizontally integrated into the overall education system, the weaker are the linkages to the labour market (Powell and Solga, 2010). The Nordic VET system evolved along different trajectories and developed different types of

20   *Christian Helms Jørgensen*

connections to the labour market and to general and higher education. In Sweden and Finland, it has been a priority to offer all young people eligibility for higher education in an integrated, full-time upper secondary school, while giving low priority to work-based learning of vocational skills. Denmark, on the contrary, maintained and expanded the apprenticeship system, where the labour market organisations have a strong position. Labour in Denmark has maintained organisations based on crafts, while industrial organisations were established early in Sweden (Dobbins and Busemeyer, 2014). The Norwegian model represents a hybrid, with two years of school-based education followed by two years of apprenticeship training or alternatively, a third supplementary school-based year qualifying for higher education.

Earlier comparative research has emphasised that different societal models of connecting VET systems with labour markets have implications (a *'societal effect'*) for the segmentation and stratification of labour markets and for the organisation of work at the organisational level (Maurice et al., 1986). Studies of the German VET system demonstrated how training based on standardised occupations corresponds with work organisations along occupational lines and high autonomy. In Germany, companies engage in broad multi-skilling that enables the 'professionalisation' of work at intermediary levels of work organisation (Deissinger, 1998). From this research, it could be assumed that the apprenticeship systems of Norway and Denmark are associated with stronger occupational labour markets and job discretion, compared to the more statist VET systems of Sweden and Finland. However, despite differences in the Nordic production regimes and VET systems, employees in all the Nordic countries generally have a high quality of work-life and a high degree of job discretion (Gallie, 2009). Work-life research has identified a common Nordic model of work-life and management (Gustavsen, 2011), characterised by flat hierarchies with low power distance and high employee involvement and autonomy (Dølvik, 2013; Gallie, 2009). The historically strong position of labour unions helps to explain the high degree of work autonomy in the Nordic countries (Edlund and Grönlund, 2010). In addition, the high levels of education and employment protection and the low wage differentials tend to facilitate non-hierarchical organisations with high levels of job discretion. Moreover, the relatively low levels of unemployment and high levels of social security associated with the Nordic welfare state has worked against authoritarian forms of management and work organisations. The gradual reduction of social security and the shift from a welfare regime towards a new workfare regime in recent decades (Kananen, 2016) is a challenge for the future of these characteristics of work in the Nordic countries.

VET between social demands and labour market requirements

All the four VET systems have developed in the field of tension between the demand for skilled labour in the labour market and the social demand for education of young people. Due to differences in the governance of the Nordic VET systems, they have given priority to one or the other of these demands. The main priority of the statist upper secondary school is to provide educational opportunities for all young people, while the systems of collective skill formation and apprenticeships are more sensitive to the requirements in the labour market. The states can adapt the Swedish and Finnish VET systems to the demands of young people leaving compulsory school. A higher proportion of 21-year-olds in these two countries has completed upper secondary education compared to the two countries with apprenticeships. The capacity of the apprenticeship systems depends on the supply of training placements offered by employers. The situation in the training market mirrors the general employment situation of the training companies and the industry. This linkage between the demand in the training market and the labour market reduces the risk of mismatch, as the number of entrants in specific occupations is linked to the employment situation and the demand for labour. However, while the apprenticeship system creates a closer link between supply and demand in the labour market, apprenticeship systems also systematically create mismatch problems. When an economic downturn hits and firms start to downsize, they normally also stop recruiting new apprentices. During recessions, the training of apprentices is reduced strongly, and an upturn is often followed by a shortage of skilled labour. This can prevail for years, as the training of new apprentices typically takes four years.

The recruitment to the VET programmes in Norway and Denmark is not regulated directly by the number of apprenticeships. All programmes start with one or two years of school-based training. In many of the most popular VET programmes in Denmark, access to the first school-based courses is limited by quotas in order to adapt the number of students to the number of apprenticeships available. In other occupations, where a shortage of labour is expected, the students are guaranteed a training placement. If apprenticeships are not available, the vocational schools in Denmark and Norway provide school-based training. In Norway, the municipalities (*'fylkeskommunene'*) are responsible for the vocational schools. Their adaptation of the enrolment level to the demand in the labour market is quite weak, as the size of the programmes is more dependent on the capacity of the schools (Høst, 2012). As a result, a deficit of students in relation to the demand for labour is common in some programmes, and a deficit of apprenticeships in relation to students' demand arises in other programmes. This is one reason why a substantial proportion of students abandon their vocational aspirations and switch to the general programmes in the third year in Norway. Until the early 1990s, the capacity of the vocational programmes in Sweden was determined by local and regional authorities, based on assessments of the demand for labour. Following the deregulation and the introduction of students' free choice of school and decentralisation, the schools primarily adjust their capacity to the students' level of demand, which tends to increase the mismatch problems in the labour market (Olofsson and Panican, 2015).

VET and the Nordic transition systems

The focus of interest in this volume is on how the Nordic VET systems manage the dual challenge of supporting the students' transition to skilled employment and to higher education. The concepts of 'transition systems' (Raffe, 2008) and 'transition regime' (Walther, 2006) are useful for exploring this issue. The concepts draw attention to the critical thresholds and points of selection in students' movements into, through and out of VET. This can elucidate the relative strengths and weaknesses of the Nordic VET systems regarding processes of selection regarding social background, ethnic origin and gender. While young peoples' agency and strategies are important for their transitions, this chapter focuses on the institutional architecture and the opportunities provided by the different Nordic VET systems. Pohl and Walther (2007) characterise the Nordic countries as representing a universalistic regime for young peoples' transition from school to work. This transition regime provides strong and multi-dimensional support that reduces the risks involved in the transition process (Walther, 2006). Governments in the Nordic countries have given high priority to offering access to post-compulsory education for all young people and to keeping youth unemployment low (Jensen, 2015).

The Nordic welfare state prioritises individual autonomy by providing social benefits independent of socio-economic status. Although it is often characterised as a collectivist regime, the universal benefit system releases the individual from dependency on the family and private charity. The high level of social security might contribute to prolonging the transitions from school to work in the Nordic countries. Young people have opportunities to try out different educations, make switches and reorientate their lives (Walther, 2006). Children in the Nordic countries move out of their parents' homes and become financially independent earlier than in other countries. In addition, the participation of women in post-compulsory education and in employment is very high in all the Nordic countries, due to the comprehensive system of care institutions for children, the sick and elderly. However, neo-liberal reforms of this model over the last two decades have reduced the level of social support for young people and placed more responsibility for a successful transition on the individual (Kananen, 2016; Angelin et al., 2014).

The highly organised Nordic labour markets constrain the development of a secondary, low-wage youth labour market (Jensen, 2015). Studies indicate that the opportunities for young people to gain access to employment in the Nordic labour markets has changed over the last decade, especially since the financial crisis (Albæk et al., 2015). Low-skilled jobs that were previously accessible for early school leavers are disappearing due to the outsourcing of labour-intensive production, new technologies and migration in the post-2004 'borderless' European labour market (Segendorf, 2013). Researchers find that in most European countries, the transition from education to a stable position in the labour market has become more demanding, prolonged and less transparent (Walther and Plug, 2006).

Vocational education and training 23

Research on transitions has emphasised that the concept of 'school to work transition' does not designate one single movement, but involves reverse transitions, from the labour market back into education, and other non-standardised, prolonged and complex movements of young people between education, work and other situations (Raffe, 2014; Walther and Plug 2006). In Norway, Sweden and Denmark, the average age of entry into the labour market has increased from around 20 years in the early 1990s, to currently 28 years. In international comparison, the employment rates of young people in the Nordic countries are high, but youth unemployment has been growing since 1998 (Albæk et al., 2015). The employment of young people in full-time permanent jobs has been reduced, and part-time employment has increased (Madsen et al., 2013; Eurofound, 2015). This has given VET a central position in policies to tackle youth unemployment and make all young people complete an upper secondary education.

The students' transitions through VET towards the labour market involve processes of choosing and the passing of thresholds of institutional selection. The organisation of these processes in the four Nordic VET systems can be examined using the concepts of 'standardisation', 'stratification' and 'vocational specificity' from comparative VET research (Allmendinger, 1989; Müller, 2005; Andersen et al., 2010). Strong *standardisation* entails a binding regulation at national or industry level of the content, duration and quality procedures for VET. Strong standardisation enhances the portability of the qualifications provided in the vocational programmes for employers, which promotes the education-to-job matching of the programmes. However, rigid centralised regulation can prevent the adaptation of the programmes to specific local requirements and reduce the scope for individual choice in education. All four Nordic countries are categorised as highly standardised in international comparisons (Pfeffer, 2008). However, the strong decentralisation and marketization of vocational education in Sweden since the 1990s, has resulted in growing disparities between the municipalities regarding educational quality and transition policies (Lundahl and Olofsson, 2014; Lundahl et al., 2013). The VET systems in Sweden and Finland have been reorganised with an individualised and modularised structure. The completion of a VET programme in these countries depends on the accumulation of a certain number of credit points, which can be attained by completing different courses. In Norway and Denmark, the students have to pass a standardised final apprenticeship exam.

The *specificity* of the vocational qualifications offered in the VET programmes differs significantly between the Nordic countries. This has shifted over time in each country. Since the 1960s, it has been a dominant argument in education policy that specific qualifications only have short-term value due to the rapidly changing skills requirement. This was a strong argument behind the reforms to integrate vocational and general education in the 1970s in all four countries. It was assumed that broad, general qualifications and generic skills prepared the students better for flexibility and life-long learning. Programmes that centre on specific skills entail a risk of locking the students into a specific

24 *Christian Helms Jørgensen*

job or occupation. Consequently, all the Nordic VET systems have reduced the specificity and the number of different programmes and specialisations (see Chapter 2).

A major difference between the Nordic VET systems is the extent of *stratification* at upper secondary level, which refers to the degree of tracking and selection of students. The comprehensive school has been realised most consistently in Sweden with the reform in 1991, although it was reversed somewhat in 2011. Finland has maintained a division of students into two tracks of upper secondary schools, but it offers all students eligibility for higher education. In 1994, Norway introduced a comprehensive school model for the first two years of upper secondary education, followed by division into two tracks: higher education preparatory programmes and apprenticeships. Denmark has maintained the strongest form of tracking between general and vocational education in upper secondary schools.

To conclude, VET plays a key position in the transition systems at the crossroad between compulsory education and higher education, and between the education system and the labour market. The VET system is also positioned in a field of tension between the social demands and educational choices of young people and the requirements of employers and the political objectives of governments. This ambiguous position gives rise to the dual challenge for VET of providing direct access to employment at the level of skilled workers and simultaneously providing access to higher education. In addition, the egalitarian aims of the Nordic countries give VET a special role in the inclusion of young people who do not opt for higher education after completing compulsory school. In order to attract and retain the students and provide access to work-based training, VET is also required to maintain high esteem among young people and employers. The focus of this book is to explore how these diverse challenges are managed by the Nordic VET systems, and to examine how the challenges are interrelated. The following chapters examine these key challenges in comparative studies of the four VET systems (Chapters 2, 3 and 4) and in the examination of selected reforms to manage the challenges (Chapter 5). In addition, the same challenges are examined in two multi-level studies of selected occupations (Chapters 6 and 7). The concluding chapter (Chapter 8) points at some lessons to be taken from the Nordic VET systems.

References

Albæk, K., Asplund, R., Barth, E., Lindahl, L., von Simson, K., and Vanhala, P. (2015) *Youth Unemployment and Inactivity*, Copenhagen, Nordic Council of Ministers.

Allmendinger, J. (1989) 'Educational systems and labour market outcomes', *European Sociological Review*, vol. 5, no. 3, pp. 231–250.

Andersen, R., and van de Werfhorst, H. G. (2010) 'Education and occupational status in 14 countries: The role of educational institutions and labour market coordination', *The British Journal of Sociology*, vol. 61, no. 2, pp. 336–55.

Angelin, A., Kauppinen, T., Lorentzen, T., Bäckman, O., Moisio, P., Dahl, E., and Salonen, T. (2014) 'Have Nordic welfare regimes adapted to changes in transitions to adulthood?' in

Antonucci, L. and Hamilton, M. (eds.) *Young People and Social Policy in Europe*, Basingstoke, Palgrave Macmillan, pp. 169–188.

Antikainen, A. (2006) 'In search of the Nordic model in education', *Scandinavian Journal of Educational Research*, vol. 50, no. 3, pp. 229–243.

Archer, M. S. (1979) *Social Origins of Educational Systems*, London, Sage Publications.

Bacchi, C. (2009) *Analysing Policy: What's the Problem Represented to Be?* Frenchs Forest, Pearson Education.

Bäckman, O., Jakobsen, V., Lorentzen, T., Österbacka, E., and Dahl, E. (2011) *Dropping Out in Scandinavia*, Stockholm, Institutet för Framtidsstudier.

Baldwin, P. (1990) *The Politics of Social Solidarity: Class Bases of the European Welfare State, 1875–1975*, Cambridge, Cambridge University Press.

BCG. (2015) *Nordic Agenda*, Boston, Consulting Group. Available at https://media-publications.bcg.com/Nordic-Agenda-2017.pdf (Accessed 18 December 2017).

Bergh, A. (2014) 'What are the policy lessons from Sweden? On the rise, fall and revival of a capitalist welfare state', *New Political Economy*, vol. 19, no. 5, pp. 662–694.

Blossing, U., Imsen, G., and Moos, L. (2014) *The Nordic Education Model*, The Netherlands, Springer.

Börjesson, M., Ahola, S., Helland, H., and Thomsen, J. P. (2014) *Enrolment Patterns in Nordic Higher Education*, Oslo, NIFU.

Bosch, G., and Charest, J. (2008) 'Vocational training and the labour market in liberal and coordinated economies', *Industrial Relations Journal*, vol. 39, no. 5, pp. 428–447.

Brandal, N., Bratberg, O., and Thorsen, D. E. (2013) *The Nordic Model of Social Democracy*, London, Palgrave Macmillan.

Buchardt, M., Markkola, P., and Valtonen, H. (2013) *Introduction: Education and the Making of the Nordic Welfare States*, Helsinki, Nordic Centre of Excellence Nordwel.

Busemeyer, M. R. (2015) *Skills and Inequality: Partisan Politics and the Political Economy of Education Reforms in Western Welfare States*, Cambridge, Cambridge University Press.

Busemeyer, M. R., and Trampusch, C. (eds.) (2012) *The Political Economy of Collective Skill Formation*, Oxford, Oxford University Press.

Campbell, J. L., and Pedersen, O. K. (2007) 'The varieties of capitalism and hybrid success: Denmark in the global economy', *Comparative Political Studies*, vol. 40, no. 3, pp. 307–332.

Deissinger, Th. (1998) *Beruflichkeit als "organisierendes Prinzip" der deutschen Berufsausbildung*, Markt Schwaben, Eusl Verlag.

Dobbins, M., and Busemeyer, M. R. (2014) 'Socio-economic institutions, organized interests and partisan politics: The development of vocational education in Denmark and Sweden', *Socio-Economic Review*, vol. 13, no. 2, pp. 259–284.

Dølvik, J. E. (2013) *Grunnpilarene i de nordiske modellene: Et tilbakeblikk på arbeidslivs-og velferdsregimenes utvikling*, NordMod2030, Oslo, Fafo.

Dumas, A., Méhaut, P., and Olympio, N. (2013) 'From upper secondary to further Education: European models of post-compulsory learning', in Janmaat, J. G., Duru-Bellat, M., Green, A., and Méhaut, P. (eds.) *The Dynamics of Social Outcomes of Education Systems*, Basingstoke, Palgrave Macmillan, pp. 47–69.

Edlund, J., and Grönlund, A. (2010) 'Class and work autonomy in 21 countries: A question of production regime or power resources?' *Acta Sociologica*, vol. 53, no. 3, pp. 213–228.

Elvander, N. (2002) 'The labour market regimes in the Nordic countries: A comparative analysis', *Scandinavian Political Studies*, vol. 25, no. 2, pp. 117–137.

Esping-Andersen, G. (1990) *The Three Worlds of Welfare Capitalism*, Cambridge, Polity Press.

Eurofound (2015) *Recent Developments in Temporary Employment: Employment Growth, Wages and Transitions*, Luxembourg, Publications Office of the European Union.

26 *Christian Helms Jørgensen*

Gallie, D. (2009) 'Institutional regimes and employee influence at work: A European comparison', *Cambridge Journal of Regions, Economy and Society*, vol. 2, no. 3, pp. 379–393.

Gonon, Ph. (2016) 'Zur Dynamik und Typologie von Berufsbildungssystemen – eine internationale Perspektiv', *Zeitschrift für Pädagogik*, vol. 62, no. 3, pp. 307–322.

Greinert, W. D. (1999) *Berufsqualifizierung und dritte industrielle Revolution*, Baden-Baden, Nomos-Verlags-Gesellschaft.

Gustavsen, B. (2011) 'The Nordic model of work organization', *Journal of the Knowledge Economy*, vol. 2, no. 4, pp. 463–480.

Hall, C. (2012) 'The effects of reducing tracking in upper secondary school evidence from a large-scale pilot scheme', *Journal of Human Resources*, vol. 47, no. 1, pp. 237–269.

Høst, H. (2012) *Tradisjonelle utfordringer-fornyet interesse: Hvordan er de nordiske landes yrkesutdanninger i stand til å møte arbeidslivets behov?* Copenhagen, Nordic Council of Ministers.

Jensen, C. S. (2015) 'The Nordic labour market (s) and the European Union', in Grøn, C. H., Nedergaard, P., and Wivel, A. (eds.) *The Nordic Countries and the European Union: Still the Other European Community?* London, Routledge, pp. 226–240.

Jónasson, Jón Torfi (2003) 'Does the state expand schooling? A study based on five Nordic Countries', *Comparative Education Review*, vol. 47, no. 2, pp. 289–203.

Jørgensen, C. H. (2015) 'Challenges for work-based learning in vocational education and training in the Nordic countries', in Bohlinger, S., Haake, U., Jørgensen, C. H., Toiviainen, H., and Wallo, A. (eds.) *Working and Learning in Times of Uncertainty*, Rotterdam, Sense Publishers.

Jørgensen, C. H. (2018) 'The modernisation of the apprenticeship system in Denmark 1945–2015', in Michelsen, S. and Stenström, M. L. (eds.) *Vocational Education in the Nordic Countries: The Historical Evolution*, Abingdon, Routledge, pp. 171–189.

Kananen, J. (2016) *The Nordic Welfare State in Three Eras: From Emancipation to Discipline*, Abingdon, Routledge.

Kettunen, P. (2013) 'Vocational education and the tensions of modernity in a Nordic periphery', in Buchardt, M., Markkola, P., and Valtonen, H. (eds.) *Education, State and Citizenship*, Helsinki, Nordic Centre of Excellence NordWel, pp. 31–55.

Kivinen, O., and Rinne, R. (1998) 'State, governmentality and education – the Nordic experience', *British Journal of Sociology of Education*, vol. 19, no. 1, pp. 39–52.

Knudsen, T., and Rothstein, B. (1994) 'State building in Scandinavia', *Comparative Politics*, vol. 26, no. 2, pp. 203–220.

Kristensen, P. H., Lilja, K., Moen, E., and Morgan, G. (2015) 'Nordic countries as laboratories for transnational learning', in Strang, J. (ed.) *Nordic Cooperation: A European Region in Transition*, London, Routledge, pp. 183–204.

Kvist, J., and Greve, B. (2011) 'Has the Nordic welfare model been transformed?' *Social Policy & Administration*, vol. 45, no. 2, pp. 146–160.

Lasonen, J., and Young, M. (1998) *Strategies for Achieving Parity of Esteem in European Upper Secondary Education*. Final Report on the Project. FIER, University of Jyväskylä.

Levels, M., Van der Velden, R., and Di Stasio, V. (2014) 'From school to fitting work: How education-to-job matching of European school leavers is related to educational system characteristics', *Acta Sociologica*, vol. 57, no. 4, pp. 341–361.

Lundahl, L., Arreman, I. E., Holm, A-L., and Lundström, U. (2013) 'Educational marketization the Swedish way', *Education Inquiry*, vol. 4, no. 4, pp. 497–517.

Lundahl, L., and Olofsson, J. (2014) 'Guarded transitions? Youth trajectories and school-to-work transition policies in Sweden', *International Journal of Adolescence and Youth*, vol. 19, sup1, pp. 19–34.

Lutz, B. (1991) 'Die Grenzen des 'effet societal' und die Notwendigkeit eioner historischen Perspektive', in Heidenreich, M. and Schmidt, G. (eds.) *International Vergleichende Organisationsforschung*, Wiesbaden, VS, Verlag für Sozialwissenschaften, pp. 91–105.

Madsen, P. K., Molina, O., Møller, J., and Lozano, M. (2013) 'Labour market transitions of young workers in Nordic and southern European countries: The role of flexicurity', *Transfer: European Review of Labour and Research*, vol. 19, no. 3, pp. 325–343.

Markussen, E. (ed.) (2010) *Frafald i utdanning for 16–20 åringer i Norden*, Copenhagen, Nordic Council of Ministers.

Maurice, M., Sellier, F., and Silvestre, J-J. (1986) *The Social Foundation of Industrial Power: A Comparison of France and Germany*, Cambridge, MA, MIT Press.

Michelsen, S., Høst, H., and Olsen, O-J. (2014) *Origins and Development of VET 1860–2010*, Nord-VET Research report, Bergen, Bergen University.

Michelsen, S., and Stenström, M. L. (eds.) (2018) *Vocational Education in the Nordic Countries: The Historical Evolution*, Abingdon, Routledge.

Müller, W. (2005) 'Education and youth integration into European labour markets', *International Journal of Comparative Sociology*, vol. 46, no. 5–6, pp. 461–485.

Nilsson, T. (1997) 'Scandinavian liberalism – prophets instead of Profits', in Sørensen, Ø. and Stråth, B. (eds.) *The Cultural Construction of Norden*, Oslo, Scandinavian University Press, pp. 206–230.

Olofsson, J., and Panican, A. (2015) *Lärlingsutbildning i skärningspunkten mellan kompetensförsörjning och socialpolitik*, Lund, Socialhögskolan.

Olofsson, J., and Persson Thunqvist, D. (2018) 'The modern evolution of VET in Sweden (1945–2015)', in Michelsen, S. and Stenström, M. L. (eds.) *Vocational Education in the Nordic Countries: The Historical Evolution*, Abingdon, Routledge, pp. 125–145.

Parker, P. D., Jerrim, J., Schoon, I., and Marsh, H. W. (2016) 'A multination study of socio-economic inequality in expectations for progression to higher education: The role of between-school tracking and ability stratification', *American Educational Research Journal*, vol. 53, no. 1, pp. 6–32.

Pfeffer, F. T. (2008) 'Persistent inequality in educational attainment and its institutional context', *European Sociological Review*, vol. 24, no. 5, pp. 543–565.

Pohl, A., and Walther, A. (2007) 'Activating the disadvantaged: Variations in addressing youth transitions across Europe', *International Journal of Lifelong Education*, vol. 26, no. 5, pp. 533–553.

Powell, J. J., and Solga, H. (2010) 'Analyzing the Nexus of higher education and vocational training in Europe: A comparative-institutional framework', *Studies in Higher Education*, vol. 35, no. 6, pp. 705–721.

Raffe, D. (2008) 'The concept of transition system', *Journal of Education and Work*, vol. 21, no. 4, pp. 277–296.

Raffe, D. (2014) 'Explaining National differences in education-work transitions', *European Societies*, vol. 16, no. 2, pp. 175–193.

Rothstein, B. (1996) *The Social Democratic State: The Swedish Model and the Beaureaucratic Problem of Social Reforms*, Pittsburgh, University of Pittsburgh Press.

SCB. (2012) *Etablering på arbetsmarknaden tre år efter gymnasieskolan*, Örebro, Statistics Sweden.

Segendorf, Å. O. (2013) *Unga i arbete i Norden. Ungas väg mot etablering på arbetsmarknaden i de nordiska länderna*, Copenhagen, Nordic council of Ministers.

Senghaas, D. (1985) *The European Experience: A Historical Critique of Development Theory*, Dover, Berg Publisher.

28 *Christian Helms Jørgensen*

Stenström, M. L., and Virolainen, M. (2018) 'The development of finnish vocational education and training in 1850–1945', in Michelsen, S. and Stenström, M. L. (eds.) *Vocational Education in the Nordic Countries: The Historical Evolution*, Abingdon, Routledge, pp. 24–45.

Telhaug, A. O., Asbjørn Mediås, O., and Aasen, P. (2006) 'The Nordic model in education: Education as part of the political system in the last 50 years', *Scandinavian Journal of Educational Research*, vol. 50, no. 3, pp. 245–283.

Thelen, K. (2004) *How Institutions Evolve: The Political Economy of Skills in Germany, Britain, the United States, and Japan*, Cambridge, Cambridge University Press.

Thelen, K. (2014) *Varieties of Liberalization and the New Politics of Social Solidarity*, Cambridge, Cambridge University Press.

Walther, A. (2006) 'Regimes of youth transitions: Choice, flexibility and security in young people's experiences across different European contexts', *Young*, vol. 14, no. 2, pp. 119–139.

Walther, A., and Plug, W. (2006) 'Transitions from school to work in Europe: Destandardization and policy trends', *New Directions for Child and Adolescent Development*, vol. 2006, no. 113, pp. 77–90.

Wiborg, S. (2009) *Education and Social Integration: Comprehensive Schooling in Europe*, New York, Palgrave Macmillan.

Wolbers, M. H. (2007) 'Patterns of labour market entry: A comparative perspective on school-to-work transitions in 11 European Countries', *Acta sociologica*, vol. 50, no. 3, pp. 189–210.

2 Transitions from vocational education to employment in the Nordic countries

Christian Helms Jørgensen and Anna Hagen Tønder

The aim of this chapter is to examine how the systems of initial vocational education and training (VET systems) in four Nordic countries connect to the labour market, and how they support students' transition to employment. The bleak prospects for young people with low levels of education and the contraction of the youth labour market has highlighted the school-to-work transition as a central concern for policy-makers. This is amplified by the demographic changes, with declining numbers of youth entering the labour market and a growing population of elderly. The declining enrolment in VET in Denmark and Sweden is accompanied by forecasts of serious shortages of skilled labour (Høst, 2012). The VET systems are receiving greater political attention, because they are seen as a key to achieving the goal of all young people completing at least an upper secondary education, and being integrated into the labour market. However, the opportunities for VET students to gain access to stable employment at a relevant level differs between the Nordic countries due to differences in the institutional linkages between the VET systems and the labour markets. This chapter explores and compares these differences and their consequences for young peoples' transition from vocational education to employment.

The data used in the chapter have been gathered and analysed in four separate country reports for each country (a total of 12 reports). They were prepared by researchers from each of the four countries in the Nord-VET project. Where no other reference is made, this chapter draws on the country reports on the current VET systems from Denmark (Jørgensen, 2014), Sweden (Persson Thunqvist and Hallqvist, 2014), Finland (Stenström and Virolainen, 2014) and Norway (Olsen et al., 2014). In addition, the chapter draws on statistical data from official sources. In order to provide a picture of the differences between the four Nordic countries, key data on youth transitions from education to the labour market in the period 2000 to 2015 are summarised in Table 2.1. The table shows that significant changes have taken place during this period, which reflect the shifts in the general economic situation of these four countries. In the period from 2000 to 2015, the total employment in Norway grew by 18%, while the figures for Sweden (10%) and Finland (9%) were lower, while in Denmark they stagnated (www.norden.org). Youth unemployment rates and the share of young people

30 Christian Helms Jørgensen and Anna Hagen Tønder

Table 2.1 Indicators of school-to-work transitions of youth

Youth unemployment below 25 years (% of active population)[1]

	2000	2005	2010	2015
Denmark	6.2	8.6	13.9	10.8
Finland	21.4	20.1	21.4	22.4
Sweden	10.5	22.6	24.8	20.4
Norway	9.8	11.4	9.2	9.9

Temporary employees age 15–29 (% of all employees)[2]

	2000	2005	2010	2015
Denmark	22.4	22.3	18.7	20.2
Finland	40.7	36.3	34.3	34.0
Sweden	32.3	40.2	42.4	41.0
Norway	22.1	23.1	21.3	19.9

Attainment below upper secondary education, age 25–34 (% of cohort)[3]

	2000	2005	2010	2015
Denmark	20	13	13	20
Finland	14	11	9	10
Sweden	13	9	9	18
Norway	7	17	17	19

Enrolment of students in upper secondary vocational education (% of all students at ISCED 3)[4]

	1998	2005	2010	2012
Denmark	51.8	47.9	46.5	46.1
Finland	52.0	63.9	69.7	70.1
Sweden	40.6	53.6	56.1	49.4
Norway	52.5	60.8	53.9	52.0

Sources of data: 1. Eurostat Une rt a, 2. Eurostat lfsa_etpga, 3. Education at a Glance 2015 Table A1.4a, 4. Eurostat [tps00055].

in temporary employment in Sweden and Finland are considerably higher than in the two other countries (Segendorf, 2013; Albæk et al., 2015). Finland tends to have higher NEET (not in education, training or employment) rates than the other countries, and in Norway and Denmark, a higher proportion of young people have not completed any post-compulsory education at age 21. Persistent findings in studies comparing the Nordic countries indicate that the transition from upper secondary education to stable employment in Norway and Denmark is smoother than in Sweden and Finland. At the same time, the drop-out rate from VET is higher in Denmark and Norway (Bäckman et al., 2015), and the completion rates in upper secondary education are higher in Sweden and Finland (Albæk et al., 2015; Segendorf, 2013).

The following sections examine how these differences can be explained by differences in the institutional architecture of the four countries. First, the different types of linkages between the VET system and the employment system are examined. Next, we explore the diverse ways of organising the choice and selection processes, and we compare employment protection in the four countries. Lastly, we examine the initiatives taken in all four countries to reinvent or enhance new forms of apprenticeships, and try to explain why this has only been successful in two countries. It should be noted that in addition to differences at the country level, we find significant differences in the school-to-work transitions between sectors and industries (Nyen et al., 2015; Jørgensen, 2013). In Sweden, for example, 74% of the students from the energy programme and only 35% from the food programme were in employment three years after completion (SCB, 2012). As a consequence, reservations must be taken for internal heterogeneity when examining the qualities of the four VET systems in general. This is clear from our case studies of the health and construction sectors in Chapters 6 and 7. They indicate that the internal differences between the two occupations within one country, are in some respects larger than the cross-country differences within a single occupation.

Linking VET and the employment system

A main purpose of VET in all the Nordic countries is to supply skilled labour for the labour market and employment opportunities for the students. However, this is only one of several aims of VET, which has different priority across the four Nordic countries. Moreover, as a result of different historical trajectories, the linkages between the Nordic VET systems and the labour market vary considerably (Michelsen and Stenström, 2018). Based on the Greinert (2008) concepts, we can distinguish between three types of coordination regimes: state planning, market-based regulation and institutionalised negotiation. The first, central state planning, relies on forecasting of skill requirements to guide educational planning in order to match the short-term and long-term supply of labour with the demands in the employment system. This approach is especially associated with the centralised planning by the Nordic Social Democratic governments in the period 1950–80s. It was based on the assumption that the capitalist economy could be controlled and regulated through state intervention with a long-term perspective. The second type of regime, market-based regulation, relies on coordination through the balancing of demand and supply of skills through the market signals of employment rates and wage levels. It assumes that young peoples' choices of education conform to a rational investment model that seeks to optimise future employment and income (Ball, 2012). This approach is associated with the deregulation and decentralisation of the education system as part of the neo-liberal policies from the 1980s onwards. It emphasises students' opportunities for choice and the vocational schools' opportunities for flexible adjustment of the programmes to the requirements in the local labour market. The third regime type, institutionalised negotiation, is associated with the tripartite collaboration between the state and the labour market organisations on collective skill formation. The corporatist institutions are mostly organised around occupations and can function at the local, regional and national levels. These three basic regimes for the matching of VET to the world of work are combined in different ways in the Nordic countries.

In Finland, nation-building has historically been a key objective for education policy (Kettunen, 2013). The Finnish VET system relies on forecasting to predict future skill demands – a 'forecast industry' (Ahola, 2012). The state-led Finnish VET system has a weak tradition for work-based occupational training, and weak institutional linkages to the labour market. Since the 1990s, reforms have tried to make the VET system more responsive to the requirements of the labour market, by organising the programmes around competencies defined by practical work tasks (outcome-based education) and assessment of competencies in collaboration between vocational schools and training companies (see Chapter 5). In order to improve the matching of VET to the labour market, the funding of the VET providers depends on the subsequent employment rates of the students. In addition, all programmes have included six months of work-based training, and the flexibility of the programmes is increased through modularisation (Ahola, 2012). Tripartite bodies have been established for each industry to plan and develop VET for that industry. The local providers of VET are responsible for adjusting the VET programmes to the local labour markets, and for having all students draw up an individual study plan (Stenström and Virolainen, 2014). The legislation for VET emphasises the students' right to choose an individual programme, which can be designed flexibly by combining study elements from different areas and from across the vocational and academic curricula. Consequently, the matching of students' skill profiles to job profiles is less standardised than is the case in the occupational VET systems in Norway and Denmark. This helps to explain why the education-to-job match of upper secondary students is lower in Finland than in Norway and Denmark (Levels et al., 2014). The Finnish 'planning machine' has a number of weaknesses according to Ahola (2012). There is a lack of reflective feedback mechanisms in the planning process, which could correct the procedures when the planning fails. The planning does not include the sometimes-contradictory policy measures in different sectors, which reduces the reliability of the planning. The financial crisis in 2008 demonstrated that long-term planning in a liberalised and volatile global economy is unreliable. Consequently, central state planning runs the risk of losing credibility when it fails and leaves young people disappointed after choosing an education that is no longer in demand in the labour market. Moreover, the non-participatory and technocratic nature of state planning tends to alienate the labour market organisations and the students (Herschbach, 2009).

The Danish apprenticeship-system is organised by tripartite collaboration between the state and the labour market organisations. The adaptation of the VET programmes to changes in the labour market is institutionalised through a complex architecture of joint committees at all levels. The central bodies are the national trade committees ('*faglige udvalg*'), who have a wide-ranging authority to organise, monitor and assess the VET programmes (Juul and Jørgensen, 2011). The self-governance of the trade committees is supervised by the state. Every year, all trade committees must submit a report to the Ministry regarding employment rates, future skills requirements and the potential demand for new programmes. The state has limited capacity to regulate the training market, but the supply of apprenticeships is subsidised through a training levy paid by all employers. In collaboration with the trade committees, the Ministry sets quotas for enrolment in the most popular programmes to tackle unemployment. The trade committees determine the national training ordinances that set uniform national standards for each programme. This standardised certification of the occupations at national level is crucial for the working of the occupational labour markets in the Danish flexicurity model, which is characterised by very high labour mobility between firms (Madsen et al., 2013; Berglund et al., 2010). Newly educated apprentices have high employment rates, which is an indication of the efficiency of this standardisation. Nine months after completion, two out of three of the former apprentices are still employed in the training company (AE, 2016). It has been argued that the high employment rates in the short-term come at the cost of lower long-term employability (Raffe, 2011; Hampf and Woessmann, 2016), because the emphasis on specific skills in apprenticeships involves a risk of locking students into a specific firm or occupation. In Denmark, however, skilled workers have a very high mobility, not only in a specific occupational field, but also across sectors, which is supported by an extensive public CVET system of further training (Trampusch and Eichenberger, 2012; Jørgensen, 2013). While the apprenticeship system performs well in education-to-job matching of the skills supplied, it is weaker in securing the volume of skilled labour on demand in the labour market. A main current problem is that the declining enrolment in VET does not match the predicted future demand for skilled labour. This is a challenge that the Danish VET system shares with the Norwegian and Swedish VET systems.

In Denmark, the state has respected the occupational self-governance of the labour market organisations. However, governments have taken an active role in the merging of the labour market training with the IVET and CVET systems and in the financing of VET (Thelen, 2014). A positive feature of this neo-corporatist system is that the close involvement of the labour market organisations provides high credibility for the certification of skills. Changes mainly take place as incremental adjustments of the programmes in the jurisdiction of each trade committee. While the regulation by institutionalised negotiations dominates in Denmark, it should be noted that the distribution of training placements mainly takes place through a training market, which tends to create problems with mismatch and to discriminate against minorities (Lancee, 2016).

While the VET systems in Norway and Denmark have many similarities, the Norwegian state took on a stronger role in VET after the VET reform of 1994. The state regulation mainly concerns the first two school-based years of VET, while the labour market organisations have more control of the last two years of apprenticeships. The Norwegian apprenticeship system is very effective in bringing the students into employment, as two thirds continue in the training company after completion (Nyen et al., 2015). A very interesting institutional innovation in the Norwegian VET system, intended to coordinate supply and demand at the local level, are the local training agencies, LTAs ('*opplæringskontor*'). These are discussed in Chapter 5 of this volume.

Mismatch in supply and demand of apprenticeships occurs regularly in Norway and Denmark due to shifts in the business cycle and young people's preferences (Brunello, 2009). In addition, structural changes in many industries tend to raise the entrance requirements set by firms for giving students access to work-based training (Jørgensen, 2015). Due to the increasing standards of efficiency and quality in production, the employers are increasing the requirements for maturity and self-regulation of the apprentices. The high investment costs per job in industry reduces the room for students' learning-by-doing. Tighter production chains and high-quality production standards reduce the room for making errors while learning. In addition, the shift towards a more short-term shareholder economy, challenges employers' commitment to collective and long-term investments in occupational training (Jørgensen, 2015).

The Swedish VET system shares a strong tradition of central state regulation with the Finnish VET system, but it has been strongly decentralised since the reform in 1991 (Lundahl et al., 2013). In a process of deregulation, control has been transferred, first to the municipalities and later to the local upper secondary schools. As a unique initiative in a Nordic context, the Swedish government allowed privatisation of upper secondary schools. Private schools enrol around one quarter of all VET students. Previously, large companies established so-called industrial schools in close connection to their production facilities (Nilsson, 2013). These industrial schools became popular because they offered smooth access to employment. The neo-liberal privatisations in the 1990s gave rise to large school corporations that can extract profits and go bankrupt (Rönnberg, 2017). One of the intentions of this marketization is to loosen the municipal control of the upper secondary schools and make them more responsive to demands in the labour market. However, the financing of the schools depends on the enrolment of students and the production of graduates, which means that the schools compete more on attracting students than on meeting the demands in the labour market. In addition, the decentralisation of the VET system means that the degree of specialisations and the links to companies differ significantly between municipalities. The local diversity of VET reduces the portability of the skills provided and makes it difficult for students and companies to assess the value of the programmes. Moreover, the transition from state to market regulation of skill production faces a collective action problem. When collective employer interest in training is not institutionalised, the individual employers tend to underinvest in training (Crouch et al., 2001). The marketization of the vocational schools has aggravated the mismatch problems in the labour market (Olofsson and Panican, 2012). In contrast, the Swedish post-secondary apprenticeship programmes in some industries demonstrate how collective interest can be organised without state support. Another promising example is the emerging 'Vocational Colleges' (*yrkescollege*), which bring together employers, vocational schools and municipalities in the regions in order to safeguard the quality and relevance of the VET system (see Chapter 5).

Choice and selection in the transition process

Students' transitions through VET and into the labour market are shaped through the interaction between the students' agency and the institutional architecture of the VET system. The Nordic model of education emphasises equality of educational opportunities for all, and the rights of the individual students to choose their own educational pathway. In spite of these egalitarian aims, students' pathways and choices are still influenced by their family background, geographical location and gender. In all the Nordic countries, the enrolment of students in upper secondary education has a persistent social bias (Blossfeld et al., 2016). The proportion of students from families with a higher education is two to three times higher in the general programmes compared to the vocational programmes. Students in peripheral areas mostly chose a local upper secondary school, and especially in Denmark and Norway, they often have a limited choice of vocational programmes in the local area. In Sweden, the educational options and the municipal support for transition differ considerably between the localities as a result of the decentralisation of educational governance (Lundahl and Olofsson, 2014). In addition, in all four countries, most of the vocational programmes are highly gendered, which mirrors the strong horizontal gender segregation, which persists in the Nordic labour markets (Jarman et al., 2012). The gendered images of occupational identities tend to shape young peoples' aspirations for an 'appropriate' choice of education. Students from ethnic minorities tend to be disadvantaged in the education system, especially in getting access to apprenticeships. Across countries, the dropout rates are higher for gender and ethnic minorities than for majority students (Hjelmér et al., 2010).

This segregation in the Nordic upper secondary schools can partly be explained by the social shaping of young peoples' choices and aspirations. It can also be explained by the processes of assessment, categorisation and selection in the school systems. One purpose of the VET systems is to guide and select students into different fields of work in accordance with the demands of the employment system. The students are assessed in tests and exams; they are given teachers' and trainers' attention and recognition; and they become part of peer groups or are excluded from these groups (Hjelmér et al., 2010; Jørgensen, 2016; Brunila et al., 2011). Furthermore, they are positioned as immigrants, boys or girls, separated into groups and classes at different levels, sanctioned for absence or arriving late, and guided into different programmes (Lappalainen et al., 2013). Some students are expelled from the vocational schools, while others feel disappointed, drop out or switch to another programme. In Norway and Denmark, students' access to apprenticeships is to a large extent an individual responsibility, and their success depends on their social and family network. While the shorter internships in the Swedish and Finnish VET programmes are organised by the vocational schools, the task of finding a post-secondary apprenticeship in Sweden lies mainly with the individual student (Fjellström, 2014). In addition to weaker social networks, ethnic minority youths encounter discrimination when they are looking for a training placement. This can explain why young immigrants have a higher risk of unemployment in countries where the education system is more vocationally oriented (Lancee, 2016).

The organisation of educational choice

A key question for all the VET systems is how to organise the processes of choice and the selection of students into different programmes. This is a particular challenge in the Norwegian and the Danish apprenticeships, which include extensive occupational specialisation (Olsen, 2013). The Danish VET system offers 106 occupations, with more than 300 specialisations, while the Norwegian VET system offers more than 50 specialisations in year 2, and around 180 in year 3 and 4. The VET programmes in Norway and Denmark are based on the occupational principle and offer an alternative work-based learning environment, compared to the more 'bookish' upper secondary school. It thereby supports the transition to employment for young people who have grown tired of school-based education. A challenge for these systems is that the students have to choose at an early age between a broad range of occupations, about which they usually have little knowledge. Some students are attracted to a specific occupation, which they expect to learn from the start of the programme, while others need to try out different occupations before they can choose.

All the Nordic VET systems have adapted to the model of gradual choice and specialisation. They start with broad introductory programmes, which qualify the students for subsequent specialisations. In 1994, the Norwegian VET system reorganised more than 100 programmes into 12 broad basic courses in the first year, and 50 specialisations in the second year. As this led to a mismatch between students' choices and labour market requirements, the reform in 2006 postponed the specialisation until the third year, when the apprenticeship started. The aim of broadening the second-year courses was to enable more vocational schools to provide the full range of courses locally, even in smaller schools. Another aim was to broaden the range of specific occupations the students could apply for, when they shifted into apprenticeships in the third year. The objective was to create a better balance between the training companies' and the students' demands for training placements. However, as a result of the broadening of the programmes, their vocational profiles became unclear and their relationship to the labour market became weaker in the two first years (Olsen, 2013). This made the programmes demotivating for some students, who were attracted by a specific occupation such as carpenter or hairdresser. Moreover, employers criticised the broad programmes for offering too little specific vocational qualifications, which impeded the students' transition

From vocational education to employment   37

to employment (Nyen and Tønder, 2014). However, the formation of coherent VET systems and their gradual integration into a national system of upper secondary education has made the VET programmes broader, more general and standardised (Olsen, 2013). In addition to bureaucratic and economic reasons, this is driven by the wish to ease the transition to higher education and increase social mobility.

In the Finnish VET system, the students have to choose between seven broad fields of study and around 120 study programmes in total. The VET programmes have a module structure and give the students the right to flexible and versatile programmes with an individual study plan. The Swedish VET system generally has broad programmes with more emphasis on general subjects than on vocational specialisation. Therefore, the students' choices here are less challenging and specific than in the Norwegian and Danish apprenticeships. However, there are significant differences between programmes and schools. In the construction programmes examined by Fjellström (2014), the process of specialisation is organised in a similar way as in the Norwegian VET system. In the first year, the students try out the various occupations ('taster' courses) and choose one of them (e.g. carpenter) for specialisation during the final two years. The specific vocational training takes place two days every week in a workshop or workplace, while the other three days are allocated for school-based teaching of general subjects.

In the Danish VET system, the early choice of occupational specialisation in apprenticeships has consistently been considered a reason for the high rate of dropout among students. The broad, one-year, school-based introductory courses were established to prepare students for a qualified choice of specialisation in an apprenticeship. However, reforms have shifted between broad and specific entrance courses. A reform in 2006 emphasised that the students should encounter a specific occupation from the first week in the vocational school in order to meet the expectations of students who had made a clear choice of occupation. The argument was that the broad and general introductory programmes demotivated this group of students. In a reform in 2014, the prevention of dropout was an argument for organising the VET system with only four broad introductory courses. The aim was to prepare the students to make a qualified choice by offering them experiences with a variety of programmes during the first six months (Jørgensen, 2016).

The oscillation of policy in Denmark and Norway indicates that policies in this field involve a trade-off between the advantages of a gradual choice of specialisation, and the advantages of the students' early engagement with specific occupational work tasks. In Norway, the trade-off was managed in 2006 by introducing internships as a new subject, the 'vocational specialisation' ('in-depth study project'), in the first two broad years of the VET programmes (Høst, 2012). In this subject, the students gain experience from in-company training in one or more specific occupations, and qualify their subsequent choice of specialisation. In addition, they become more motivated and can make contacts that may subsequently result in an apprenticeship contract. Since the reform

38   *Christian Helms Jørgensen and Anna Hagen Tønder*

in 2014 in Denmark, the trade-off is managed through practical, theme-based and project-based teaching. The students have the opportunity to become acquainted with selected specific occupations and, at the same time, obtain a broader knowledge of the whole industry. They get hands-on experience from occupational work and become better prepared to make a qualified choice of a specific vocational programme.

Employment protection and students' transitions to work

Newly graduated VET students' access to employment depends very much on the general employment situation, as young people entering the labour market are most severely affected by rising unemployment. The transition to the labour market also depends on the structure and functioning of the labour market. Strong occupational labour markets that correspond to specific VET programmes, tend to make transitions easier (Müller, 2005; Raffe, 2014). Occupational labour markets are more predominant in countries with VET systems with relatively high specificity of vocational qualifications, like Norway and Denmark. Differences in employment protection is another explanation for the diversity in young peoples' transitions to the labour market (Breen, 2005; Noelke, 2015; Wolbers, 2007). The negative consequences of employment protection for young people entering the labour market has been emphasised in an insider-outsider perspective (Barbieri and Cutuli, 2015). However, a number of positive wider benefits of employment protection have been identified in relation to vocational education.

Estevez-Abe et al. (2001) emphasise the role of employment protection for the protection of individuals' and companies' investment in skills. Employment protection reduces employers' opportunistic hiring and firing practices, improves employees' job security and contributes to labour market stability. In addition, employment protection features as a 'beneficial constraint' (Streeck, 1989) that increases employers' incentives to invest in their employees in order to raise their internal flexibility, instead of the 'hire and fire' practices of external flexibility. The standardised certification of vocational education helps to protect the value of occupational skills in the labour market, and enhances the matching of education and jobs (Levels et al., 2014). The strong involvement of the labour market organisations in quality control, examination and certification processes, provides the journeyman's certificate with a high level of legitimacy in the labour market and reduces the risk of unemployment after completing a VET programme (Müller, 2005). Employment protection reduces the likelihood of newcomers in the labour market becoming unemployed, once they have entered their first significant job (Wolbers, 2007).

Labour market protection legislation has been a part of the Social Democratic policy to increase social security for workers and reduce the instability of the capitalist economies. The strength of employment protection differs significantly between the Nordic countries, with Sweden (3.0) having the strongest protection, Finland (2.6) and Norway (2.5) medium, and Denmark (1.5) the lowest protection (OECD, 2012). While temporary employment in Sweden is weakly regulated, the Swedish labour market regulations impose extensive restrictions of employers' dismissal practices. The Danish labour market regulation has very few restrictions (Emmenegger, 2010), which form part of the Danish 'flexicurity' regime, which combines relatively generous (though declining) unemployment benefits and liberal dismissal regulations, with a strong active labour market policy (Madsen et al., 2013). As a consequence, the Danish labour market has one of the highest rates of job mobility in Europe. This is an advantage for newcomers to the labour market, as it creates many job openings (Berglund et al., 2010). Comparing the Nordic labour markets, Svalund (2013) finds that strict regulations of temporary employment transfer unemployed youth into the labour market through safe, permanent employment contracts. To conclude, the considerable differences in employment protection, especially between Sweden and Denmark, can help to explain the differences in the transition from VET to employment.

Reviving apprenticeships in the Nordic countries

Apprenticeships had little relevance for the new unified and non-selective upper secondary school system established in the 1960s and 1970s in accordance with the ideals of the Nordic model of education. Apprenticeship appeared to be an institution of the past that should be discarded due to its narrow and firm-specific training, early tracking and the exploitation and abuse of young people (Nilsson, 2013; Michelsen and Stenström, 2018). The apprenticeship contract tied the apprentice to a specific company for years. Moreover, apprenticeships were associated with traditional, artisan work practices that were being displaced by new technologies and modern forms of production. As apprenticeships mainly convey specific vocational skills, they were inadequate for preparing young people for mobility and flexibility in the labour market of the future. These were the most common arguments against apprenticeships in the decades when the Nordic type of comprehensive school was extended to the upper secondary level. The disapproval of apprenticeships came from all sides, both the employers' and the employees' organisations (Lundahl, 1997).

Apprenticeships only survived in a very marginal position in Sweden and Finland following the educational reforms of the early 1970s. Even in Denmark, a coalition of the dominant labour market organisations and the government agreed in 1976 to abolish apprenticeships (*mesterlæren*). Due to a change in the political climate, a modernised form of apprenticeship has developed as the core of the VET system in Denmark. In successive reforms, the apprenticeship system was standardised and extended into new fields to cover the entire labour market, including health, services, administration and retail. In Norway, school-based VET was integrated with general education in 1975 in a new comprehensive upper-secondary school system. Apprenticeships were left outside as a separate institution governed by the labour market organisations. It had its own law in 1981, which included adults, and employers in Norway continued to embrace apprenticeships as an important source for the supply of skilled labour (Olsen et al., 2014). This was not the case in Sweden and Finland, where the state did not support a modernisation of apprenticeships, which gradually eroded.

From the 1980s, the mainly negative image of apprenticeships changed among policy-makers. A rehabilitation took place in education policy in all the Nordic countries, not only of apprenticeship, but also of new forms of work-based training. Many factors were involved in this shift. One of them was the collapse of many traditional industries and the soaring levels of youth unemployment in the 1980s and 1990s. The apprenticeship model was associated with a smooth transition to stable employment and low levels of youth unemployment for young people who were not continuing to higher education (Müller, 2005; Raffe, 2014; Andersen and Werfhorst, 2010; Bol and Werfhorst, 2013). In research, four social mechanisms are emphasised to explain the quality of apprenticeships. One is the gradual socialisation to work life that takes place as an integral part of training in the workplace (Jørgensen, 2013). The workplace training provides occupational skills that are portable in an occupational labour market beyond the company. Another mechanism is the transparency of the system for young people. The choice of an apprenticeship is known to provide access to a specific type of occupation, which has the role of a 'sign post', guiding young people's transition to employment (Heinz, 2009). For the apprentices, learning a vocation is a process of becoming and belonging (Chan, 2013). Thirdly, the close involvement of the labour market organisations in the governance of the VET system guarantees a high degree of legitimacy and recognition of apprenticeship (Streeck, 1989). Lastly, many companies regard recruitment as an important motive for training apprentices. Two thirds of apprentices in Norway and Denmark continue as regular employees in the training company after completion. In many cases, the apprentices do not experience this shift in status as a significant transition (Jørgensen, 2013; Nyen et al., 2015). This is a great advantage in comparison to school-based VET systems, even if they include shorter work-based training periods.

Since the early 1990s, all four Nordic countries have taken initiatives to strengthen or revive apprenticeship programmes. The following section explores why these initiatives have been successful in Norway and Denmark, but not in Finland or Sweden.

The reform in Norway in 1994 established a standard model for VET, which integrated school-based VET and apprenticeships into a hybrid system of two years of comprehensive, school-based courses followed by two years of work-based apprenticeships. Young people were given priority, as they were given a statutory right to an upper secondary education. While school-based VET and apprenticeships had previously been competitors, they were now merged into a system that combined the advantages of equity of the comprehensive school with the employability provided by apprenticeships. The state could guarantee the first two years in a school, but providing apprenticeships became a key challenge. A variety of measures were taken. The training companies were awarded

From vocational education to employment 41

substantial state subsidies. This was used to finance the local training agencies (LTAs) that took on a coordinating and monitoring role, and relieved the companies of administrative burdens. Corporatist collaboration on apprenticeships was strengthened in order to commit employers to establish training placements. Students who were unable to obtain an apprenticeship were offered a third year of school-based training, leading to the journeyman's certificate. And to make it less risky to choose a vocational programme, students were given the opportunity to shift to an academic programme after two years, without extension of the programme. Measured by enrolments, the new VET system became a success, as the number of students tripled after the reform (Olsen et al., 2014). This increase was partly due to the expansion of the system into sectors like health care and social work, cleaning services, commerce and office work. As shown in Chapter 6, the new apprenticeship system is less successful in the health sector, where the recruitment of experienced adults continues, and in retail and office work, where few skilled job positions are available for the VET students (Reegård, 2017).

In Sweden, the reintroduction of apprenticeships took place in 2011 in connection with a major reform of upper secondary education. The reform was part of a broader shift of VET policy towards the world of work. It was intended as a systemic shift and a reversal of the reform in 1991 that linked VET closer to higher education. The reform in 2011 introduced a new apprenticeship programme in upper secondary education, where more than half of the time must be devoted to work-based training. In addition, the vocational schools had to establish local programme committees for cooperation with work life. However, the apprenticeship programme has been a limited success, as it has attracted far fewer students than expected by the initiators of the reform and the dropout rate is high (Skolverket, 2013). The main reason is that the apprenticeship programme does not provide eligibility for higher education. Similar weaknesses characterise the adult apprenticeship programme (*'yrkesvux'*), which gives priority to applicants with the weakest employment chances who have little and weakly regulated work-based learning (Olofsson and Panican, 2012). The main motive for introducing apprenticeships in Sweden was to reduce the rate of dropout from upper secondary schools and to offer early school leavers and low-performing students an alternative pathway to employment. From the start, apprenticeships appeared to be more a tool for social policy than for meeting the skill requirements of the labour market. The apprenticeships were mainly an initiative organised by the state with low employer involvement. Students in this programme are not employed by the training company, and the programme does not have the qualities to be categorised as an 'apprenticeship' by Cedefop (2016). Despite the reform in 2011, the links between the Swedish VET system and the labour market are significantly weaker than in Norway and Denmark (Persson Thunqvist and Hallqvist, 2014). In this respect, the state-led apprenticeship programme differs significantly from the Swedish employer-driven post-secondary apprenticeships (*'färdigutbildning'*, see Chapter 7). This scheme demonstrates a weakness of the comprehensive

Nordic Model of upper secondary education. Because of its weak links to the labour market, employers in some industries have maintained an independent, post-secondary apprenticeship programme outside the public upper secondary school system, for example for construction workers, plumbers, hairdressers and electricians. These apprenticeship programmes are controlled by a trade committee ('*Yrkesnämnd*') for each occupation, with representatives of the labour market organisations. The programmes have a duration of one to two years and are completed with a journeyman's certificate that gives access to skilled employment. Although these post-secondary apprenticeships are only institutionalised in some areas, they demonstrate three points. The first is the significance of collective skill formation (Busemeyer and Trampusch, 2012), even in Sweden, where there is a strong tradition for state-organised VET. The second is the importance for employment of having specific vocational skills, acquired through work-based learning. The third is the significance of standardisation and certification of these skills by an institution with high credibility in the labour market.

In Finland, apprenticeships have mainly been intended for adults. The employers have taken no responsibility for the initial training of newcomers to their field of industry, and training has been left to the state and the municipalities. In the early 1990s, apprenticeship training was promoted as an alternative for young people, but it did not have the expected success (Stenström and Virolainen, 2014). In 2014, apprenticeship was presented as part of a 'youth guarantee' that was targeted at youth without any upper secondary qualifications, but it only has a marginal position today.

In order to increase the opportunities for work-based learning, the governments in all the Nordic countries offer subsidies to raise the quantity and quality of internships and apprenticeships in the VET programmes. State funding was important for the exceptional growth in apprenticeships in Norway since 1994, and for the operation of the Norwegian training agencies. When the new apprenticeship programme was introduced in Sweden in 2011, a state subsidy was included to improve the cooperation between vocational schools and training companies (Olofsson and Panican, 2012). In Denmark, the employers' payment of a training levy depends on the number of training placements offered by the company in relation to quotas set by the state. In Finland, providers of education can pay employers a sum for the guidance given to students in internships.

The examination of Nordic initiatives to promote apprenticeships shows that they have been successful in Norway and Denmark, but not in Sweden and Finland. The Norwegian case in particular demonstrates that education policy has the capacity to successfully expand enrolment levels in the apprenticeship system and extend apprenticeship into new sectors. However, the fulfilment of a set of institutional conditions are required in order to successfully develop apprenticeships (Ryan, 2012). Apprenticeship schemes are not likely to gain high esteem among students or employers, if they are initiated by the state as a social policy measure. Employer organisations must be strongly involved in

From vocational education to employment   43

the design and organisation of apprenticeships in order to guarantee the quality of the programmes. Viable apprenticeship systems require a complex institutional framework, which includes collective employer engagement in training, occupational labour markets and the protection of vocational skills. Moreover, the Nordic apprenticeship systems rely on state subsidies (and in Denmark, on a training levy) that distribute the costs of training among all employers. In addition, collective agreements must set apprentices' wage high enough to limit employers' exploitation of their cheap labour, yet low enough to make apprentices attractive for employers.

Conclusions

The examination of the connections between VET and the world of work in the Nordic countries has demonstrated the different systems of coordination regimes. Their strengths and weaknesses are summarised here. The central state planning can take a holistic perspective that addresses long-term shifts in the labour market through forecasting and planning, as demonstrated in Finland. However, this is not very reliable in a period of political instability, rapid technological shifts and volatile markets. State initiatives to rationalise and integrate upper secondary education in a coherent system tend to crowd out the employers and to be insensitive to the specific requirements of individual occupations. This weakens the coordination between education and work and tends to make the students' transition from VET to employment difficult and prolonged.

The decentralised and market-based regulation of the relations between VET and the employment system can provide flexible VET programmes adjusted to local requirements, which can ease the students' access to the local labour market. However, the weak standardisation of skills tends to aggravate matching problems by reducing the portability of skills in the labour market and by making school-to-work transitions demanding. The decentralisation and marketization of education tends to increase inequalities between schools, due to the polarising effects of free school choice, as has been demonstrated in Sweden (Lundahl and Olofsson, 2014; Rudolphi and Erikson, 2016).

The dual-corporatist regime provides a strong institutional framework for cooperation between the state and the labour market organisations for the adaptation of VET to the demands in the labour market. It gives priority to occupational skills and a strong national standardisation of skills, which improves the portability of skills and the mobility in occupational labour markets. The certification of skills has high validity due to the high involvement of the employers in the plural governance structure of VET (Høst, 2012). The students' transition from VET to employment is integrated into the vocational programmes, and after completion, the majority of apprentices in Norway and Denmark progress seamlessly into ordinary employment. However, this regime is associated with tracking of upper secondary education, social inequality and diversion of students from higher education (Müller, 2005).

The comparison of transitions from VET to the labour market in four Nordic countries has identified some general trends and many differences. All four VET systems have become more school-based and more separated from work-life. Preparatory school-based education of one to three years' duration has been included in the programmes before the students get experience from internships or apprenticeships. In all four countries, young peoples' school-to-work transitions tend to become prolonged and non-linear, and the completion of upper secondary education and the transition to work is postponed until a later average age of the students. Considerably more young people in Sweden and Finland take the direct route through the school-based upper secondary school and complete their training within the expected time compared to Norway and Denmark, where more young people drop out of VET, but where more are also in employment and fewer are unemployed (Albæk et al., 2015). This indicates that the transition through the VET systems with apprenticeships is more difficult, but that the transition to employment is easier. One reason is the challenges for students associated with obtaining an apprenticeship contract, and their shift from school to work-based training and to a new social environment in a training company, which involves an increased risk of dropping out. In contrast, students in the Swedish school-based VET programmes follow the same peer group through three years in age-homogeneous classes. The drop-out rates from school-based programmes are generally lower than from work-based programmes (Segendorf, 2013), even when the effects of the differences in the social background of the students in the VET programmes is taken into account (Markussen, 2010). However, work-based training can engage young people who have grown tired of schools and are focused on finding a job. Apprenticeships improve the transition to work of students who acquire a training placement and complete the programme. However, apprenticeships are demanding for young people, and they are generally not a tool for reducing early school leaving (Bäckman et al., 2015).

It is a general trend that the qualifications provided by the Nordic VET systems have become broader and less specific, especially in the first years of the programmes. However, we have found oscillations between making the programmes broader and more specific. VET has been integrated into a comprehensive upper secondary school system in all countries, except Denmark. VET in Sweden is preparatory and postpones more of the specific training until after the transition to the labour market. In Norway and Denmark, the initial school-based courses have become broader, while the subsequent apprenticeships are still highly specialised (180–300 specialisations). In all countries, the VET systems have expanded into new sectors, although with varying success. The initiatives in Norway to establish new apprenticeship programmes in the service sector (health, retail, office work) have demonstrated the limits of political intervention, if the programmes do not give access to full-time skilled jobs (Reegård, 2017).

Work-based learning had a very limited role in the ideal of the Nordic model of comprehensive schooling in the 1970s. The dominant assumption was that broad and general qualifications were essential, both for citizenship, promoting

From vocational education to employment   45

equal access to higher education and for achieving long-term employability (Lundahl, 1997; Ledman, 2014). In addition, the employers' control of the training opportunities for young people was not consistent with the Social Democratic idea of public provision of education for all. Apprenticeship programmes involve a conflict between the principle of free and equal access to upper secondary education, and the distribution of apprenticeships in a training market, which is selective and dependent on the business cycle. However, the Swedish employer-driven post-secondary apprenticeship programme (*'färdigutbildning'*) demonstrates the engagement of the employers in some industries in collective skill formation. The last two decades have witnessed growing political recognition of working life as an important learning environment for acquiring multiple types of generic, social, personal and specific skills that are difficult to provide in a school. However, all the Nordic countries find the provision of access to high-quality training placements or internships to be a challenge.

Policy-makers have increasingly regarded VET as an option for early school leavers and disadvantaged youth. VET is identified as a solution to the challenge of having all young people complete an upper secondary education programme. Consequently, there is a conflict between the employers' increasing requirements when recruiting for apprenticeships, and governments' education policy using work-based learning for social inclusion in VET. In all four countries, governments have tried to reinforce the link between VET and the labour market in order to improve the employability of the students (Raffe, 2011). However, there can be a trade-off between short-term and long-term employability. High specificity of the vocational qualifications in the VET programmes improves the students' rapid and direct access to employment, but entails a risk of lower long-term mobility in the labour market (Bol and de Werfhorst, 2013). However, the Danish case demonstrates that this risk can be offset by a flexible labour market and a strong public system of CVET and adult education (Jørgensen, 2013; Trampusch and Eichenberger, 2012).

The comparison shows that the diverging institutional architectures of the Nordic transition systems locate the risks at different points in the transition process. In Sweden and Finland, the choice of a vocational programme at upper secondary level offers direct progression to higher education, unlike the situation in Denmark and Norway. However, this risk of VET as a 'dead end' is reduced in Norway due to the opportunity to shift horizontally into a general programme after the second year. In Finland, general and vocational education are separated into different schools, but they all offer access to higher education, as they do in Sweden. In Sweden, however, more than half of the VET students do not attain eligibility for higher education. In the Norwegian and the Danish apprenticeship systems, the highest risks are located inside the programmes, in the transition from school-based training to work-based apprenticeships. This transition is strongly regulated and supported by the education system – and in Norway by the training agencies (see Chapter 5). This contrasts with the school-based systems of Sweden and Finland, where the highest risks occur after completion, in the transition from education to the labour market.

The apprenticeship programmes in Norway and Denmark offer clear alternatives to the academic upper secondary school. The standardised apprenticeship programmes offer distinct occupational identities that assist young peoples' educational choices. The apprenticeship programmes support the social inclusion of youth from disadvantaged social backgrounds. However, these programmes also tend to exclude minorities, due to the strong gender segregation in VET and the disadvantage of ethnic minorities in their access to training placements. Moreover, in the predominantly male apprenticeship programmes, practical skills tend to be positioned in opposition to academic education as part of a traditional culture of masculinity. Thus, the general-vocational divide is reproduced, and youths from lower educated families are diverted from academic education (Brockmann and Laurie, 2016).

The chapter's examination of the Nordic VET systems indicates a number of trade-offs for policy and didactics. The organisation of choice and specialisation in VET involves contradictory effects of both early and late specialisation. School-based systems can be more caring and inclusive for vulnerable youths, but can have high dropout rates for students who are tired of school. Systems based on apprenticeships are more inclusive for young people from families with low levels of education, but tend to be more gender segregated and less inclusive for ethnic and gender minorities. Such systems provide high short-term employment rates, but tend to have lower long-term employment rates. The school-based and comprehensive upper secondary school that offer eligibility for higher education promotes educational equality, but tend to be less inclusive for students from families with low levels of education. A basic lesson is that VET is a complex field with multiple interests and diverse policy aims, and policy making therefore tends to involve trade-offs. Managing the complex trade-offs calls for an approach to policy-making other than the widespread interest in 'best practices' to optimise performance indicators one at a time. Managing trade-offs requires systematic considerations of the potential unintended consequences of policy measures and the diverse effects of these measures for different groups of students and programmes. In addition to deliberate considerations of the contradictory effects of political interventions, policies can search for opportunities to circumvent the trade-offs through innovations of institutions and practices in VET, as shown in Chapter 5.

References

AE. (2016) *8 ud af 10 virksomheder beholder lærlingen efter endt uddannelse*, Copenhagen: Arbejderbevægelsens Erhvervsråd.

Ahola, S. (2012) 'Finsk yrkesfagutdanning (VET) og arbeidslivets behov', in Høst, H. (ed.) *Tradisjonelle utfordringer – fornyet interesse*, TemaNord 2012:503, Copenhagen, Nordic Council of Ministers.

Albæk, K., Asplund, R., Erling, B., Lindahl, L., von Simson, K., and Vanhala, P. (2015) *Youth Unemployment and Inactivity: A Comparison of School-to-Work Transitions and Labour Market Outcomes in Four Nordic Countries*, Copenhagen, Nordic Council of Ministers.

Andersen, R., and Van de Werfhorst, H. G. (2010) 'Education and occupational status in 14 countries: The role of educational institutions and labour market coordination', *The British Journal of Sociology*, vol. 61, no. 2, pp. 336–355.

Bäckman, O., Jakobsen, V., Lorentzen, T., Österbacka, E., and Dahl, E. (2015) 'Early school leaving in Scandinavia: Extent and labour market effects', *Journal of European Social Policy*, vol. 25, no. 3, pp. 253–269.

Ball, S. J. (2012) *Politics and Policy Making in Education: Explorations in Sociology*, London, Routledge.

Barbieri, P., and Cutuli, G. (2015) 'Employment protection legislation, labour market dualism, and inequality in Europe', *European Sociological Review*, vol. 32, no. 4, pp. 501–516.

Berglund, T., Aho, S., Furåker, B., Lovén, K., Madsen, P. K., Nergaard, K., and Virjo, I. (2010) *Labour Market Mobility in Nordic Welfare States*, Copenhagen, Nordic Council of Ministers.

Blossfeld, H., Buchholz, P. S., Skopek, J., and Triventi, M. (eds.) (2016) *Models of Secondary Education and Social Inequality: An International Comparison*, Northampton, Edward Elgar Publishing.

Bol, T., and van de Werfhorst, H. (2013) 'Educational systems and the trade-off between labour market allocation and equality of educational opportunity', *Comparative Education Review*, vol. 57, no. 2, pp. 285–308.

Breen, R. (2005) 'Explaining cross-national variation in youth unemployment: Market and institutional factors', *European Sociological Review*, vol. 21, no. 2, pp. 125–134.

Brockmann, M., and Laurie, I. (2016) 'Apprenticeship in England – the continued role of the academic – vocational divide in shaping learner identities', *Journal of Vocational Education & Training*, vol. 68, no. 2, pp. 229–244.

Brunello, G. (2009) 'The effect of economic downturns on apprenticeships and initial workplace training: A review of the evidence', *Empirical Research in Vocational Education and Training*, vol. 1, no. 2, pp. 145–171.

Brunila, K., Kurki, T., Lahelma, E., Lehtonen, J., Mietola, R., and Palmu, T. (2011) 'Multiple transitions: Educational policies and young people's post-compulsory choices', *Scandinavian Journal of Educational Research*, vol. 55, no. 3, pp. 307–324.

Busemeyer, M. R., and Trampusch, C. (2012) *The Political Economy of Collective Skill Formation*, Oxford, Oxford University Press.

Cedefop. (2016) *Governance and Financing of Apprenticeships*, Luxembourg, Publications Office of the European Union.

Chan, S. (2013) 'Learning through apprenticeship: Belonging to a workplace, becoming and being', *Vocations and Learning*, vol. 6, no. 3, pp. 367–383.

Crouch, C., Finegold, D., and Sako, M. (2001) *Are Skills the Answer? The Political Economy of Skill Creation in Advanced Industrial Countries*, Oxford, Oxford University Press.

Emmenegger, P. (2010) 'The long road to flexicurity', *Scandinavian Political Studies*, vol. 33, no. 3, pp. 271–294.

Estevez-Abe, M., Iversen, T., and Soskice, D. (2001) 'Social protection and the formation of skills: A reinterpretation of the welfare state', in Hall, P. and Soskice, D. (eds.) *Varieties of Capitalism: The Institutional Foundations of Comparative Advantage*, Oxford, Oxford University Press, pp. 145–183.

Eurostat. (2017) Available at http://ec.europa.eu/eurostat/

Fjellström, M. (2014) 'Vocational education in practice: A study of work-based learning in a construction programme at a Swedish upper secondary school', *Empirical Research in Vocational Education and Training*, vol. 6, no. 1, pp. 1–20.

Greinert, W-D. (2008) *Steuerungsformen von Erwerbsqualifizierung und die aktuelle Perspektive europäischer Berufsbildungspolitik*, Gütersloh, Bertelsmann Stiftung.

48 *Christian Helms Jørgensen and Anna Hagen Tønder*

Hampf, F., and Woessmann, L. (2016) *Vocational vs. General Education and Employment Over the Life-Cycle: New Evidence from PIAAC*, London, Centre for Vocational Educational Research.

Heinz, W. R. (2009) 'Structure and agency in transition research', *Journal of Education and Work*, vol. 22, no. 5, pp. 391–404.

Herschbach, D. R. (2009) 'Planning for Education and Work: Alternatives and Issues', in Maclean, R. and Wilson, D. (eds.) *International Handbook of Education for the Changing World of Work*, Dordrecht, Springer, pp. 939–959.

Hjelmér, C., Lappalainen, P. A., and Rosvall, P. Å. (2010) 'Time, space and young people's agency in vocational upper secondary education: A cross-cultural perspective', *European Educational Research Journal*, vol. 9, no. 2, pp. 245–256.

Høst, H. (2012) *Tradisjonelle utfordringer-fornyet interesse: Hvordan er de nordiske landes yrkesutdanninger i stand til å møte arbeidslivets behov?* Copenhagen, Nordic Council of Ministers.

Jarman, J., Blackburn, R. M., and Racko, G. (2012) 'The dimensions of occupational gender segregation in industrial countries', *Sociology*, vol. 46, no. 6, pp. 1003–1019.

Jørgensen, C. H. (2013) 'The role and meaning of vocations in the transition from education to work', *International Journal of Training Research*, vol. 11, no. 2, pp. 166–183.

Jørgensen, C. H. (2014) *The Current State of the Challenges for VET in Denmark*, Roskilde, Roskilde University. Available at www.Nord-VET.dk

Jørgensen, C. H. (2015) 'Challenges for work-based learning in vocational education and training in the Nordic countries', in Bohlinger, S., Haake, U., Jørgensen, C. H., Toiviainen, H., and Wallo, A. (eds.) *Working and Learning in Times of Uncertainty*, Rotterdam, Sense Publishers.

Jørgensen, C. H. (2016) 'Shifting problems and shifting policies to reduce students' dropout: – the case of vocational education policy in Denmark', in Bohlinger, S., Dang, K. A., and Klatt, G. (eds.) *Education Policy: Mapping the Landscape and Scope*, Bern, Peter Lang, pp. 325–353.

Juul, I., and Jørgensen, C. H. (2011) 'Challenges for the dual system and occupational self-governance in Denmark', *Journal of Vocational Education & Training*, vol. 63, no. 3, pp. 289–303.

Kettunen, P. (2013) 'Vocational education and the tensions of modernity in a Nordic periphery', in Buchardt, M., Markkola, P., and Valtonen, H. (eds.) *Education, State and Citizenship*, Helsinki, NordWel, pp. 31–55.

Lancee, B. (2016) 'The negative side effects of vocational education: A cross-national analysis of the relative unemployment risk of young non-western immigrants in Europe', *American Behavioral Scientist*, vol. 60, no. 5–6, pp. 659–679.

Lappalainen, S., Mietola, R., and Lahelma, E. (2013) 'Gendered divisions on classed routes to vocational education', *Gender and Education*, vol. 25, no. 2, pp. 189–205.

Ledman, K. (2014) 'Till nytta eller onytta: Argument rörande allmänna ämnen i ungas yrkesutbildning i efterkrigstidens Sverige', *Nordic Journal of Educational History*, vol. 1, no. 1, pp. 21–43.

Levels, M., Van der Velden, R., and Di Stasio, V. (2014) 'From school to fitting work How education-to-job matching of European school leavers is related to educational system characteristics', *Acta Sociologica*, vol. 57, no. 4, pp. 341–361.

Lundahl, L. (1997) *Efter svensk modell: LO, SAF och utbildningspolitiken 1944–90*, Umeå, Boréa.

Lundahl, L., Arreman, I. E., Holm, A. S., and Lundström, U. (2013) 'Educational marketization the Swedish way', *Education Inquiry*, vol. 4, no. 3, pp. 497–517.

Lundahl, L., and Olofsson, J. (2014) 'Guarded transitions? Youth trajectories and school-to-work transition policies in Sweden', *International Journal of Adolescence and Youth*, vol. 19, sup1, pp. 19–34.

Madsen, P. K., Molina, O., Møller, J., and Lozano, M. (2013) 'Labour market transitions of young workers in Nordic and southern European countries: The role of flexicurity', *Transfer: European Review of Labour and Research*, vol. 19, no. 3, pp. 325–343.

Markussen, E. (2010) *Frafall i utdanning for 16–20 åringer i Norden*, Copenhagen, Nordic Council of Ministers.

Michelsen, S., and Stenström, M-L. (2018) *Vocational Education in the Nordic Countries: The Historical Evolution*, London, Routledge.

Müller, W. (2005) 'Education and youth integration into European labour markets', *International Journal of Comparative Sociology*, vol. 46, no. 5–6, pp. 461–485.

Nilsson, A. (2013) 'Lärlingsutbildning – ett alternativ I yrkesutbildningen', in Håkansson, P. and Nilsson, A. (eds.) *Yrkesutbildningens formering i Sverige 1940–1975*, Lund, Nordic academic Press, pp. 87–120.

Noelke, C. (2015) 'Employment protection legislation and the youth labour market', *European Sociological Review*, vol. 32, no. 4, pp. 471–485.

Nyen, T., Skålholt, A., and Tønder, A. H. (2015) 'Vocational education and school to work transitions in Norway', in Bohlinger, S., Haake, U., Jørgensen, C. H., Toiviainen, H., and Wallo, A. (eds.) *Working and Learning in Times of Uncertainty*, Rotterdam, Sense Publishers.

Nyen, T., and Tønder, A. H. (2014) *Yrkesfagene under press*, Oslo, Universitetsforlaget.

OECD. (2012) *OECD Indicators on Employment Protection*, Paris, OECD Publishing.

Olofsson, J., and Panican, A. (2012) 'Den svenska yrkesutbildningsmodellen', in Høst, H. (ed.) *Tradisjonelle utfordringer – fornyet interesse*, Copenhagen, Nordic Council of Ministers.

Olsen, O. J. (2013) 'Bredde og fordypning i norsk fag-og yrkesopplæring – Spenninger i/mellom utdanning, arbeidsliv og perspektiver på læring', *Norsk pedagogisk tidsskrift*, vol. 97, no. 2, pp. 141–153.

Olsen, O. J., Høst, H., and Tønder, A. H. (2014) *Key Challenges for Norwegian VET: The State of Play*, Roskilde, Roskilde University. Available at www.Nord-VET.dk

Persson Thunqvist, D., and Hallqvist, A. (2014) *The Current State of the Challenges for VET in Sweden*, Roskilde, Roskilde University. Available at www.Nord-VET.dk

Raffe, D. (2011) 'Cross-national differences in education-work transitions', in London, M. (ed.) *The Oxford Handbook of Lifelong Learning*, New York, Oxford University Press, pp. 312–328.

Raffe, D. (2014) 'Explaining national differences in education-work transitions', *European Societies*, vol. 16, no. 2, pp. 175–193,

Reegård, K. (2017) 'Contrasting prospects: The institutionalisation of VET for retail and office work in Norway', *Journal of Vocational Education & Training*, vol. 69, no. 4., pp. 558–575.

Rönnberg, l. (2017) 'From national policy-making to global edubusiness: Swedish edupreneurs on the move', *Journal of Education Policy*, vol. 32, no. 2, pp. 234–249.

Rudolphi, F., and Erikson, R. (2016) 'Social selection in formal and informal tracking in Sweden', in Blossfeld, H. P., Buchholz, S., Skopek, J., and Triventi, M. (eds.) *Models of Secondary Education and Social Inequality: An International Comparison*, Cheltenham, Edward Elgar, pp. 165–179.

Ryan, P. (2012) 'Apprenticeship: Between theory and practice, school and workplace', in Pilz, M. (ed.) *The Future of Vocational Education and Training in a Changing World*, Dordrecht, Springer, pp. 402–432.

SCB. (2012) *Establishment on the Labour Market Three Years After Upper Secondary School*, Örebro, Statistics Sweden.

Segendorf, Å. O. (2013) *Unga i arbete i Norden. Ungas väg mot etablering på arbetsmarknaden i de nordiska länderna*, Copenhagen, Nordic Council of Ministers.

Skolverket. (2013) *Utvecklingen av lärlingsutbildningen*, Rapport 397, Stockholm, Skolverket.

50 *Christian Helms Jørgensen and Anna Hagen Tønder*

Stenström, M-L., and Virolainen, M. (2014) '*The Current State and Challenges of Vocational Education and Training in Finland*, Roskilde, Roskilde University. Available at www.Nord-VET.dk

Streeck, W. (1989) 'Skills and the limits of neo-liberalism: The enterprise of the future as a place of learning', *Work, Employment & Society*, vol. 3, no. 1, pp. 89–104.

Svalund, J. (2013) 'Labor market institutions, mobility, and dualization in the Nordic countries', *Nordic Journal of Working Life Studies*, vol. 3, no. 1, pp. 123–144.

Thelen, K. (2014) *Varieties of Liberalization and the New Politics of Social Solidarity*, Cambridge, Cambridge University Press.

Trampusch, C., and Eichenberger, P. (2012) 'Skills and industrial relations in coordinated market economies – continuing vocational training in Denmark, the Netherlands, Austria and Switzerland', *British Journal of Industrial Relations*, vol. 50, no. 4, pp. 644–666.

Wolbers, M. H. (2007) 'Patterns of labour market entry: A comparative perspective on school-to-work transitions in 11 European Countries', *Acta sociologica*, vol. 50, no. 3, pp. 189–210.

3 Progression to higher education from VET in Nordic countries

Mixed policies and pathways

Maarit Virolainen and Anna Hagen Tønder

Introduction: redefinitions of the universal policy and VET–HE relations

In the Nordic countries, general upper secondary education and initial VET constitute a particularly important selection process toward higher education (HE), especially as compulsory education (up to the completion of Grade 9 or Grade 10) in Nordic countries is comprehensive rather than stratified. Thus, the *unitary* compulsory school system in the Nordic countries can be contrasted with *stratified* compulsory education systems like the one in Germany. In the Nordic countries, the upper secondary education systems are stratified in the sense that the general upper secondary programmes and routes offer the most common and direct access to HE (Shavit and Müller, 2000). The Nordic countries' higher education systems have been associated with Social Democratic welfare states. In such welfare states, higher education is characterised by a relatively high share of public expenditure, high enrolment rates per age cohort, low or no student fees, generous grants and loans, and a low level of differentiation (Willemse and de Beer, 2012, p. 115). The Nordic higher education systems are binary in the sense that traditional science universities exist in parallel to the non-university sector of polytechnics or colleges (Jóhannsdóttir and Jónasson, 2014; Kyvik, 2004).

The education policies of the Nordic Social Democratic welfare states differ from those of other countries with either more conservative or liberal welfare regimes. On the one hand, in countries with more liberal regimes, like Australia, Canada, Ireland, New Zealand, the UK and the US, the share of public spending is relatively low, tuition fees are high and the level of vocational specificity in the programmes offered is low. On the other hand, more conservative regimes, such as Austria, Belgium, France, Germany, Italy, the Netherlands, Portugal, Spain and Switzerland, offer low-cost or free tuition but scant student grants or loans and are characterised by high levels of differentiation and high vocational specificity in their HE (Willemse and de Beer, 2012).

In recent decades, the Nordic countries have changed from their 'classical period' of the Social Democratic compromise toward more individualisation, decentralisation and education policies inspired by neo-liberal ideas. The classical period, which prioritised social equality in its educational policies, lasted from 1945 until around 1970 (Telhaug et al., 2006; Ahonen, 2002). In the last few decades, policies have put a stronger emphasis on economic competition between nations and on technical and instrumental goals. In accordance, policies have increasingly favoured efficiency, output management and adjustments to international resolutions on school reform while downplaying state control (Telhaug et al., 2006; Ahonen, 2002). With respect to the relation between VET and HE, this has meant a shift from 'widening participation' in HE to an emphasis on quality, the introduction of steering mechanisms, increased competitiveness of academic professionals, and elite orientation at traditional science universities associated with the discourse on globalisation (Pinheiro et al., 2014; Berggren and Cliffordson, 2012).

The binary structure of Nordic HE has resulted in transitions from VET to HE having steered mostly toward the more vocationally oriented universities of applied sciences (formerly called 'polytechnics') or colleges. The uncertainty regarding the labour market value of new programmes in HE has also contributed to changing transitional patterns, while a wider array of opportunities has challenged youths' choice making. It has become more difficult to forecast the benefits of various HE programmes for future careers. In the Nordic countries, delayed transitions to HE have been more common than in many other countries (Hauschildt et al., 2015, p. 35; Walther, 2009). In parallel, the role of HE with respect to equality has changed due to HE systems' massification in the Nordic countries. Once a HE system has become massified and universalised through expansion, it has lost part of its prominent role as a scapegoat to be blamed for limited access, increasing inequalities and elite favouritism (Brennan and Naidoo, 2008; Levin, 2003). At the same time, internal competition between HE institutions has emerged to spearhead academic stratification.

From HE institutions' perspective, the combination of decreased public funding and increased student participation has led to many kinds of responses internationally, such as a reduction in study programmes and greater emphasis on activities that increase revenues (Levin, 2003). Some HE institutions have also expressed disinterest in promoting equity while demonstrating an active willingness to limit access. In Finland, for example, some universities of applied sciences (UAS) have introduced entrance examinations for students with a VET background in the 2010s. Internationally, limiting access to HE for those with a VET background has been argued as being rational from the perspective of HE institutions for various reasons: social inclusion is not their primary responsibility, promoting wider inclusion threatens academic standards, and they cannot afford increasing their student intake via inclusion policies (see Brennan and Naidoo, 2008). The ongoing discussion about the access to HE via the VET route has involved various interest groups and stakeholders. It has become evident that this is an important area of educational policy, subject to continuous renegotiations. Transitioning from VET to HE has been a longstanding topic of concern, not only in connection with national education policies but also more internationally within the European Union and in the general research community (see, e.g., OECD, 2010; Hoelscher et al., 2008; Stenström and Lasonen, 2000; Trant, 1999; Lasonen and Young, 1998).

While VET's relationship with HE has been ambiguous and contested, VET has often been perceived as a choice for less ambitious youths or for those with lower career expectations (see, e.g., Brunila et al., 2011; Lahelma, 2009; Silver and Brennan, 1988). On the one hand, the opportunity to progress to HE has improved VET's status in Finland and Sweden since the 1990s, but not without those in favour of it having faced opposing policy discussions (Virolainen and Persson Thunqvist, 2017). The appreciation for practical training has a long history in the Nordic countries, with its cultural origin dating back to the 19th century. 'Learning by doing' has been characteristic in the progressivism of Nordic education (Thorsteinsson et al., 2016; Telhaug et al., 2006; Heikkilä, 2003). In recent years, international World Skills competitions, popular culture and TV shows have projected images of knowledgeable, competent, competitive, developing and highly skilled practitioners (e.g., chefs, carpenters, technicians) from a variety of occupational fields (Ruohotie et al., 2008). Furthermore, changes in the working world have increased the need for combining the skills of various formerly separate occupations in a hybrid way as part of new singular occupations. Accordingly, a sharp division between blue-collar and white-collar jobs has become rather outdated as skill demands have increased and become more complex across the board (e.g., Della Porta et al., 2015; Marcoux, 2010; Goos et al., 2009).

Changes in the working world and the development of new job profiles have led to the redefining of competence needs. The need to support the development of poly-contextual and boundary-crossing skills involving critical thinking, problem solving, communication, collaboration, creativity, controlling, evaluating, self-direction and digital literacy has been brought up to define targets for 21st century education (Winch, 2015; Trilling and Fadel, 2009; Guile, 2002). These shifts in the demand for skills have also addressed the need to rethink VET–HE relations. Wide unanimity prevails internationally concerning the need for lifelong learning competences as well as career management skills (see, e.g., European parliament, 2012; OECD, 2007). Altogether, changes in the labour market have accelerated the demand for opportunities to continue from VET to further and higher education. This chapter aims to provide knowledge on education policy and to help education planners consider the relations between VET and HE for future developments, particularly by reviewing the history of the Nordic VET–HE relationship.

Decisive turns of educational policy constructing transitions from VET to HE

This section describes, in broad terms, the decisive turning points by which transitional routes from VET to HE have been significantly altered in Nordic education systems since the 1960s. Since the Second World War, all Nordic countries (except Denmark as there presently is no VET to HE route there) have faced HE expansion to the extent of universal access (Börjesson et al., 2014). The transformation of HE systems has been a crucial part of changing VET-to-HE transitional patterns, particularly since vocational education and universities had very little interconnection prior to the Second World War. While the Nordic HE systems are relatively extensive compared to those of many other European countries, the expansion has led to student recruitment patterns having become more diverse. There has been a shift from cohesive and standardised systems administered by nation states toward more diverse, competitive, market- and efficiency-oriented international-style HE systems (Börjesson et al., 2014). Whereas the expansion of Nordic HE systems in the 1960s was related to demographic and economic growth, the expansion during the 1990s took place in circumstances of a declining youth population and economic crisis or stagnation (Börjesson et al., 2014).

Nordic HE institutions adopted the Bologna model at a different pace and their degree programmes vary in length and diversity. The Danish HE system has clear divisions between three main types of institutions: First, there are the academic- and research-based universities, which include two old universities and the younger regional universities established in the 1970s. Then, secondly, there are the university colleges (UC) that have been merged and strengthened over the last two decades. The UCs primarily provide education for students preparing for specific professions and only offer degrees up to the Bachelor's degree level. Finally, the third type is represented by the new vocational academies offering short-cycle and Bachelor's degrees, mainly in the fields of technological and business education (see Börjesson et al., 2014).

In parallel, in Norway, the HE system comprises universities, specialised university institutions and university colleges. In general, a higher education entrance qualification is required in order to enter any higher education institution. This qualification is obtained through a general study programme in upper secondary education. Some programmes, mainly in engineering, are open to students from vocational programmes through the vocational pathway ('Y-veien', in Norwegian). In these programmes, admission is based on a relevant craft or journeyman's certificate. Vocational colleges ('fagskoler', in Norwegian) offer post-secondary vocational education outside the higher education sector. The vocational colleges offer short programmes (between six months and two years of study) that are based on upper secondary education and work experience.

In Sweden, the HE institutions include universities, specialised institutions, art institutions, university colleges and health colleges. They offer a large diversity of degrees with various durations compared to HE institutions in the other Nordic countries (Börjesson et al., 2014). In Finland, the HE system consists of traditional science universities and universities of applied sciences (UAS) ('ammattikorkeakoulut – AMKs', in Finnish), the latter of which were established on the basis of the former vocational colleges in the 1990s (Böckerman et al., 2009). In general, Norway and Denmark offer more HE in specialised HE institutions than is the case in Finland and Sweden (Börjesson et al., 2014).

Progression to higher education from VET 55

Nordic countries have emphasised universal access to HE and promoted VET and general upper secondary education be given equal status due to the increasing emphasis on societal equality and in reaction to an increasingly knowledge-driven economy. In accordance, each Nordic country has developed bridging solutions to provide high-performing VET graduates access to HE. At times, these measures have had unintended consequences that have worked against the intensions and aims of policy-makers. The measures taken to provide access to HE via VET as well as their outcomes are described in more detail per Nordic country as follows. The description starts with the countries that have constructed more stratified systems, Denmark and Norway, and continues with Sweden and Finland, which although having built more unified systems have recently also been reformed further in regard to VET–HE transitional options.

Denmark

In Denmark, a crucial post-war turning point for access from VET to HE was in the 1960s, when the number of applicants to the apprenticeship system declined and the drop-out rate increased (Albæk, 2004; Betænkning, no. 612, 1971). The crisis of the apprenticeship system created demand for a reform. Reducing social inequality in connection with the limited access to HE was an explicit objective of the reform proposals (Juul, 2006). While a reform proposal suggested the coordination of the general and vocational upper secondary education routes, detracking upper secondary education was opposed by the right wing of the parliament and major labour market organisations (Christensen, 1978). The outcome of the modified reform in 1976 was that a new programme, Initial Vocational Education ('*Erhvervsfaglig Grunduddannelse* – EFG', in Danish) was introduced parallel to the traditional apprenticeship system. It started with a one-year basic course including 40% general subjects. The resulting parallel programmes – apprenticeships and EFG programmes – were combined in consecutive reforms, one in 1991 and another in 2000, where the separation of VET from the gymnasium, the major route of general upper secondary education, was maintained (Jørgensen, 2018).

Alongside the apprenticeship track and EFG programmes, two types of Vocational gymnasiums were introduced in the 1980s with the aim of improving the progression rate to HE, each building on different traditions (Jørgensen, 2018). These two formats, the business gymnasium (HHX) and technical gymnasium (HTX), eventually failed to create a connection between apprenticeships and HE and did not raise the esteem of VET offered through apprenticeships. Rather, they attracted the most ambitious learners from the apprenticeship scheme and contributed to the falling status of the other, ordinary VET programmes. Since 1995, the HHX and HTX have enabled access to HE and their separation from the apprenticeship route was maintained in a later reform that took place in 2005. By 2013, the vocational gymnasiums grew, annually recruiting more than 15% of the eligible youth cohorts (Statistics Denmark, 2015). However, they do not enable access to the skilled labour market. A reform introduced in 2000 has allowed VET students to choose additional general subjects as part of their VET programme in order to be able to apply for higher education. However, very few students have taken advantage of this opportunity.

Traditionally, Danish VET graduates' typical higher education route steered toward short-cycle programmes below the Bachelor's degree level, which are presently offered by Vocational Academies (*'Erhvervsakademier'*, in Danish). These institutes offer programmes that had previously been offered by vocational and professional schools. They were established as the result of a reform conducted in 2007 in order to provide better opportunities for educational progression to VET students. However, since the 1990s, the rate of progression from VET to HE has decreased, and the majority of graduates from VET who continue in HE pursue Bachelor's degree programmes at university colleges. For example, during 2009–2012, only 13% of the students at Vocational Academies had an upper secondary VET educational background (Jørgensen, 2017).

In sum, in Denmark, a dual system of VET forms a minor alternative route to HE, while transitions from VET to the labour market are relatively successful. Medium-cycle tertiary education mainly attracts participants from vocational gymnasiums (HHX, HTX; Jørgensen, 2018). Since 2011, the hybrid eux programme is offered as a solution to prevent youngsters in VET from entering blind alleys, to improve the status of the VET route and to attract also high-performing students to vocational education. The eux programme integrates academic subjects into the apprenticeship programmes through a new approach that combines subject- and problem-based work. As almost one third of the students enrolling in VET applied for eux in 2017, it can be considered a success. However, it is a very demanding programme, so it is expected that many students may not complete the programme.

Norway

In Norway, in connection with a government committee known as the Steen Committee, there was a strong discussion about the need for changes to the education system at the beginning of the 1960s (Michelsen et al., 2018). There was a need to create a more coherent education system to replace the former heterogeneous school structure that had developed on the basis of local initiatives. The Steen Committee suggested increasing the integration of the general and vocational upper secondary education tracks. The committee supported students being free to choose an educational track, and based this on the principle that the completion of an upper secondary education with satisfactory results should enable access to HE. While a reform of the upper secondary education system was being planned, the apprenticeship system was being contested. The youth organisation of the Labour party wanted to abolish apprenticeship training, claiming that economic and legal conditions for apprentices were unfavourable compared to those of ordinary pupils in vocational schools (Michelsen, 1993). As a response to the criticism, the apprentice system was revitalised in the 1970s by measures taken to improve it. School-based initial VET was integrated in the general upper secondary education system and thus formed a more unified upper secondary educational path in 1975. The apprenticeship system was further strengthened by a new, separate law given in 1980 (Michelsen et al., 2018).

The reformed upper secondary education system was criticised as being outdated already later in the 1980s (Michelsen et al., 2018). The perceived status of VET was still low compared to that of the general academic track in upper secondary education. There was a structural mismatch between the number of study places and employment opportunities; educational contents were seen to be outdated and too specific in relation to the demands of the labour market. In 1994, Reform '94 was implemented to grant all 16–19-year-olds the right to three years of upper secondary education. The policy's aim was to abolish youth unemployment and improve the inclusion of youths in society. The reform recombined school-based and apprentice training through the '2+2 model', where two years of upper secondary education in school was to be followed by two years as an apprentice in a firm. The 2+2 system, however, blocked opportunities for the horizontal transfer between trades. The former 101 foundational courses were reformed into 12 broader, theoretically oriented initial courses which combined several related trades into different vocational tracks. While the provision and availability of apprenticeships was a major challenge, it was decided, through implementing and trying various measures, that students who cannot find an apprenticeship after the two-year training period can complete a third, supplementary year of practical training at school. Also, it became possible for VET students to transfer back to the general education track by completing a third supplementary year of studies enabling access to HE. The most recent demands for further reforms have concerned the increased need for individual flexibility in combining school-based and work-based learning as well as for improved learning arrangements in general (Michelsen et al., 2014).

At present, the opportunities to continue in post-secondary education vary considerably between the vocational programmes in Norway (Olsen et al., 2014). There are educational programmes whose pathways to post-secondary education are well established, mainly in the area of technical trades, but there are also programmes where direct opportunities for transitioning to HE do not exist. Students who are not formally qualified to enter HE typically continue their studies at post-secondary vocational colleges (*'fagskoler'* – ISCED 4). Entry requirements for vocational colleges are either a vocational upper secondary education, a general upper secondary education or an assessment of relevant practical skills or non-formal competences. The term 'higher vocational education' has recently, in 2017, been established as an official term for the vocational college programmes. The share of students continuing at vocational colleges varies from field to field, but it is highest for the field of technical and industrial production (16% of students three years after the completion of VET, Olsen et al., 2014).

Sweden

In Sweden, the provision of vocational education increased considerably in the 1950s (Olofsson and Persson Thunqvist, 2018). In the early 1960s, the need to better coordinate the provision of VET programmes was reflected in several reform initiatives, and the Commission on Vocational Education was appointed in 1963. The commission suggested decreasing the number of former vocational education programmes and developing them into broader, two-year study programmes. The Swedish parliament ultimately decided to merge the former general upper secondary school system with the commercial and technical upper secondary school systems and coordinated their provision as part of post-compulsory, two-year continuation schools and vocational schools. The greatest changes, however, concerned the regulation of content and scheduling; these were reformed to create an integrated upper secondary school system. In the 1960s, a shift in regulating educational contents took place when syllabuses based on local governance and initiatives were replaced by centrally determined syllabuses. When a reform was established in 1971, the new vocational programmes were to be broadly oriented toward their relevant branch of study and a new VET programme-based upper secondary school system was implemented in the same spirit. The new vocational study programmes were to provide a basic vocational education, while the adoption of working life competences was to take place later. The reform led to an expansion of interest in establishing vocational school programmes parallel to decreasing workplace training across the total study time in vocational programmes. During the school year 1983–1984, only 6% of these type of students' studies took place at a workplace (Olofsson and Persson Thunqvist, 2018).

In 1991, the upper secondary education system was further reformed to comprise 17 educational programmes, 14 of which were vocationally oriented. All upper secondary education was extended to last three years. Third, a theoretical year was embedded in the upper secondary vocational education's curriculum to enable eligibility for HE. At the same time, the governance of education was decentralised (Lundahl and Olofsson, 2014). In 1992, a reform of the private school system took place as well, which led to further liberalisation and emphasised that initiatives should be taken at the local level (Olofsson and Persson Thunqvist, 2018). Even though the upper secondary education system enabled a general eligibility for higher education, many students, particularly those in vocational programmes, did not complete their studies satisfactorily. For example, in 2012, 23% of students did not gain their final certificate and 36% did not achieve eligibility for HE (Olofsson and Persson Thunqvist, 2018). The increased regulation directed at the provision of general subjects with the aim of easing the eligibility for HE led to a further weakening of work-based learning. This effect was addressed by a reform introduced in 2011.

This most recent Swedish reform, in 2011, aimed to counterbalance the academic drift by creating a stronger division between higher education preparatory programmes and respective vocational programmes. The Swedish upper secondary education system, at present, comprises three pathways to gaining an upper secondary diploma: (1) general education as the major route to HE, (2) school-based vocational programmes and (3) apprenticeships – with the latter two giving priority to work-based learning. The school-based vocational system provides 18 national programmes, 12 of which are vocational programmes placing more emphasis than previously on specific vocational knowledge and skills (Olofsson and Persson Thunqvist, 2018).

As an outcome of the reforms, the present Swedish system of initial VET is rather heterogenous in contrast to its unified past that had become the norm since the 1990s. A review of the effects of the reform pilot from 1990 did not indicate a clear increase in the participation rate of former VET students in HE (Olofsson and Persson Thunqvist, 2018; Statistics Sweden, 2013, p. 14; Hall, 2013, 2012). The general HE participation rate has increased. Among vocational students, 6–7 out of 10 of the students finished their upper secondary education and were qualified for HE (Statistics Sweden, 2013). At the same time, enrolment in VET programmes in general has declined from 50% in the 1990s to 27% in 2013, and Swedish VET has had to struggle against the academic drift (Virolainen and Persson Thunqvist, 2017; Skolverket, 2013). The need to counteract the academic drift in order to meet the needs of the labour market as well as to decrease youth unemployment has raised renewed interest in promoting apprenticeship training in Sweden.

Finland

In Finland, vocational education expanded remarkably in the 1960s due to the creation of a network of vocational schools established to meet the demands of the growing population after Second World War (Laukia, 2013). The shift from an agricultural to an industrial society and further on to a service society was also more rapid in Finland than in other European countries (Haapala, 2006). Since the expansion of VET in the 1960s, the next ground-breaking reforms in Finnish VET's relation to HE took place in the 1980s and 1990s, whereas the 1970s saw the establishment of the nine-year comprehensive school system. In the upper secondary school reform during 1982–1988, a general education component was enhanced in the VET qualifications. Despite the hierarchical and stratified structure of VET programmes, the reform initiated a route to higher education via so-called college institutions ('*Opistoaste*', in Finnish). Thus, it changed the status of VET from being an educational dead end with no prospect of progressing to HE, which was previously only possible along the general upper secondary education route (Laukia, 2013; Numminen, 2000; Salminen, 1999; Väärälä, 1995).

In the 1990s, the reforms of the Finnish education system took advantage of experience gained from the youth education and polytechnics experiments, and the vocational qualification structure was developed further. The stratified structure of VET was replaced by a consecutive educational structure, curricula were modularised, the number of qualifications was reduced and the accreditation of prior learning was to be emphasised. Through these VET reforms, local education providers gained more responsibility for planning curriculum contents, while the duration of education programmes, the qualification structure of education and the national aims were still decided at the national level (Stenström and Virolainen, 2016; Laukia, 2013; Numminen, 2000; Salminen, 1999; Väärälä, 1995).

The reforms of the 1990s improved young people's eligibility for HE, and as part of these reforms all VET qualification programmes were extended to last three years. In parallel, vocational colleges (Opistoaste) were abolished once the universities of applied sciences (UAS) were permanently established on the basis of the former vocational colleges following the *polytechnics experiment*. In addition to extending the duration of VET qualification programmes, work-based learning was given greater emphasis in VET by incorporating obligatory on-the-job learning periods (about six months). Furthermore, at the beginning of the 2000s, a Finnish system of skills demonstrations was adopted as a new pedagogical approach emphasising educational collaboration with the working world. As an outcome of the so-called *youth education experiment*, many cities continued to offer dual qualifications in order to widen the bridge from VET to HE. This enabled students to complete the matriculation examination of their general upper secondary education and their VET qualification in parallel. In 2012, the share of young VET graduates among matriculated students (i.e., completers of the dual qualification) was 7.6% (Kumpulainen, 2014, pp. 78, 81).

The latest Finnish VET reform introduced during 2015–2018 emphasised individual study progress and the competence-based approach. Even though the national curriculum framework is committed to equal opportunities and provides access to HE, the decreased funding of both the VET and HE system has led to the weakening of VET graduates' position vis-à-vis general upper secondary school graduates in competition for study places in HE. Some UAS have adopted entrance examinations for VET graduates as of the 2010s. In general, VET graduates' entrance to traditional science universities has not changed from the 2%–3% rate seen in 1995 and during 2008–2009, even though field-specific exceptions with higher participation rates exist (Kumpulainen, 2009; Ahola, 1997). Around one third of applicants to UAS have a VET background, and they make up around 20%–80% of entrants, varying between study programmes (Hintsanen et al., 2016). The funding models of the Ministry of Education underline study progress, and VET graduates' rate of dropping out of UAS studies has been higher than for general upper secondary students in some fields of education (Halonen, 2015; Stenström et al., 2012). In sum, access to HE is highly competitive in Finland despite the introduction of opportunities for eligibility via the VET route (see also Kilpi-Jakonen et al., 2016).

Comparison of transitions to higher education

In the previous sections, we have described how transitions to HE via the VET route have been developed in the Nordic education systems. The comparison of the Nordic education systems' developments highlights how decisions on the organising of VET's relationship with the general upper secondary education system and on the provision of general subject contents have been key issues in reforms and in anchoring the institutional development of VET's relation to HE. Over the years, this has led to the establishing of education systems with deeper stratification (Denmark), integrated programmes and the reintroduction of apprenticeships (Swedish 'Gy-11' reform), binary and combinatory solutions (Finland, ordinary VET and experimental reform of youth education and dual qualifications), and consecutive optional routes (Norway, '2+2' vs. '2+1'). Since the 1990s, all countries have had policy discussions to settle the issue of enabling progress from VET to HE; Norway, Sweden and Finland have developed distinct bridging solutions to offer young VET graduates pathways to HE. The outcomes of these polices are, however, somewhat difficult to compare, because, despite the policy attempts for universal HE access, their definitions and categorisations of HE differ substantially and there are also significant differences between the categorisations of the occupational fields of these countries.

An unintended side-effect of the variety of opportunities on offer has been that Nordic youths transit relatively slowly to HE, but the systemic reasons for delayed transitions and critical transition points vary from country to country (cf., Walther, 2009, 2006). Denmark offers only limited opportunities for progressing from VET to HE, and Norway offers several but not all particularly explicit routes, whereas these are quite clear in Sweden and Finland. In Sweden and Finland, however, formal eligibility is moderated later down the line through competitive HE entrance examinations and requirements. In general, Danish VET students have not acquired eligibility for higher education. The recent introduction of eux programmes, since 2011, has promised some improvements to this pattern and an easier route to both HE and the working world (see Chapter 5). Since Danish VET graduates do have direct access to some short-cycle programmes of HE (Vocational Academies), these would be their primary route to further education. However, even some of these require additional qualifications that can only be achieved through supplementary preparatory courses (typically lasting one year). For Danish VET graduates, the path from VET to higher education thus normally weaves via preparatory courses or adult education ('higher preparatory exam', HF), or via the eux programme. Since 2011, the eux programme has offered direct routes to both HE and the working world (see Chapter 5).

In contrast, in Norway, access to HE is possible via several routes alongside internationally well-known 2+2 system. The most common route is the third supplementary year in upper secondary school that qualifies students for admission to higher education, but this option runs parallel to apprenticeship training and tends to complicate the progression. The third supplementary year is quite demanding, and a large share of students do not pass their exams. VET students also have the opportunity to enter HE via one of these four routes: (1) By following a special integrated track, TAF/YSK ('teknisk allmennfag/ yrkes- og studiekompetanse', in Norwegian; lit. translation: 'technical general or vocational and academic qualifications'), which combines VET with general education and leads to a trade certificate as well as a general university admission certification within four years. (2) By following the VET route to higher education ('*Y-veien*', in Norwegian; lit. translation: 'Y-road'). These are programmes adapted to VET graduates, offered by higher education institutions, in particular to meet the demands of the labour market in engineering. The Ministry of Education and Research wants to open up the possibility for VET-route programmes for further fields. Also, (3) the holders of a trade or journeyman's certificate may pursue further studies (duration from six months to two years) in tertiary vocational education ('fagskole', in Norwegian; lit. translation: 'vocational school') at the EQF-level 5. The completion of a two-year post-secondary (non-tertiary) programme qualifies students for admission to higher education, provided the applicants can demonstrate a sufficient academic level in Norwegian language. Furthermore, (4) applicants aged 25 years or more can apply for admission to higher education based on the recognition of their prior learning, RPL.

In Sweden, the qualification structure provides access to HE for VET students, but not all students achieve the targeted level in order to qualify for HE. The share of qualified students varies by programme. For instance, in the school year 2014–2015, it varied from 20% of students in the Energy study programme to 60% of those in the Health Care programme gaining eligibility for HE (Skolverket, 2016). In Finland, completing all three years of the VET programme successfully yields general eligibility for HE by law; however, VET graduates' access to HE is still complicated by highly competitive entrance requirements, with eligibility ultimately also depending on students' final grades (Numerus Clausus) and individual HE institutions' entrance examinations. Often, Finnish VET students willing to ensure their eligibility for HE are on firmer ground if they have completed a so-called dual qualification, that is, the matriculation examination of general upper secondary school and a VET qualification. Furthermore, the recent trend in VET reforms, during 2015–2018, steering toward the competence-based approach, as well as the existing variety of general studies depending on education providers' preferences, have caused regional differences in opportunities among youths in Finland.

In sum, Nordic VET systems have developed various bridging solutions to enable VET graduates' eligibility for HE. While the pathways leading to such eligibility are more or less direct and explicit, the complexity of the various conditions for eligibility make youths dependent on guidance counselling regarding the progression opportunities. Finland and Sweden have a more integrated system, while Norway and Denmark have more auxiliary routes. The progression routes for Norwegians have been more systematic and embedded in the education structure than has been the case for the Danish routes until the introduction of the eux system. In general, the differences between the Nordic HE systems complicate the comparison of the success rates of Nordic students' transitioning from VET to HE.

Differences between Nordic HE systems

The differences between how Nordic HE systems enable VET graduates' eligibility are reflected in the number of entrants to HE (see Table 3.1) and seen implicitly in the general rate of the different age groups of adults who have completed a tertiary education (see Table 3.2). The figures in Table 3.1 show how the eligibility for entrance to HE with a VET background varies between Nordic countries and their occupational fields. However, these figures have to be interpreted with precaution, firstly as they do not present the HE entrance numbers for the same year per country (see footnote of Table 3.1), and secondly as the numbers for the time passed since the HE entrants' graduation from VET up to starting HE vary between the countries. Furthermore, the categorisations of the VET occupational fields represented differs between the countries. In general, the number of entrants to HE would be higher if students' whole life span were to be taken into account, but getting access to such representative data was not targeted by the research. Thus, the presented numbers are only an example intended to show how, for instance, progress from Danish VET to HE is on average more rare than in other Nordic countries that have more established routes to HE. The differences reflect country-specific cultures in regard to the intertwinement of education systems and labour market relations, employment situations, occupational hierarchies, demand for labour, and the specific needs of occupations in each field.

The share of Finnish VET graduates among all young applicants to UAS was 27% in 2013, on average per UAS (Hintsanen et al., 2016), while the share of those who had started their studies in VET in 2004 and progressed to UAS by 2008 (within the typical four-year follow-up period) varied between 4% and 15%, depending on the field of study (see Table 3.1). In Sweden, the share of VET graduates studying in HE programmes varies likewise from field to field, ranging from 2% of students in Vehicle Engineering having a VET background to around 30% in Health Care in the school year 2006–2007 (Skolverket, 2016). In Norway, the highest participation rate of VET students in 'fagskoler' has been in the field of Technical and Industrial Production, where 16% of participants were VET graduates in 2011 (Nyen et al., 2013). In all Nordic countries, entrance to traditional science universities with a VET background is much rarer. In Finland, the rate in 2001 was 0%–13%, depending on the field (Vuorinen-Lampila and Valkonen, 2012), and in Norway, around 1%–9% in 2011 (Nyen et al., 2013).

In Table 3.2, the varying outcomes of HE structures become explicit; although, whether the HE entrants stemmed from a general upper secondary school or a VET programme is not differentiated. The figures in Table 3.2 show that the provision of short-cycle education is strongly represented in the HE structures of Denmark and Norway. It is also the main destination for VET graduates in Norway. In Denmark, however, VET graduates increasingly opt for Bachelor's degree programmes at university colleges and in an occupational field different to their VET programme (Frederiksen et al., 2012). Swedish VET

Table 3.1 Transitions from VET to higher education in the four Nordic countries by field of education

Denmark[1]		Norway[2]		Finland[3]		Sweden[4]	
Apprenticeship programmes' VET graduates who entered HE 5 years after completion of VET	Cohort 2006, %	VET graduates registered in HE within 5 years after completion of VET	Cohort 2007, %	VET graduates who entered UAS 1–2 years after completion of VET	2008, %	VET graduates who entered HE 3 years after completion of VET	2006–2007, %
Business & Retail	10.7	Design, Arts & Crafts	14	Humanities & Education	12.8	Business & Admin.	15.1
Construction	3.0	Building & Construction	10	Culture	14.7	Building & Construction	2.3
Metal & Mechanical	1.9	Electricity & Electronics	21	Social Sciences, Business and Administration	13.6	Media	8.2
Media & Graphics	3.3	Technical & Industrial Production	13	Natural Sciences	15.0	Electricity	9.6
Technical & Industry	4.7	Restaurant & Food Processing	18	Technology, Communication & Transport	5.3	Energy	6.1
Social Services	2.0	Service & Transport	32	Natural Resources & Environment	6.9	Industry	5.2
Restaurant & Catering	2.0	Health Care, Child Care & Youth Development	22	Social Services, Health and Sport	9.9	Food	8.2
Transport	4.8			Tourism, Catering & Domestic Services	7.3	Vehicle Engineering	1.9
Health	3.8			Other	3.6	Child Care & Recreation	24.3
						Handicraft	13.8
						Hotel & Restaurant	9.8
						Food	8.2
						Media	30.2
						Agriculture	18.0
						Health Care	28.7

1 Denmark: Progression to higher education within five years of completion of an apprenticeship in Denmark, real (not estimated) transition rates. Source: Frederiksen et al. (2012). Muligheder og barrierer på erhvervsuddannede unges vej til videregående uddannelse [Opportunities and Barriers in Journeymen's Progression to Higher Education]. Roskilde: Roskilde Universitet. http://rucforsk.ruc.dk.

2 Norway: VET graduates who entered higher education within five years after completion. The table includes only those who were 21 years old or younger when completing VET. Source: Nyen et al. (2015).

3 Finland: VET Graduates' progression to UAS by field of education (within one to two years after completion). Source: Stenström et al. (2012, p. 83).

4 Sweden: Transition from upper secondary VET to higher education within three years after completion, by VET programme and cohort, 2006/07. (Skolverket, 2016).

Progression to higher education from VET 65

Table 3.2 Adults who have attained tertiary education, by type of programme and age group

Education and age group	Finland (FI) %	Denmark (DK) %	Norway (NO) %	Sweden (SE) %	Germany (DE) %	United Kingdom (UK) %
Short cycle						
25–34	0	4	14	10	0	8
55–64	17	4	9	11	1	11
Bachelor's						
25–34	26	22	22	22	14	31
55–64	7	18	16	9	14	16
Master's						
25–34	14	15	12	13	13	10
55–64	9	7	6	9	10	7

Source of data: Adopted from OECD, 2015, p. 41.

Note: The OECD's data refer to ISCED 2011. Definitions and categorisations have changed in recent decades and therefore comparisons of age groups are somewhat problematic.

graduates also continue mostly in higher vocational education ('*yrkeshögskolor*', in Swedish; lit. translation: 'professional colleges'). In Finland, in contrast, short-cycle HE is only beginning to emerge, as suggested by recent experiments (Aittola et al., 2016). A significant proportion of the younger Finnish age groups completed their Bachelor's degree at a UAS. Increased rates of the completion of UAS studies is the reason why the share of those who completed Bachelor's and/or Master's degrees has been relatively high in Finland compared to other Nordic countries (Hagensen, 2014; Virolainen and Stenström, 2014). However, the statistics for 2015 and 2016 on 25–34-year-olds' completion of HE show that the number of students who completed HE in that period was actually higher per other Nordic country than in Finland (OECD, 2017, p. 51).

In sum, participation in HE varies in all of the Nordic countries from field to field. While Finland is the only Nordic country where VET participation has increased since the 1990s by at least 10% (Stenström and Virolainen, 2016), the shift in its educational transition pattern from VET to HE has also been significant. This is not only an outcome of HE eligibility. The policies on how UAS choose their students and assess students' VET background depend on their autonomous choice. Finnish UAS have the right to organise entrance examinations and reserve study places for VET graduates. They may also consider work experience as part of their entrance criteria. The expansion of HE via the introduction of UAS is the second main reason for Finnish VET's increased attractiveness. Also, the Finnish educational transition pattern may in future change toward favouring the academic over the VET route as a result of the latest education policies' emphasis on general upper secondary education and the matriculation examination as the basis for student selection at traditional science universities (Stenström and Virolainen, 2016). At the same time, Finnish VET graduates' employment rate has been weaker than that of VET graduates in other Nordic countries. Their lower employment rate is not explained only by the prolonged recession since 2008, but also by the slow recovery from the previous recession in the 1990s as well as by the high rate of HE completion in the overall population having led to increased competition in the labour market (Stenström and Virolainen, 2018; Julkunen and Nätti, 1999). In Sweden, recent policies have placed increased emphasis on the links between VET and the working world in order to improve and increase youth employment, and the changes in VET have been reflected in the diminishing transitions to HE (Persson Thunqvist and Hallqvist, 2014). In Sweden, the general situation has been that transitions to HE have been less common via male-dominated VET programmes aimed at specific occupations such as building and construction than via female-dominated VET programmes broadly oriented toward occupational fields such as the arts and media (Virolainen and Persson Thunqvist, 2017).

Conclusions

In the Nordic countries, higher education systems have significant similarities, in broad terms, such as public funding and related state control, tuition-free education and very high rates of enrolment despite the introduction of marketisation and managerialism in recent decades. In contrast to other countries, the Nordic systems of higher education have been characterised as less market-oriented and less hierarchical than the Anglo-American systems as well as less academically focused than the continental European systems (Antikainen, 2016). Still, from the perspective of VET graduates and their opportunities to progress to HE, the Nordic systems of HE also have major differences between each other. First of all, the eligibility requirements for VET graduates to enter HE differ, and there are also general differences between the HE systems. In particular, the provision of professionally oriented HE makes each Nordic HE system distinct. What Nordic countries have in common is that creating a parity of esteem between VET graduates and graduates of general upper secondary programmes in regard to gaining access to HE is still a challenge.

As for learning policies, it is, firstly, notable that the Nordic attempts to bridge VET and HE have developed at a different pace and the relation between their respective VET and national education systems varies. On the one hand, the Danish hybridisation strategy and Norwegian VET system have intended to integrate apprenticeships and HE preparation (eux and YSK). On the other hand, since 2011, Sweden has offered unified upper secondary education and enhanced work-based learning in integrated vocational programmes. Finland has based its approach to bridging on enhancing the general subject content in school-based vocational education but emphasises individual choice in this in the most recent reform covering 2015–2018. Every Nordic VET–HE bridging model that has been established at some point in time has been reconsidered, renegotiated or reformed.

Secondly, the provision of short-cycle HE has different roles in various Nordic education systems. In Denmark, historically, it has held a strong position in contrast to Finland, where it has not yet established itself. Thirdly, the

Progression to higher education from VET 67

adoption of the Bologna structure of HE has not had similar effects in the Nordic countries in regard to the transitioning from VET to HE. While HE entrance requirements have been formalised, the interpretation of HE institutions' autonomy to decide on them have varied across the Nordic countries. In Denmark, the adoption of the Bologna structure has caused a growing time gap in these transitions, probably also due to a weak VET–HE bridging model. Fourthly, based on the experienced decline in the enrolment rate for VET in Norway, Denmark and especially Sweden after 2011, it seems that clear progression routes to HE are required to make VET an attractive alternative to the academic programmes of upper secondary education. However, the experience in Sweden since 1991 demonstrates that including academic subjects in all VET programmes in order to provide eligibility for higher education to everyone tends disadvantage students from non-academic backgrounds. In this respect, the Finnish strategy of combining skills demonstrations and enhanced on-the-job learning in addition to offering academic subjects appears to be a promising development concerning VET graduates' options for gaining eligibility for HE. Fifthly, in Finland, the UAS reform has succeeded in creating clear progression routes from VET to HE, and this has contributed to raising the attractiveness of VET. Even though a similar effect is not visible in Denmark following the establishment of Vocational Academies there, the Danish outcome reflects that VET graduates in Denmark tend to be already employed in the labour market by the time they have completed their VET programme, and it is thus less of an incentive for them to continue in or re-enter the education system. In Finland, the high level of unemployment compared to other Nordic countries has hampered youths' transition from VET to the labour market and thus made it an incentive to continue along the educational path.

Our descriptions of the Nordic VET systems' developments with respect to transitioning to HE have portrayed the diversity and dynamics of the systemic development in each of the Scandinavian countries. The secondary data derived from the project Nord-VET have enabled us to sketch some of the dynamics of the systemic developments as well as their recent outcomes. These findings give support to what has been found, namely, 'generic conditions for successful transitions'. Successful transitions are generally supported by "a healthy economy, well-organised pathways that connect initial education with work and further study, widespread opportunities for workplace experience to be combined with education, tightly knit safety nets for those at risk, good information and guidance, and effective institutions and processes" (Raffe, 2008, p. 291). Previous research has also shown that transition systems' many dimensions are interconnected and embedded in their national contexts, which makes their comparison challenging. As one kind of data typically only reflects some aspects of a systemic change, only a partial view of the complete picture can be gained – which has also been the case for this study. Our secondary data enabled identifying key turning points in education policy and their outcomes in terms of HE participation rates. As eligibility for HE has been an organisational challenge for all Nordic countries and has had an effect on transition patterns and education policies, it deserves further investigation. The differences between the occupational fields of education, their relations to the dominant forms of production in the labour market of each country, as well as the aspect of vulnerability within the present global economy all deserve more attention. Furthermore, the relevance of short- versus long-cycle HE qualifications as forms of further education for VET graduates also deserves further research. The modifications that Busemeyer (2015) has suggested, to theories explaining institutional diversity of education and training systems further highlight one particular trait of education policies that should be examined further: the policy processes by which educational goals are defined and negotiated. In regard to transitions to and from VET, the processes by which curricular aims are defined are particularly interesting as the general content and adequacy of general competencies with respect to demands in further and higher education are defined in these processes. In particular, the polarisation and the hybridisation of job profiles in the labour market invite researchers and policy makers to rethink the education systems' affordances concerning lifelong learning and further education opportunities. During career changes, people need career management skills, abilities and affordances to learn on the job, and they should be able to combine new learning taking place on the job with knowledge and skills learned in the past. A challenge for VET communities of practitioners is not to lose their field-specific knowledge, skills and competence when additional skills are demanded.

A deeper understanding of curricular processes would also be helpful as significant changes in the labour market can even stir up panic among policy makers, and modifications made to the education system in such circumstances are bound to lead to fragmented solutions. For example, Busemeyer's study in 2015 brought up the temporality of educational reforms, remarking: long-term changes demand long-term commitment. Further comparative analyses of the educational experiences of youths would also be useful as interpreters of national transition systems since transitions to HE are relatively lengthy and complex in Nordic countries (despite their differences) compared to other countries. More information about the reasons for the slow transitioning is needed to assess whether, for example, these involve a lack of guidance counselling and information which would help students in making career choices; a lack of transparency regarding educational outcomes in terms of employment; and a lack of independence from economic pressures, the insecurity of careers, the current cultural changes in society, a combination of these or something else.

References

Ahola, S. (1997) '"Different but equal": Student expectations and the Finnish dual higher education policy', *European Journal of Education*, vol. 32, no. 3, pp. 291–302.

Ahonen, S. (2002) 'From an industrial to a post-industrial society: Changing conceptions of equality in education', *Educational Review*, vol. 54, no. 2, pp. 173–181.

Progression to higher education from VET   69

Aittola, H., Laine, K., and Välimaa, J. (2016) *Tärkeintä on, että kehittyy ja oppii – titteli ei ole niin tärkeä: Korkeakouludiplomikoulutuskokeilun seuranta- ja arviointitutkimuksen loppuraportti*, Jyväskylä, Jyväskylän yliopisto, Koulutuksen tutkimuslaitos, 53.

Albæk, K. (2004) *Om lærepladsspørgsmålet*, København, Økonomisk Institut, 212.

Antikainen, A. (2016) 'The Nordic model of higher education', in Côté, J. E. and Furlong, A. (eds.) *Routledge Handbook of the Sociology of Higher Education*, Milton Park, Routledge, pp. 234–240.

Berggren, C., and Cliffordson, C. (2012) 'Widening participation trends in Sweden: Regulations and their effects, intended and unintended', in Hinton-Smith, T. (ed.) *Widening Participation in Higher Education: Casting the Net Wide?* Basingstoke, Palgrave Macmillan, pp. 197–212.

Betænkning nr. 612. (1971) *Betænkning om erhvervsfaglige grunduddannelser*, København, Statens Trykningskontor.

Böckerman, P., Hämäläinen, U., and Uusitalo, R. (2009) 'Labour market effects of the polytechnic education reform: The Finnish experience', *Economics of Education Review*, vol. 28, no. 6, pp. 672–681.

Börjesson, M., Ahola, S., Helland, H., and Thomsen, J. P., (2014) *Enrolment Patterns in Nordic Higher Education, ca 1945–2010. Institutions, Types of Education and Fields of Study*, Working Paper, 15, Oslo, NIFU, 2014 [Online]. Available at http://forskning.ku.dk/find-en-forsker/?pure=da/publications/enrolment-patterns-in-nordic-higher-education-ca-19452010-institutions-types-of-education-and-fields-of-study(8d6f868a-5928-4708-b37f-fd8af23d82b0).html (Accessed 13 March 2018).

Brennan, J., and Naidoo, R. (2008) 'Higher education and the achievement (and/or prevention) of equity and social justice', *Higher Education*, vol. 56, no. 3, pp. 287–302.

Brunila, K., Kurki, T., Lahelma, E., Lehtonen, J., Mietola, R., and Palmu, T. (2011) 'Multiple transitions: Educational policies and young people's post-compulsory choices', *Scandinavian Journal of Educational Research*, vol. 55, no. 3, pp. 307–324.

Busemeyer, M. R. (2015) *Skills and Inequality: Partisan Politics and the Political Economy of Education Reforms in Western Welfare States*, Cambridge, Cambridge University Press.

Christensen, E. (1978) *Konflikter mellem faglærte og ufaglærte arbejdere*, Aalborg, Aalborg Universitetsforlag.

Della Porta, D., Hänninen, S., Siisiäinen, M., and Silvasti, T. (eds.) (2015) *The New Social Division: Making and Unmaking Precariousness*, Basingstoke, Palgrave MacMillan.

European Parliament. (2012) *European Parliament Resolution of 20 April 2012 on Modernising Europe's Higher Education Systems* [Online]. Available at www.europarl.europa.eu/sides/getDoc.do?type=TA&reference=P7-TA-2012-0139&format=XML&language=EN (Accessed 15 November 2017).

Frederiksen, J. T., Jensen, H. H., and Jørgensen, C. H. (2012) *Muligheder og barrierer på erhvervsuddannede unges vej til videregående uddannelse*, Roskilde, Roskilde Universitet.

Goos, M., Manning, A., and Salomons, A. (2009) 'Job polarization in Europe', *American Economic Review*, vol. 99, no. 2, pp. 58–63.

Guile, D. (2002) 'Skill and work experience in the European knowledge economy', *Journal of Education and Work*, vol. 15, no. 3, pp. 251–276.

Haapala, P. (2006) 'Suomalainen rakennemuutos', in Saari, J. (ed.) *Historiallinen käänne: Johdatus pitkän aikavälin historian tutkimukseen*, Helsinki, Gaudeamus, pp. 91–124.

Hagensen, K. M. (ed.) (2014) *Nordic Statistical Yearbook 2014*, vol. 52., Copenhagen, Nordic Council of Ministers [Online]. Available at http://norden.diva-portal.org/smash/get/diva2:763002/FULLTEXT07.pdf (Accessed 15 November 2017).

70 *Maarit Virolainen and Anna Hagen Tønder*

Hall, C. (2012) 'The effects of reducing tracking in upper secondary school: Evidence from a large-scale pilot scheme', *Journal of Human Resources*, vol. 47, no. 1, pp. 237–269.

Hall, C. (2013) *Medförde längre och mer generella yrkesprogram en minskad risk för arbetslöshet?* Institutet för arbetsmarknads-och utbildningspolitisk utvärdering, Uppsala, IFAU, 16.

Hauschildt, K., Gwosć, C., Netz, N., and Mishra, S. (2015) *Social and Economic Conditions of Student Life in Europe, EUROSTUDENT V 2012–2015* [Online], Bielefeldt, DZHW. Available at www.eurostudent.eu/download_files/documents/EVSynopsisofIndicators. pdf (Accessed 15 November 2017).

Heikkilä, D. (2003) 'Käsityön ammatillinen opetus Suomessa 1700-luvulta nykypäiviin', in Anttila, P., Heikkilä, D., and Ylönen, I. (eds.) *Suomalaisen käsityökoulutuksen vaiheita 1700-luvulta 2000-luvulle*, Jyväskylä, Suomen käsityön museo, 22, pp. 7–48 [Online]. Available at www.craftmuseum.fi/kassaatko/julkaisut.htm (Accessed 15 November 2017).

Hintsanen, V., Juntunen, K., Kukkonen, A., Lamppu, V-M., Lempinen, P., Niinistö-Sivuranta, S., Nordlund-Spiby, R., Paloniemi, J., Rode, J-P., Goman, J., Hietala, R., Pirinen, T., and Seppälä, H. (2016) *Liikettä niveliin: Ammatillisesta koulutuksesta ammattikorkeakouluun johtavien opintopolkujen ja koulutusasteiden yhteistyön toimivuus*, Helsinki, Kansallinen koulutuksen arviointikeskus.

Hoelscher, M., Hayward, G., Ertl, H., and Dunbar-Goddet, H. (2008) 'The transition from vocational education and training to higher education: a successful pathway?' *Research Papers in Education*, vol. 23, no. 2, pp. 139–151.

Jóhannsdóttir, G., and Jónasson, J. T. (2014) 'External and internal influences on the development of Icelandic higher education', *Nordic Studies in Education*, vol. 34, no. 3, pp. 153–171.

Jørgensen, C. H. (2017) 'From apprenticeship to higher vocational education in Denmark – building bridges while the gap is widening', *Journal of Vocational Education & Training*, vol. 69, no. 1, pp. 64–80.

Jørgensen, C. H. (2018) 'The modernisation of the apprenticeship system in Denmark 1945–2015', in Michelsen, S. and Stenström, M-L. (eds.) *The Historical Evolution of Vocational Education in the Nordic Countries*, Milton Park, Routledge, pp. 171–190.

Julkunen, R., and Nätti, J. (1999) *The Modernization of Working Times: Flexibility and Work Sharing in Finland* [Online], Jyväskylä, University of Jyväskylä. Available at www.jyu.fi/ ytk/laitokset/yfi/en/sophi/publications/sophi46 (Accessed 15 November 2017).

Juul, I. (2006) 'Den danske velfærdsstat og uddannelsespolitikken', *Uddannelseshistorie*, vol. 40, pp. 71–98.

Kilpi-Jakonen, E., Erola, J., and Karhula, A. (2016) 'Inequalities in the haven of equality? Upper secondary education and entry into tertiary education in Finland', in Blossfeld, H-P., Buchholz, S., Skopek, J., and Triventi, M. (eds.) *Models of Secondary Education and Social Inequality: An International Comparison*, Cheltenham, Edward Elgar Publishing, pp. 181–196.

Kumpulainen, T. (2009) *Koulutuksen määrälliset indikaattorit 2009*, Helsinki, Opetushallitus.

Kumpulainen, T. (2014) *Koulutuksen tilastollinen vuosikirja 2014*, Helsinki, Opetushallitus, 10.

Kyvik, S. (2004) 'Structural changes in higher education systems in Western Europe', *Higher Education in Europe*, vol. 29, no. 3, pp. 393–409.

Lahelma, E. (2009) 'Dichotomized metaphors and young people's educational routes', *European Educational Research Journal*, vol. 8, no. 4, pp. 497–507.

Lasonen, J., and Young, M. (eds.) (1998) *Strategies for Achieving Parity of Esteem in European Upper Secondary Education*, Jyväskylä, Institute for Educational Research.

Laukia, J. (2013) *Tavoitteena sivistynyt kansalainen ja työntekijä: Ammattikoulu Suomessa 1899–1987*, Ph.D thesis, Helsinki, University of Helsinki.

Levin, B. (2003) *Approaches to Equity in Policy for Lifelong Learning*, A paper commissioned by the Education and Training Policy Division, OECD, for the Equity in Education

Thematic Review [Online]. Available at www.oecd.org/education/innovation-educa
tion/38692676.pdf (Accessed 26 September 2017).

Lundahl, L., and Olofsson, J. (2014) 'Guarded transitions? Youth trajectories and school-to-
work transition policies in Sweden', *International Journal of Adolescence and Youth*, vol. 19,
no. 1, pp. 19–34.

Marcoux, G. (2010) 'L'expérience de travail en centre d'appels: Aux confins de l'engagement
et de la distanciation', *Relations Industrielles*, vol. 65, no. 4, pp. 654–672.

Michelsen, S. (1993) *Utdanningspolitikk og utdanningsekspansjon*, Unpublished manuscript
Department administration and organization, Bergen, University of Bergen.

Michelsen. S, Olsen, O.J. and Høst, H. (2014) *Origins and development of VET 1850–2008 –
An Investigation into the Norwegian Case*. Roskilde University. Research report Nord-VET –
The future of VET in the Nordic Countries [Online]. Available at http://nord-vet.dk/
indhold/uploads/report1a_no.pdf (Accessed 13 March 2018).

Michelsen, S., Olsen, O. J., and Høst, H. (2018) 'The Norwegian VET model and social
democracy', in Michelsen, S. and Stenström, M-L. (eds.) *The Historical Evolution of Vocational Education in the Nordic Countries*, Milton Park, Routledge, pp. 146–170.

Numminen, U. (2000) 'Strategies for improving vocational education: The Finnish case', in
Stenström, M-L. and Lasonen, J. (eds.) *Strategies for Reforming Initial Vocational Education and
Training in Europe*, Jyväskylä, Institute for Educational Research, pp. 74–91.

Nyen, T., Skålholt, A., and Tønder, A. H. (2013) 'Overgangen fra fagopplæring til arbeidsmarkedet og videre utdanning', in Høst, H. (ed.) *Kvalitet i fag- og yrkesopplæringen: Fokus på
skoleopplæringen: Rapport 2*, Oslo, NIFU, 23, pp. 159–202.

Nyen, T., Skålholt, A., and Tønder, A. H. (2015) 'Fagopplæring som vei inn i arbeidslivet', in
Høst, H. (ed.) *Kvalitet i fag- og yrkesopplæringen: Sluttrapport*, Oslo, NIFU, 14, pp. 169–228.
Available at www.udir.no/globalassets/upload/forskning/2015/nifu-rapport-14-12.mai-
2015.pdf (Accessed 26 September 2017).

OECD. (2007) *Qualifications Systems: Bridges to Lifelong Learning: Executive Summary*, pp. 9–16
[Online]. Available at www.oecd.org/edu/skills-beyond-school/38465471.pdf (Accessed
15 November 2017).

OECD. (2010) *Learning for the Jobs: Synthesis Report of the OECD Reviews of Vocational Education and Training*, Paris, OECD Publishing [Online]. Available at www.oecd.org/edu/
skills-beyond-school/Learning%20for%20Jobs%20book.pdf (Accessed 10 May 2016).

OECD. (2015) *Education at a Glance 2015: OECD Indicators*, Paris, OECD Publishing.

OECD. (2017) *Education at a Glance 2017: OECD Indicators*, Paris, OECD Publishing.

Olofsson, J., and Persson Thunqvist, D. (2018) 'The modern evolution of VET in Sweden
(1945–2015)', in Michelsen, S. and Stenström, M-L. (eds.) *The Historical Evolution of Vocational Education in the Nordic Countries*, Milton Park, Routledge, pp. 46–65.

Olsen, J. O., Høst, H., and Tønder, A. H. (2014) *Key Challenges for Norwegian VET: The State
of Play*, Research report published 2014 by Nord-VET – the future of Vocational Education in the Nordic countries, Roskilde, Roskilde University [Online]. Available at http://
nord-vet.dk/indhold/uploads/report1b_no.pdf (Accessed 15 November 2017).

Palonen, M., and Halonen, P. (2015) *Higher Education in Finland* [Online]. Available at
www.arene.fi/sites/default/files/PDF/2015/Chile%20Visit/Tomi_Halonen_Maarit_
Palonen_%20HE%20in%20Finland.pdf (Accessed 12 March 2018).

Persson Thunqvist, D., and Hallqvist, A. (2014) *The Current State of the Challenges for VET
in Sweden*, Research report published 2014 by Nord-VET – the future of Vocational
Education in the Nordic countries, Roskilde, Roskilde University [Online]. Available at http://nord-vet.dk/indhold/uploads/report1b_se.pdf (Accessed 15 November
2017).

72 Maarit Virolainen and Anna Hagen Tønder

Pinheiro, R., Geschwind, L., and Aarrevaara, T. (2014) 'Nested tensions and interwoven dilemmas in higher education: The view from the Nordic countries', *Cambridge Journal of Regions, Economy and Society*, vol. 7, no. 2, pp. 233–250.

Raffe, D. (2008) 'The concept of transition system', *Journal of Education and Work*, vol. 21, no. 4, pp. 277–296.

Ruohotie, P., Nokelainen, P., and Korpelainen, K. (2008) 'Ammatillisen huippuosaamisen mallintaminen: Teoreettiset lähtökohdat ja mittausmalli', *Ammattikasvatuksen aikakauskirja*, vol. 10, no. 1, pp. 4–16.

Salminen, H. (1999) 'Ammattikorkeakoulu-uudistuksen ja keskiasteen tutkinnonuudistuksen yhteneväisyyksiä ja eroja', *Kasvatus*, vol. 30, no. 5, pp. 472–490.

Shavit, Y., and Müller, W. (2000) 'Vocational secondary education, tracking, and social stratification', in Hallinan, M. T. (ed.) *Handbook of the Sociology of Education*, New York, Kluwer Academic, pp. 437–438.

Silver, H., and Brennan, J. (1988) *A Liberal Vocationalism*, London, Methuen.

Skolverket. (2013) *Utvecklingen av lärlingsutbildningen*, Stockholm, Skolverket, 397.

Skolverket. (2016) *Uppföljning av Gymnasieskolan*, Stockholm, Skolverket.

Statistics Denmark. (2015) *Statistical Yearbook 2015*, Copenhagen, Statistics Denmark.

Statistics Sweden. (2013) *Övergång från gymnasieskola till högskola, läsåret 2010/11: Elever som slutför naturvetenskapsprogrammet påbörjar oftast högskolestudier*, Örebro, Statistiska centralbyrån.

Stenström, M-L., and Lasonen, J. (eds.) (2000) *Strategies for Reforming Initial Vocational Education and Training in Europe*, Jyväskylä, Institute for Educational Research.

Stenström, M-L., and Virolainen, M. (2016) 'Towards the enhancement of school-based VET in Finland', in Berner, E. and Gonon, P. (eds.) *History of Vocational Education and Training in Europe: Cases, Concepts and Challenges*, Bern, Peter Lang, 14, pp. 327–348.

Stenström, M-L., and Virolainen, M. (2018) 'The modern evolution of the Finnish vocational education and training (1945–2015)', in Michelsen, S. and Stenström, M-L. (eds.) *The Historical Evolution of Vocational Education in the Nordic Countries*, Milton Park, Routledge, pp. 102–123.

Stenström, M-L., Virolainen, M., Vuorinen-Lampila, P., and Valkonen, S. (2012) *Ammatillisen koulutuksen ja korkeakoulutuksen opintourat*, Jyväskylä, Jyväskylän yliopisto, Koulutuksen tutkimuslaitos, 45.

Telhaug, A. O., Mediås, O. A., and Aasen, P. (2006) 'The Nordic model in education: Education as part of the political system in the last 50 years', *Scandinavian Journal of Educational Research*, vol. 50, no. 3, pp. 245–283.

Thorsteinsson, G., Olafsson, B., and Yokoyama, E. (2016) 'Examining the literature on basic educational ideas established by the initiators of the English Art and Craft Movement and the Scandinavian Sloyd', *Bulletin of Institute of Technology and Vocational Education*, vol. 15, no. 10, pp. 94–101.

Trant, A., Branson, J., Frangos, C., Geaney, F., Lawton, D., Mäkinen, R., Moerkamp, T., Donnabhain, D., Vuorinen, P., Voncken, E., and Walsh, P. (1999) *Reconciling Liberal and Vocational Education: Report of the European Union Leonardo da Vinci Research Project on Promoting the Attractiveness of Vocational Education (PAVE)*, Dublin, Curriculum Development Unit.

Trilling, B., and Fadel, C. (2009) *21st Century Skills: Learning for Life in Our Times*, San-Fransisco, Jossey-Bass.

Väärälä, R. (1995) *Ammattikoulutus ja kvalifikaatiot*, Ph.D thesis, Rovaniemi, University of Lapland.

Virolainen, M., and Persson Thunqvist, D. (2017) 'Varieties of universalism: Post-1990s developments in the initial school-based model of VET in Finland and Sweden and implications for transitions to the world of work and higher education', *Journal of Vocational Education & Training*, vol. 69, no. 1, pp. 47–63.

Virolainen, M., and Stenström, M-L. (2014) 'Finnish vocational education and training in comparison: Strengths and weaknesses', *International Journal for Research in Vocational Education and Training*, vol. 1, no. 2, pp. 81–106.

Vuorinen-Lampila, P., and Valkonen, S. (2012) 'Yliopisto-opiskelijoiden opintourat', in Stenström et al. (eds.) *Ammatillisen koulutuksen ja korkeakoulutuksen opintourat*, Jyväskylä, Jyväskylän yliopisto, pp. 191–268.

Walther, A. (2006) 'Regimes of youth transitions: Choice, flexibility ans security in young people's experiences across different European contexts', *Young*, vol. 14, no. 2, pp. 119–139.

Walther, A. (2009) '"It was not my choice, you know?" Young people's subjective views and decisionmaking processes in biographical transitions', in Schoon, I. and Silbereisen, R. K. (eds.) *Transitions from School to Work: Globalization, Individualization and Patterns of Diversity*, New York, Cambridge University Press, pp. 121–144.

Willemse, N., and De Beer, P. (2012) 'Three worlds of educational welfare states? A comparative study of higher education systems across welfare states', *Journal of European Social Policy*, vol. 22, no. 2, pp. 105–117.

Winch, C. (2015) 'Towards a framework for professional curriculum design', *Journal of Education and Work*, vol. 28, no. 2, pp. 165–186.

4 Balancing the esteem of vocational education and social inclusion in four Nordic countries

Lene Larsen and Daniel Persson Thunqvist

Introduction

The Nordic countries share a long-term commitment in education to equality, social justice and social inclusion, but it has also become apparent that it is a major challenge to maintain the high esteem of VET and simultaneously include all students, regardless of social background. The key topic for this chapter is how these two policy-objectives have been balanced in VET. Attempts in the Nordic countries since the 1990s to improve the esteem of VET relative to general education can be framed in the context of the egalitarian Nordic model of education. The chapter shows how different educational systems – especially in Denmark and Sweden – respond to this challenge, and we argue that esteem must be discussed in a varied way. While acknowledging that education policies have partly converged with international trends, the comparative analysis also demonstrates significant differences across the Nordic VET systems in promoting social inclusion and counterbalancing exclusion in education and working life. Linking policy-analysis to a youth research perspective, the multifaceted nature of esteem is further illustrated through the role and meaning that VET has for various groups of students. When young people with few resources become dominant in VET, the status of VET tends to fall, which increases dropout rates and social problems. Although the esteem of vocational training is declining, VET remains an active choice for many students. They find it meaningful to participate in the practical work in workshops, and they get along with the teachers in a better way than in primary school. VET provides alternative learning paths and attractive vocational identities. So, vocational training makes many students feel included in various ways in the different Nordic VET systems.

Esteem and social inclusion: policy, transitions and participation

Today, the Nordic VET is required to pursue a wide range of (sometimes contradictory) goals of educating skilled professionals and including socially disadvantaged young people (Nyen and Tønder, 2014; Larsen, 2012; Jørgensen,

2011). This raises the issue of esteem, which is not always clear-cut. Some vocational programmes provide access to attractive opportunities for employment and further education, as well as the development of a strong professional identity, which contributes to high levels of esteem (Koudahl, 2004). Some trades have high status among some groups of men and women respectively (Korp, 2013; Præstmann Hansen, 2009), and the esteem of an education is often closely linked to the status of the work it gives access to (Persson Thunqvist and Axelsson, 2012). The status of some subject areas changes over time due to media-created images of specific trades (Steno, 2015), and changes in the VET's target groups may affect VET's overall status. In all the Nordic countries, VET plays a vital role in achieving the goal of education for all young people. This should be seen in conjunction with a shift in political strategies, away from focusing on *equal access to education*, towards a much more intense focus on *education for all* in order to reduce residual group in education (Juul, 2012) and the resulting focus on inclusion.

The aim of this chapter is to explore how the challenges involved in improving the esteem of VET, while simultaneously promoting social inclusion goals, have been approached in the Nordic countries in the field of tension between macro-policies and the micro-level of young people's lived experiences. We focus on three interconnected questions: First, esteem and social inclusion are examined as a *political challenge*, comparing how the issue of parity of esteem between general and vocational education has been placed at the centre of public education reforms from 1990 to the present. Secondly, we focus on how the esteem question intersects with the social inclusion goals in VET in line with the notion of *education for all* that is associated with the Nordic model of education. In this part, conditions and measures to counteract social exclusion in terms of early school dropout are described and compared across the countries. The third and final section discusses the notion of *participation*, and how social inclusion invokes the students' perspectives and the meaning of VET for the students.

In the course of the analysis, Denmark and Sweden are particularly highlighted as representing opposite ways to maintain or improve the esteem of VET. Explanations of these differences, we argue, are connected to the two different VET systems, i.e. a dual system distinguished by apprenticeship oriented toward skilled employment (Denmark), vis-à-vis a school-based system of VET (e.g. Sweden), as described in the preceding chapters (Chapters 1 and 2). The country comparisons also raise further questions about self-reinforcing dynamics and unintended consequences of reforms directed at achieving higher esteem for VET and social inclusion goals by bringing VET closer to higher education. In addition, from a youth research perspective, we discuss institutional and cultural dimensions of social inclusion in the context of young people's multiple transitions from VET to working life, and in relation to social class and gender. We argue that linking the analysis of macro-policies to the people's lived experiences of their transitions may contribute to uncovering the differentiated nature of esteem. VET may have low prestige within general education

76 *Lene Larsen and Daniel Persson Thunqvist*

hierarchies (e.g. Billett, 2014; Mäkinen and Volanen, 1998). However, VET and skilled employment may also be a respected route associated with high esteem among students from various locations and non-academic homes.

Theoretically and conceptually, the analysis is based on classical education sociology. We draw particularly on Bourdieu's understanding of education as an unequal hierarchy of possibilities, and the transition research's concepts of young people's choices and transitions as being less linear (Walther, 2006). In addition, we draw on Willis's concept of anti-school culture in order to understand why and how the VET provides new and different opportunities for participation for some young people, not least for boys. The comparison of how esteem and inclusion has been handled on the policy level draws on a problem-based comparative approach used in the Nord-VET project. This approach focuses on how education policies are shaped in negotiations between the concerted interests (e.g. the state, the unions and the employers' organizations) in the field of VET (see the introductory chapter).

The esteem of VET as a policy challenge

For a rather long period of time, VET has attracted at least half of a youth cohort in the Nordic countries (Table 2.1, this volume; Virolainen and Stenström, 2014) and has been a vital component in skill formation. However, in the past decade, enrolment rates in initial VET are falling in all the Nordic countries (except for Finland). At present, the major policy-challenge is to make VET a more attractive choice for young people and counteract the dual problem of youth unemployment and labour shortages in skilled occupations. Similar discussions have also been highlighted in several other countries, such as the UK (Fuller and Unwin, 2009), US and Canada (Lehmann et al., 2014). A long-term perspective on the esteem of VET is relevant, since this issue has been framed differently in education policies over time in the Nordic countries, partly linked to fluctuations in enrolment rates in VET.

Internationally, the concept of *parity of esteem* is often used nowadays in policy discussions. Previous research on VET systems in different European countries (Deissinger et al., 2013; Lasonen and Manning, 2001; Lasonen and Young, 1998) reveals a multitude of policy-strategies in the context of national education reforms that have been used to improve the esteem of VET relative to general education. Overriding societal sources of the *disparity of esteem* between general and vocational education have been discussed as well. The lower status of VET is partly due to dominant perceptions in society about VET as less prestigious than academic education, articulated over centuries by power elites with a rather distant relationship to skilled labour and apprenticeship (Billett, 2014). Such discourses are linked to the labour market subordination of manual work in relation to the leading, planning and symbolic work. The fundamental contradiction within democratic market societies between the principle of equal opportunities and the scarcity of recognized social positions in society (Walther, 2006, p. 122) also matters. When the policy problem is articulated in terms of a "surplus of academic students", as in some previous education reforms in Finland and Sweden (Mäkinen and Volanen, 1998), it may refer to worries about a decrease of the quality and exclusivity of higher education. It can also refer to requests for institutional mechanisms that "cool down" or "re-direct" the aspirations of young people who lack privileged social and cultural capital. On the contrary, among the social partners involved in VET, it may refer to concerns about a drift of ambitious young people away from vocational tracks to academic tracks that undermine the quality and legitimacy of VET as a vital part in collective skill formation.

Improving the esteem of VET: different policy-strategies in the post-1990 reforms

Education policies for improving the esteem of VET in relation to general education from 1990 onwards may to some extent represent an extension of previous social democratic–inspired policies for equality and equal access to higher education within the framework of the egalitarian Nordic Welfare regime (Antikainen, 2006). Previous historical comparisons of the post-war Nordic VET systems (Michelsen and Stenström, 2018) have extensively described how the strong political efforts of the Social Democratic Party across the Nordic countries have struggled to reduce the distance between vocational education and general education, and to promote equal access to further studies for all students, regardless of their social backgrounds.

However, there are significant differences in the policy strategies used to maintain or improve the esteem of VET across the different countries. School-based VET systems in Sweden and Finland are generally distinguished by political attempts to integrate vocational education and general education. However, apprenticeship-based VET systems, such as in Denmark, have been characterized by attempts to modernize and enhance the quality of VET, while protecting the specific nature of VET (Persson Thunqvist and Jørgensen, 2015).

Sweden represents the most clear-cut example of the "unification-strategy": VET was integrated into a new upper secondary school in 1971. Largely oriented towards progression in the education system, this model remains intact in 2017, despite the fact that different education reforms (1991 and 2011) have drawn the system in different directions (Olofsson and Persson Thunqvist, 2018). In addition to partisan politics, an important reason for the strong continuity of the Swedish model is that the employer organizations and unions at central level, and the export industries dominating the Swedish economy, have all largely supported the generalist nature of school-based VET (Dobbins and Busemeyer, 2014; Lundahl, 1997; Lundahl et al., 2010).

However, post-1990 education reforms in the Nordic countries have also converged with international neo-liberal trends in educational policy, emphasizing individual choice and employability, to make VET more attractive for young people. The VET systems have been decentralized, diversified and made more flexible to respond to the diverse demands of individual students

78 *Lene Larsen and Daniel Persson Thunqvist*

(Jørgensen, 2011). A common feature for several upper secondary reforms in Sweden (1991), Norway (1994), Finland (1995) and Denmark (2000) was curriculum changes aimed at promoting individual choice and enhancing the links between VET and higher education institutions. All the reforms added more academic courses into the vocational tracks in order to create more options and educational opportunities for vocational students. In Denmark, however, a reform in 2007 reduced the extent of the general subjects in the basic courses, and a reform in 2014 reversed this policy and the higher level was required in the general subjects.

The impact of strategies has varied. One trade-off for such institutional individualization is that the more theoretically demanding tracks benefit strong groups of students who are capable of managing individually, but it risks increasing the drop-out rates among students from non-academic backgrounds (Jørgensen, 2011). The Swedish upper secondary reform of 1991 extended the two-year vocational lines to a third year of mainly higher education preparatory studies. Formally, this gave VET students eligibility for higher education, but only a minority of students in industrial and technical VET programmes attain this eligibility and then continue to higher education after completion (Persson Thunqvist and Hallqvist, 2014). As shown in Chapter 3 (this volume), transitions from initial VET to higher education is also rather limited in Finland.

The Norwegian reform in 1994 introduced a "2+2" model for vocational courses that allowed students, after two years of school-based vocational studies, to choose between one year of academic preparation or two years of apprenticeship. While this reform has proved successful in promoting flexibility, among other things, it remains a challenge to attract students to choose an apprenticeship during the final two years (Olsen et al., 2014). Finnish post-1990 upper secondary reforms generally aim to achieve a greater degree of curriculum integration and *mutual enrichment* (Lasonen and Young, 1998) of academic and vocational curricula. This is different to Norway and Sweden, where upper secondary curricula mix general and vocational courses, but do not usually blur the boundaries between them.

While reforms in the Nordic countries have repeatedly aimed to improve equal access to higher education, post-1990-reforms also reflect repeated efforts to counteract inbuilt weaknesses in the school-based VET systems in terms of weak connections to working life. Since 2000, Finland has launched several education reforms to reinforce the connection between school and working life. This includes the establishment of a new workplace learning system and new forms of assessment (skills demonstration), and the promotion of the image of VET to change negative attitudes, such as VET as a "second choice" and the "stepchild" in relation to academic education (Virolainen and Stenström, 2014, pp. 15–17). The Norwegian upper secondary reform of 1994 succeeded in expanding apprenticeship into (several) new occupational fields through close collaboration between the state and the labour market partners (Olsen et al., 2014). This also improved direct access to working life, particularly for those

Balancing the esteem of vocational education   79

students who continue their apprenticeship after two years in upper secondary school.

Denmark and Sweden as opposites

Once again, Denmark and Sweden represent two opposite cases regarding different policy strategies to improve the esteem of VET. These strategies can also be examined as policy strategies to manage unintended consequences of previous education reforms. In Sweden, attempts to improve the esteem of VET have shifted twice since 1990, affecting the overall composition between VET and general education (Persson Thunqvist, 2015). While the 1991-reform prioritized higher education preparation in vocational tracks, the 2011-reform, driven by a centre-right political alliance, prioritized a stronger demarcation between higher education preparatory programmes and vocational programmes: the amount of specific vocational content increased at the expense of higher education preparatory courses (Olofsson and Persson Thunqvist, 2018). The quality of higher education preparatory programmes was expected to increase, as they became more exclusively associated with higher education. By building new formal frameworks for cooperation between initial VET and the labour market at central and local levels, the quality and efficiency of the vocational tracks were also expected to increase. In addition, a new apprenticeship track was launched as an alternative to school-situated VET programmes. Indeed, the 2011-reform has been contested in public political debates. The Social Democratic Party (returning to power 2014), in alliance with the Green Party and with support from the trade unions and the Left Party in educational matters, have pushed for a return of equal access to higher education in VET. Declining rates of enrolment in VET (from 36% in 2007 to 27% in 2017; Skolverket, 2017) have also contributed to adjustments in school-based VET in order to facilitate higher education preparations.

During the new millennium, urgent skills shortages in large industrial sectors in Sweden have also been a decisive factor for the stronger involvement of companies and unions to initiate measures (e.g. vocational colleges, see Chapter 5) to improve the prestige of VET and to attract more young people. Other measures have been directed towards campaigning and influencing public opinion concerning attitudes to the skilled occupations. Given that craft identification has generally been rather weak in Sweden (e.g. compared to Denmark and Norway), various industrial occupations have a rather low status among young people (Ferm et al., 2017).

By contrast to Sweden, post-1990 education reforms in Denmark have been characterized by a broad consensus amongst most political parties and the dominant labour market partners to update and prioritize vocational education and apprenticeship as a track separate from the gymnasium, in order to retain the strong labour market value of the dual VET system. However, like in Sweden, the strong academic drift among young people to the gymnasium and higher education has repeatedly called for policy objectives to *build bridges* from apprenticeship to higher education (Jørgensen, 2013b). These policy attempts represent ways of addressing inbuilt challenges in the VET system in terms of weak connections to higher education. They include the establishment of a Swedish-style, full-time, school-based vocational gymnasium (introduced in the 1980s) which provides both vocational education and support progression to higher education. By contrast to apprenticeship, the vocational gymnasiums do not qualify for skilled employment.

Previous research (Jørgensen, 2013b) reveals several challenges and unintended consequences associated with such policy attempts in recent decades. Some barriers to improving the esteem of apprenticeship in Denmark by bringing it closer to higher education are related to the strong connections between VET and the labour market. The active involvement of the labour market partners in VET contributes to maintaining a strong standing of apprenticeship from a labour market perspective. Apprenticeship has remained a respected alternative in relation to general education because it offers a rather safe route for young people to skilled employment and, in many cases, high introductory wages (Jørgensen, 2013b). At the same time, extended periods of workplace learning make it difficult for students to qualify for higher education. Early establishment in the labour market and economic independency are not in themselves incentives for investments in further education. Moreover, the social background of most of the vocational students often makes the vocational route more attractive than academic studies. Therefore, VET has also played an absolutely vital role for the policy-strategy to promote "education for all".

Dropout, inclusion and exclusion

The strategy that all young people should complete a youth education has been prioritized as an inclusion challenge in all four Nordic countries. This has meant that in recent years, VET has had to educate a far more academically and socially differentiated target group than previously, including young people with social and mental issues. This inclusion task has led to declining student numbers, challenges in attracting talented and ambitious young people, large drop-out rates and (as a consequence) declining esteem.

Previous comparative Nordic research on social inclusion provides a multifaceted picture of different causes, as well as a combination of causes (Bäckman et al., 2011) for non-completion and dropout from upper secondary vocational education (Jørgensen, 2011; Engberg and Melin, 2014). In general, the dropout issue may be viewed in a holistic perspective and not as isolated phenomena, since dropout patterns are linked to overriding questions about the esteem of VET, quality and labour market connections. As shown in Chapter 2 (this volume), difficulties obtaining access to training placements for workplace learning constitute important barriers for students' completion in Denmark and Norway, with a strong apprenticeship component in VET. At the same time, in Finland and Sweden, increased academic content in VET programmes have often been suggested as a potential cause of increased dropout rates, since VET students with a non-academic background mostly prefer a shorter route to working life, and not academic studies (Olofsson and Panican, 2008).

A comparative study (Bäckman et al., 2011) on dropout patterns in upper secondary schools and VET in the Nordic countries (based on the period 1995–2007) reveals that VET tracks in Norway have the highest dropout rates (about 37%–45%) and Finland has the lowest (about 15%) during the relevant period. According to the study, the dropout rate in Danish vocational tracks fluctuates between 17% and 25%, and is close to Sweden (approximately 20%–25% drop out in the vocational tracks). Furthermore, the results of the comparative study show that *native-born* Swedish young people who follow a regular vocational track came out best among the Nordic countries *in a seven-year follow-up* from school start (Bäckman et al., 2011). This suggests that the "dropout-problem" in Swedish upper secondary school should rather be located in the academic tracks, where Sweden lags behind the other Nordic countries considerably regarding high dropout rates.

The quite positive picture on school completion for native Swedish VET students in a seven-year follow-up may be further explained by age restrictions in upper secondary school, in combination with the social inclusive function of the *second chance system*. The current increase in immigration in the Nordic countries raises questions about how the whole support system, including the school system, adult education and labour market policy, can be used and combined to support young immigrants through their studies and transitions to work.

Over the past decade, Denmark, Finland and Sweden have developed a diverse set of youth-oriented active labour market policy measures (ALMPs). They cover subsidized employment, labour market services, job seeking guidance and labour market training (Tosun et al., 2017) to support early school leavers and unemployed people, including recently arrived immigrants. While Finland and Sweden comprise rather similar cases regarding the composition of such measures, Denmark stands out since its ALMP measures concentrate more heavily on youth activation in vocational training (Tosun et al., 2017). It is relevant to also mention that Swedish initial VET (typically targeting 16–19-year-olds) is more age-homogeneous than Danish VET. The majority of youth-oriented ALMP measures in Sweden are intended for young adults (plus 20-year-olds). In Denmark, early school leavers have been extensively activated in VET, while in Sweden since early 1990, they have been allocated to separate preparatory programmes intended to enable students to transfer into regular upper secondary school programmes.

Several measures for social inclusion that have been developed in the Nordic countries relate to how young people with incomplete grades from compulsory schooling can reach the upper secondary level or find employment. Differences between the Nordic countries occur when it comes to how entrance requirements are regulated in the education systems. In Norway, all students have a statutory right to upper secondary education. While VET in Norway does not require passed exams or grades at lower secondary level in order to

82 *Lene Larsen and Daniel Persson Thunqvist*

access initial VET, access to VET in Denmark (from 2015) and to (regular) upper secondary school VET programmes in Sweden requires passed exams at lower level in eight subjects, e.g. Swedish, Mathematics and English (Nevøy et al., 2014, p. 195). Since the latest 2011 reform in Sweden and 2014 reform in Denmark, the requirements are lower in the VET programmes than in the higher education preparatory programmes. This, in combination with higher requirements for eligibility to higher education, probably affects falling enrolment rates in Swedish upper secondary school VET in recent years (Skolverket, 2017). At present, the Introduction Programme (IP) is one of the four largest upper secondary school programmes, including five different tracks for students who do not have the passing grades required for regular programmes, including VET (Lundahl, 2012). Language introduction aimed at immigrant youth who have recently arrived in Sweden is the largest track.

Denmark and Norway have developed comparable, irregular programmes. Examples in Denmark are Schools of Production (tailored for students who are not motivated by the traditional types of education) and Youth Education Adapted for Young People with Special Needs (established in 2007 for young people who have cognitive or physical disabilities). Since the 1994-reform in Norway, counties in the country provide a multitude of alternative pathways, with various connections to regular programmes, for students who are not keeping pace, or who are dropping out of regular programmes. A common feature for the irregular programmes across the three countries is that the students are in school, but they do not award any formally recognized upper secondary qualifications. Research on the impact of these programmes is scarce, but available figures suggest that the irregular programmes have limited effect: between one third and half of the students enter a regular programme (Nevøy et al., 2014, pp. 204–205). Among young immigrants in Sweden who participate in language introduction, only about 36% of the students continue to a national programme within five years (Skolverket, 2017). The latest 2011 reform in Sweden also re-introduced school-organized apprenticeship, tailored for students categorized as at risk of marginalization and, although this track was not a success, it is still in progress, but on a reduced scale (see Chapter 5; Skolverket, 2017). Given that the irregular programmes do not require reorganization or improvements of the regular programmes, a trade-off is that they contribute to maintaining the legitimacy of regular, national VET programmes, and thus also a division between "normal" and "special" tracks.

In Denmark, the inclusion challenge has resulted in various initiatives such as the establishment of special classes and courses for diverse groups of students in the vocational educations. This may entail positive experiences that can contribute to more students completing, because the programme is adapted to the individual student, but it can also increase the risk of drop-out due to stigmatization of special programmes for disadvantaged students (Jørgensen, 2011). In addition, many resources have been invested in establishing special support functions such as increased guidance, drop-out coordinators, mentors and psychological schemes (Larsen, 2012). This raises the question of what it means

Balancing the esteem of vocational education   83

for the vocational education programmes that they are increasingly challenged on their core task – training of skilled labour – and now also have to take on a host of other functions that originally and traditionally belong to other systems and institutions. In Denmark, this inclusion task has led to a discourse on the fact that education is increasingly similar to social work, and teachers question whether they are teachers or social workers (Larsen, 2012). In addition, it is also being discussed whether providing a trade or care that is the core service, i.e. whether VET should be "a place to learn" or "a place to be"? (Lippke, 2013). In the Swedish upper secondary school, it has been observed as a problem that much of the responsibility for vocational training in practice is placed on individual teachers, with weak institutional support (Fejes and Köpsén, 2012). Ultimately, these teachers, often working on their own, must deal with and make sense of the various goals stipulated by the educational policy. An education policy change in Denmark in 2014 meant, for example, that the prioritization of social inclusion was replaced by a prioritization of exclusion/selection in the form of admission requirements and increased consideration of the needs of the labour market. Thus, a significant political goal in Denmark at present is that 30% of a youth cohort should choose a vocational education (rather than upper secondary school) after primary school in 2025 (Government, 2014), which places a major strain on some adolescent's transition from primary to (lower/upper) secondary education.

Transitions to educational hierarchies

The question of how the esteem of VET can be balanced with social inclusion is intrinsically interconnected with the capacity of VET to support young people in their transitions through educational hierarchies and to working life. While education policy often focuses on school-to-work transitions in terms of efficiency and economic effects (i.e. system integration), when linked to social inclusion it is equally important to consider both the institutional and cultural dimensions of such transitions. The former dimension concerns, in our case, how different institutional architectures of the Nordic VET systems (see the introductory chapter) enable or constrain social integration in skilled employment and working life (Raffe, 2008). Departing from a sociological youth research perspective on school-to-work transitions (e.g. Walther, 2006), we argue that a discussion of the esteem of VET also needs to address issues about overriding cultural shifts in young people's transitions. For example, drop-out rates are not only a manifestation of the shortcomings and problematic behaviour of some young people, but must also be seen in conjunction with young people's general orientation, choice patterns and coping with transitions.

The Danish education system requires young people to make a very early choice between an academic preparatory or vocational secondary education, which means that a large number of young people (about 75%) choose upper secondary school as the first priority in order to postpone making a more final decision for another three years. It is therefore also referred to as "the safe choice" or "the natural choice" (EVA, 2013). The Swedish VET, on the other hand, focuses more on ensuring that young people acquire broader and more general competencies, while at the same time acquiring practical skills. In this way, early focus on employment is reduced in favour of an integration of vocational and general education, but with a correspondingly weaker link to the labour market. Therefore, young people in Sweden do not perceive vocational education in the same way as "closing doors" as they do in Denmark (Persson Thunqvist and Hallqvist, 2014).

When comparing young people's transitions from compulsory school to vocational education at upper secondary level and subsequent transitions from VET to stable employment in the labour market, significant differences appear between the Nordic countries. As demonstrated in Chapter 2 (this volume), transitions from VET to the labour market are generally smooth in Denmark and Norway, with strong apprenticeship traditions compared to the school-based systems in Finland and Sweden. On the contrary, the transition through the education system is more difficult in the former countries. This difference in upper secondary school systems is reflected in higher non-completion rates in Denmark (39%) and Norway (occasionally reaching 32%) than in Sweden (17%) and Finland (close to 20%) (comparative figures based on 1998 student cohort; Albæk et al., 2015, pp. 273–274; see also public statistics about early school leavers in Table A4.1 in the appendix). However, during the financial crisis in the early 1990s, Finland and Sweden faced serious problems with large proportions of young people with prolonged withdrawal from both education and work, the so-called NEET-group (Virolainen and Persson Thunqvist, 2017). Weak connections between the school world and the labour market contributed to high unemployment. The financial crisis has also affected the size of the NEET-group in other Nordic countries. For example, the NEET-group in Denmark increased more strongly after 2008 than in Sweden (see Table A4.1 in the appendix). It is a major challenge for apprenticeship programmes in Denmark and Norway that the supply of training placements in companies depends on the economic conditions in the labour market.

Public statistics of youth unemployment in the Nordic countries (Nordic statistics, 2017) also indicate that across the shifts in the labour market over more than two decades, there are consistent patterns in these official figures. These patterns can be explained by the stronger connections between VET and working life in Denmark and Norway compared to Finland and Sweden (Table A4.1 in the appendix). In the European context, Sweden also has one of the EU's highest percentages of 15–24-year-olds in temporary employment (60%, while the EU average was just over 40%, European Commission, 2012). According to the OECD (2016), the liberal legislation regarding temporary employment in Sweden (by contrast to the more rigid employment protection of permanent and full-time employment in the Swedish labour market) represents an important explanation for the high proportion of young people in temporary employment.

To sum up, the comparison above highlights that differences in young people's transitions through the education system and into working life is partly dependent on the institutional design of the different Nordic VET systems. Difficulties in respective VET systems are related to different phases in the transition process, i.e. inside the education system or in the transition from school to work (Jørgensen, 2006). It is also important to put the question of the esteem of VET into the general picture in youth research of transitions becoming more prolonged and complex due to shifts in the culture of young people, as well as conditions for socialization and identity formation in "late modernity" (Jørgensen, 2013b; Walther, 2006; Wyn and Dwyer, 2000; Beck, 1992). In a general sense, in order to attract young people, VET must be in touch with such cultural shifts. This has partly to do with the fact that young people spend longer periods of time in formal education institutions together with other young people before they enter the labour market. Even if class and gender distinctions prevail as an "objective reality" (e.g. Bourdieu and Passeron, 1997) and continue to separate young people in terms of access to different career pathways and life opportunities, social identities and the scope of different imagined futures has become a more open affair. This means, for example, that VET programmes in many European countries that do not open doors to further studies, risk to being regarded as a "blind alley" (e.g. Raffe, 2008; Deissinger et al., 2013). Transition is thus no longer a transition between two defined life stages but consists of many different parallel and staggered transitions, and thus has become complex and non-linear (Jørgensen, 2006; Larsen, 2003; Heinz, 2001; Wyn and Dwyer, 2000).

In general, the transition regime in the Nordic countries compared to other European countries can be presented in a positive light due to coherent school systems and good educational and social conditions and offers (Walther, 2006). This is an image which must be refined, however, as many young people experience unstable family relationships, abuse, mental problems and peripheral attachment to education (Lundahl, 2012). This depends e.g. on the relationship between choice-biography and normal-biography, where some young people fail to live up to the expectations of both managing their own choice-biography and conforming to the norms of a normal-biography (Pless, 2009). Gender also emerges as an important, but also differentiated, marker, in that all four countries display a lower completion rate among young men, and men generally have higher NEET rates (Albæk et al., 2015). Both the labour market and the education system are gendered and reproduce gendered patterns, where the Nordic countries are highly horizontally gender-segregated, despite political objectives of equality (Jørgensen, 2013a). Gender segregation in the labour market is both vertical and horizontal, and this affects which kind of education young people are oriented towards and their career opportunities in general (Niemi and Rosvall, 2013; Nielsen and Sørensen, 2004). In Denmark, the strong division between education for young people contributes to a predominance of girls in the upper secondary education programmes and a large predominance of boys in technical vocational educations. The young people who in Denmark choose a vocational education must already choose a specific occupation at the age of 15–16 and have few experiences with the labour market, so they often orient themselves towards some stereotypical gendered identity figures (Jørgensen, 2013a).

Esteem and inclusion as negotiated participation

The link between masculinity and class – and, partly, gender – is described well within classical education culture studies and masculinity (Jørgensen, 2013a; Frosh et al., 2002; Kryger, 1988; Willis, 1977). Trouble – and in more established institutional contexts, also including resistance and opposition – are classical issues, which are at stake in the struggle to secure access and the right to participation and recognition. Disadvantaged young people often seek recognition in arenas other than education and through different forms of resistance and opposition to the "system" and institutional practices (Connell, 2000, p. 137). Such oppositional practices can find expression through sub-cultural and youth-cultural forms of language, style and images – such as symbolic creativity, which shows how young people specifically work to create a sense of belonging, place and space in education (Williams, 2011; Willis, 1990). For many young people, VET constitutes a positive alternative to the school-based form of education they have experienced earlier in their schooling, while in VET they experience being practical and part of a community that offers new and different opportunities for participation (Korp, 2013). The theoretical orientations of practice theory in recent years has opened up new understandings of young people's participation in education, where practical work and craftsmanship are attributed a potential as the solution to some young people's challenges within school and education. The importance of becoming part of a community of practice (Wenger, 1998) allows some young people to experience meaningful participation in education, because they are seen and recognized as competent apprentices/colleagues, where not least the role of the teacher is important in order to establish a safe learning environment (Pless, 2009). Here, masculinity, the physical and the aesthetic are of immense importance for the development of enjoyment at school and the negotiation of identities, but where the hierarchy of the masculine over the feminine and the hierarchy of different masculinities creates some special inclusion and exclusion processes (Præstmann Hansen, 2013). Often, the Danish alternating training have been criticized for a lack of social contexts and communities and as being opposed to the emphasis of the general youth education on this aspect (Steno, 2015, 2016). Nevertheless, many VET students emphasize the social community among the students as the being the most positive aspect of a vocational education, where they experience being accepted, making friends, helping one another and enjoying a place where the general tone is humorous. In addition, it is meaningful to manufacture products and provide services and the related material and bodily sensory processing. Thus, VET is regarded as a counter-weight, or a form of counter culture in relation to primary and upper secondary education (Jørgensen, 2013a; Korp, 2013). Nevertheless, separate groups of students are formed in the form of institutional divisions into different cohorts (e.g. those who have clear career plans and those who have not) and by the students' own mutual positioning (e.g. goody-goodies and troublemakers) and who are strongly reproducing and playing a significant role in connection with drop-out. In this way, the relationship between esteem and inclusion is not just an education policy issue, it is also very much something that is negotiated in and through the vocational educations' specific cultural practices.

In the context of school-based VET in Sweden, Finland and Norway, students in the male-dominated, technically oriented VET programmes commonly prefer an early entrance into working life (Virolainen and Persson Thunqvist, 2017; see also Chapter 7 in this volume). Dissertations based on close-up descriptions of vocational students' participation in the general subjects (Kärnebro, 2014; Högberg, 2009) reveal how students recurrently resist subjects that they perceive as not immediately relevant for their future profession. However, the dissertations also show that vocational students generally want to get good grades (to pass the courses), since they assume that poor grades will negatively affect their chances to get a job. The results from previous studies on vocational students' participation in workplace-based training in Swedish industrial VET programmes (Ferm et al., 2017; Berner, 1989, 2010) reveal that such training is quite demanding. The implications of this research demonstrate that active learning strategies among students to become skilled industrial workers are particularly interesting in the light of universal school-based VET systems, where workplace-based training is increasingly used nowadays as a social political measure to combat dropping out and social problems (Olofsson and Panican, 2008, 2012). To put it somewhat incisively: advertising apprenticeship as a route for school-wary young people tends to reduce its status among youth and their parents in general. However, for those young people who manage to complete a full VET programme, workplace-based training may represent an attractive learning career. Previous research also shows that most of the students who completed an apprenticeship in the technical area in Danish VET found employment in the targeted occupation. Afterwards they also have a high mobility across sectors and industries, despite the fact that the VET programmes are focused on specific skills (Jørgensen, 2013b).

How to combine high esteem and social inclusion

By examining how the challenges involved in improving the esteem of VET and promoting social inclusion goals have been approached in the Nordic countries in the field of tensions between macro-policies and micro-level of young people's lived experiences, the chapter provides a multifaceted and varied picture. The Swedish-style unification strategy to improve equal access to higher education and social inclusion at the same time became a role model for many other countries. Hence, it comprises a kind of "natural experiment".

By requiring that all young people (16–19 years old) study general subjects, including higher education preparatory courses at the same level, programme supporters believe that the system best promotes opportunities for individuals in society in a long-term perspective. However, a trade-off is that those students who do not intend to pursue higher education lose their possibility to follow a more practical oriented VET programme. Moreover, it is quite evident that the boundaries and social inequalities between students in vocational programmes relative to general programmes have not disappeared, despite previous reforms (Persson Thunqvist and Hallqvist, 2014, pp. 16–17). A major challenge for Swedish school-based VET over time has been that the strong educational logic in initial VET has weakened the direct links to the labour market. A central concern for VET policy in recent decades has therefore been to bridge the gap between upper secondary school and the world of work. Denmark can be seen as an opposite to the Swedish case: policy strategies have been more oriented to the modernization of the dual system of VET. Trade unions and social democrats have come to recognize the benefits of a dual system and therefore support apprenticeship. The strong ties between the dual VET system and the labour market are a major strength, but the failure of persistent policy attempts to improve the weak connections to higher education have remained a policy-dilemma. Compared to Sweden, the early division of students into different education pathways in upper secondary education (the dual system) makes it difficult for young people to progress to higher education from VET. On the other hand, the Danish VET system has proved more successful than Sweden over time, by including non-academic students in skilled employment and supporting career developments in the labour market (Olofsson and Panican, 2012). This success also comprises a barrier to higher education. These different and somewhat contradictory movements in VET policies in Denmark and Sweden illustrate a notorious policy-dilemma within the framework of the Nordic, universalistic welfare regime to simultaneously provide dual-access to skilled employment and higher education. Attempts to improve the esteem of VET in relation to general education have in various ways been linked to policy-attempts to manage this dual challenge. VET policy, then, is not just about rational educational planning, but also about political processes and negotiations fraught with tensions and contradictions (Raffe et al., 1998). Reforms are shaped by institutional dynamics in the interplay between a multitude of stakeholders in VET (Streeck and Thelen, 2005). They include the state, the employers, the unions and other stakeholders at central and local levels, including students "voting with their feet" (Billett, 2014).

The esteem of VET is also closely connected to issues of social inclusion and exclusion. In addition, "the drop-out problem" has often been framed as a deviation from a normal linear route through compulsory education and upper secondary education. When vocational education is now presented in education policy as a measure to handle drop-outs and non-completion, it is likely to affect the status of vocational education negatively, since most young people do not want to be associated with problematic social categories. Importantly, however, this does not indicate a contradiction in terms between social inclusion and esteem per se. The dominant historical discourse of the academic-vocational divide (for a critical discussion, see e.g. Billett, 2014) often neglects VET students' perspectives and experiences, dismisses vocational choices and presents young people as second-chance learners (Brockmann, 2012). Indeed, social class and gender contribute to the lower esteem of VET in the dominant perception of prestige, since young people from working-class backgrounds commonly prefer a faster route to working life than through the academic route (Lappalainen et al., 2013). As illustrated above, vocational education and apprenticeship may, in social and pedagogical practices, have important inclusive functions in providing alternative learning careers, supporting study motivation and vocational identities. Apprenticeship, therefore, may be a positive choice connected with high esteem during young people's participation in communities of practice and negotiation of social identities, career pathways and life opportunities.

Appendix

Table A4.1 Indicators of social inclusion of youth

NEET rates 15–34 years (% of population)[1]

	2000	2005	2010	2015
Denmark	6.9	6.6	8.0	8.4
Finland	13.0	10.6	11.5	13.1
Sweden	7.0	10.2	8.3	7.4
Norway	20.4	10.0	7.6	8.1

Early school leavers 18–24 years (% of population)[2]

	2000	2005	2010	2015
Denmark	11.7	8.7	11.0	7.8
Finland	9.0	10.3	10.3	9.2
Sweden	7.3	10.8	6.5	7.0
Norway	12.9	4.6	17.4	10.2

Youth unemployment below 25 years (% of active population)[3]

	2000	2005	2010	2015
Denmark	6.2	8.6	13.9	10.8
Finland	21.4	20.1	21.4	22.4
Sweden	10.5	22.6	24.8	20.4
Norway	9.8	11.4	9.2	9.9

Sources of data: Eurostat 1. edat lfse 21, 2. edat_lfse_14, 3. Une rt a.

References

Albæk, K., Asplund, R., Erling, B., Lindahl, L., von Simson, K., and Vanhala, P. (2015) *Youth Unemployment and Inactivity: A Comparison of School-to-Work Transitions and Labour Market Outcomes in Four Nordic Countries*, Copenhagen, Nordic Council of Ministers.

Antikainen, A. (2006) 'In search for the Nordic model in education', *Scandinavian Journal of Educational Research*, vol. 50, no. 3, pp. 229–43.

Bäckman, O., Jakobsen, V., Lorentzen, T., Österbacka, E., and Dahl, E. (2011) *Dropping Out in Scandinavia: Social Exclusion and Labour Market Attachment among Upper Secondary School Dropouts in Denmark, Finland, Norway and Sweden*, Stockholm, Institute for Futures Studies.

Beck, U. (1992) *Risk Society: Towards a New Modernity*, London, Sage Publications.

Berner, V. B. (1989) *Kunskapens vägar: Teknik och lärande i skola och i arbetsliv*, Lund, Arkiv Förlag.

Berner, V. B. (2010) 'Crossing boundaries and maintaining differences between school and industry: Forms of boundary-work in Swedish vocational education', *Journal of Education and Work*, vol. 23, no. 1, pp. 27–42.

Billett, S. (2014) 'The standing of vocational education: Sources of its societal esteem and implications for its enactment', *Journal of Vocational Education & Training*, vol. 66, no. 1, pp. 1–21.

Bourdieu, P., and Passerson, J-C. (1997) *Reproduction in Education, Society and Culture*, London, Sage Publications.

Broockmann, M. (2012) *Learning Biographies and Learning Cultures: Identity and Apprenticeship in England and Germany*, London, The Tufnell Press.

Connell, R. (2000) *The Men and the Boys*, Cambridge, Policy Press.

Deissinger, Th., and Aff, J., Fuller, A., and Jørgensen, C. H. (2013) *Hybrid Qualifications – structural and Political Issues in the Context of European VET-Policy*, Zürish, Peter Lang.

Dobbins, M., and Busemeyer, M. (2014) 'Socio-economic institutions, organized interests and partisan politics: The development of vocational education in Denmark and Sweden', *Socio-Economic Review*, vol. 13, no. 2, pp. 259–284.

Engberg, J., and Melin, G. (2014) *Rekrytering, genomströmning och relevans: En studie av yrkes-och lärlingsutbildningssystemen i Norden*, Copenhagen, Nordic Council of Ministers.

EVA. (2013) *Veje og omveje: Studenters valg af uddannelse*, Copenhagen, Danmarks Evalueringsinstitut.

Fejes, A., and Köpsén, S. (2012) 'Vocational teachers' identity formation through boundary crossing', *Journal of Education and Work*, vol. 27, no. 3, pp. 265–283.

Ferm, L., Persson Thunqvist, D., Svensson, L., and Gustavsson, M. (2017) 'Students' strategies for learning identities as industrial workers in a Swedish upper secondary school VET programme', *Journal of Vocational Education and Training*, vol. 70, no. 1, pp. 1–19.

Frosh, S., Phoenix, A., and Pattman, R. (2002) *Young Masculinities*, Basingstoke, New York, Palgrave Macmillan.

Fuller, A., and Unwin, L. (2009) 'Continuity and change in 40 years of school to work transitions', *Journal of Education and Work*, vol. 22, no. 5, pp. 405–416.

Heinz, W. (2001) 'Transition, discontinuities and the biographical shaping of early work careers', *Journal of Vocational Behaviour*, vol. 60, no. 2, pp. 220–240.

Högberg, R. (2009) *Motstånd och konformitet: om manliga yrkeselevers liv och identitetsskapande i relation till kärnämnena*, Linköping, Linköping University.

Jørgensen, C. H. (2006) 'Fra uddannelse til arbejde: Ikke kun en overgang', *Tidsskrift for Arbejdsliv*, vol. 11, no. 1, pp. 67–86.

Jørgensen, C. H. (2011) *Frafald i erhvervsuddannelserne*, Frederiksberg, Roskilde University Press.

92 Lene Larsen and Daniel Persson Thunqvist

Jørgensen, C. H. (2013a) 'Kom du på taberholdet?' – om hvorfor nogle drenge taber I uddannelserne', in Jørgensen, C. H. (ed.) *Drenge og maskuliniteter i ungdomsuddannelserne*, Frederiksberg, Roskilde University Press, pp. 259–281.

Jørgensen, C. H. (2013b) 'Linking the dual system with higher education in Denmark – when strength become weakness', in Deissinger, Th., Aff, J., Fuller, A., and Jørgensen, C. H. (eds.) *Hybrid Qualifications – structural and Political Issues in the Context of European VET-Policy*, Zürich, Peter Lang.

Juul, I. (2012) 'Ligeværd mellem ungdomsuddannelserne – realistisk mulighed eller utopi?' *Dansk Pædagogisk Tidsskrift*, vol. 2012, no. 1, pp. 14–26.

Kärnebro, K. (2014) *Plugga stenhårt eller vara rolig: Normer om språk, kön och skolarbete i identitetsskapande språkpraktiker på Fordonsprogrammet*, Umeå, Umeå University.

Korp, H. (2013) 'Hvem regnes for dygtige her? – intelligens og maskulinitet i erhvervsuddannelserne', in Jørgensen, C. H. (ed.) *Drenge og maskuliniteter i ungdomsuddannelserne*, Frederiksberg, Roskilde University Press, pp. 103–124.

Koudal, P. (2004) *Den gode erhvervsuddannelse*, Ph.D. thesis, Department of Psychology and Educational Studies, Roskilde University.

Kryger, N. (1988) *De skrappe drenge*, Copenhagen, Unge Pædagoger.

Lappalainen, S., Mietola, R., and Lahelma, E. (2013) 'Gendered divisions on classed routes to vocational education', *Gender and Education*, vol. 25, no. 2, pp. 189–2005.

Larsen, L. (2003) *Unge, livshistorie og arbejde*, Ph.D. thesis, Department of Educational Studies, Roskilde University.

Larsen, L. (2012) 'Når uddannelse bliver til socialt arbejde', *Dansk Pædagogisk Tidsskrift* vol. 2012, no. 1, pp. 30–40.

Lasonen, J., and Manning, S. (2001) 'How to improve the standing of Vocational compared to General Education', in Descy, P. and Tessaring, M. (eds.) *Training in Europe, Second Report on Vocational Training Research in Europe 2000 – background report Volume I*, Paris, CEDEFOP, pp. 115–167.

Lasonen, J., and Young, M. (eds.) (1998) *Strategies for Achieving Parity of Esteem in European Upper Secondary Education*, Jyväskylä, University of Jyväskylä.

Lehmann, W., Taylor, A., and Wright, L. (2014) 'Youth apprenticeship in Canada: On their inferior status despite skilled labour shortages', *Journal of Vocational Education & Training*, vol. 66, no. 4, pp. 572–589.

Lippke, L. (2013) *En erhvervsskole for alle? Professionelle deltagelsesformer og spændingsfelter mellem faglighed og omsorg*, doctoral dissertation, Institut for Kommunikation, Aalborg, Aalborg University.

Lundahl, L. (1997) 'A common denominator? Swedish employers, trade unions and vocational education', *International Journal of Training and Development*, vol. 1, no. 1, pp. 91–103.

Lundahl, L. (2012) 'Leaving school for what? Notes on school-to-work transitions and school dropout in Norway and Sweden', in Strand, T. and Roos, M. (eds.) *Education for Social Justice, Equity and Diversity*, Zürich, LIT Verlag, pp. 85–108.

Lundahl, L., Erixsson Arreman, I., Lundström, U., and Rönnberg, L. (2010) 'Setting things right? Swedish secondary school reform in a 40-year perspective', *European Journal of Education*, vol. 45, no. 1, pp. 46–59.

Mäkinen, R., and Volanen, M. (1998) 'Improving parity of Esteem as a policy goal', in Lasonen, J. (ed.) *Reforming Upper Secondary Education in Europe: The Leonardo da Vinci Project Post- 16 Strategies*, Juväskylä, University of Juväskylä.

Michelsen, S., and Stenström, M. L. (eds.) (2018) *Vocational Education in the Nordic Countries: The Historical Evolution*, Abingdon, Routledge.

Nevøe, A., Rasmussen, A., Ohna, S-E., and Barow, T. (2014) 'Nordic upper secondary school: Regular and irregular programmes – or just one irregular school for all?' in Blossing, U.,

Imsen, G., and Moos, L. (eds.) *The Nordic Education Model: 'A School for All' Encounters Neo-Liberal Policy*, London, Springer, pp. 191–210.

Nielsen, S. B., and Sørensen, A. (2004) *Unges valg af uddannelse og job – udfordringer og veje til det kønsopdelte arbejdsmarked*, Center for Ligestilling, Roskilde, Roskilde University.

Niemi, A. M., and Rosvall, P. Å. (2013) 'Framing and classifying the theoretical and practical divide: How young men's position in vocational education are produced and reproduced', *Journal of Vocational Education & Training*, vol. 65, no. 4, pp. 445–460.

Nordic Statistics. (2017) Available at www.dst.dk/nordicstatistics

Nyen, T., and Tønder, A. H. (2014) *Yrkesfagene Under Press*, Oslo, Universitetsforlaget.

OECD. (2016) *OECD Employment Outlook 2016*, Paris, OECD Publishing.

Olofsson, J., and Panican, A. (2008) *Ungdomars väg från skola till arbetsliv, Nordiska erfarenheter*, TemaNord 2008.584, Copenhagen, Nordic Council of Ministers.

Olofsson, J., and Panican, A. (2012) 'Lärlingsutbildning- aktuella erfarenheter och framtida möjligheter, Stockholm', *RATIO: Rapport* vol. 2, no. 2, pp. 3–65.

Olofsson, J., and PerssonThunqvist, D. (2018) 'The modern evolution of VET in Sweden (1945–2015)' in Michelsen, S. and Stenström, M. L. (eds.) *Vocational Education in the Nordic Countries: The Historical Evolution*, Abingdon, Routledge, pp. 124–145.

Olsen, O. J., Høst, H., and Hagen Tønder, A. (2014) *Key Challenges for Norwegian VET: The State of Play*. Research Report. NordVET. Roskilde, Roskilde University [Online]. Available at http//nord-vet.dk/ (Accessed 13 March 2018).

Persson Thunqvist, D. (2015) *Bridging the Gaps: Recent Reforms and Innovations in Swedish VET to Handle the Current Challenges*, Roskilde, Roskilde University [Online]. Available at www.Nord-VET.dk (Accessed 13 March 2018).

Persson Thunqvist, D., and Axelsson, B. (2012) "Now it's not school, it's for real!': Negotiated participation in media vocational training', *Mind, Culture, and Activity*, vol. 9, no. 1, pp. 29–51.

Persson Thunqvist, D., and Hallqvist, A. (2014) *The Current State of the Challenges for VET in Sweden*, Roskilde, Roskilde University [Online]. Available at www.nord-vet.dk (Accessed 13 March 2018)

Persson Thunqvist, D., and Jørgensen, H. C. (2015) 'Inclusion and equal access at the same time – comparing VET in Sweden and Denmark', *Conference-article ECER 2015 VET-NET Conference Budapest 8–11 2015.*

Pless, M. (2009) *Udsatte unge på vej i uddannelsessystemet*, Ph.D. thesis, Danmarks Pædagogiske Universitetsskole, Aarhus University.

Præstmann Hansen, R. (2009) *Autoboys.dk: En analyse af maskulinitets- og etnicitetskonstruktioner i skolelivet på automekanikeruddannelsen*, Ph.D. dissertation, Det Humanistiske Fakultet, University of Copenhagen.

Præstmann Hansen, R. (2013) 'Håndens maskuline arbejde – problem og potentiale: Drenges kønsforhandlinger på mekanikeruddannelsen', in Jørgensen, C. H. (ed.) *Drenge og maskuliniteter i ungdomsuddannelserne*, Frederiksberg, Roskilde University Press, pp. 87–103.

Raffe, D. (2008) 'The concept of transition system', *Journal of Education and Work*, vol. 21, no. 4, pp. 277–296.

Raffe, D., Arnman, G., and Bergdahl, P. (1998) 'The strategy of a unified system: Scotland and Sweden', in Lasonen, J. and Young, M. (ed.) *Strategies for Achieving Parity of Esteem in European Upper Secondary Education*, Juvaskyla, University of Jyvaskyla, pp. 135–159.

Skolverket. (2017) 'Uppföljning av gymnasieskolan', in *Rapport 2017*, Stockholm, Skolverket.

Steno, A. M. (2015) *Ungdomsliv i en uddannelsestid – kønnede, klassede og tidsbundne driblerier i og mellem erhvervsuddannelser*, Ph.D. dissertation, Roskilde University.

Steno, A. M. (2016) 'Om sociale fællesskabers svære betingelser på EUD', *Dansk Pædagogisk Tidsskrift*, vol. 2016, no. 4, pp. 40–49.

94 *Lene Larsen and Daniel Persson Thunqvist*

Streeck, W., and Thelen, K. (eds.) (2005) *Beyond Institutional Change in Advanced Political Economies*, Oxford, Oxford University Press.

Tosun, J., Unt, M., and Wadensjö, E. (2017) 'Youth-oriented active labour market policies: Explaining policy effort in the Nordic and the baltic states', *Social Policy & Administration*, vol. 51, no. 4, pp. 598–616.

Virolainen, M., and Stenström, M. L. (2014) 'Finnish vocational education and training in comparison: Strengths and weaknesses', *International Journal for Research in Vocational Education and Training*, vol. 1, no. 2, pp. 81–106.

Virolainen, M., and Persson Thunqvist, D. (2017) 'Varieties of universalism: Developments in initial school-based model of VET in Finland and Sweden post-1990s and transitions to the world of work and higher education', *Journal of Vocational Education and Training*, vol. 1, no. 69, pp. 47–63.

Walther, A. (2006) 'Regimes of youth transitions: Choice, flexibility and security in young people's experienced across different European contexts', *Young*, vol. 14, no. 2, pp. 119–139.

Wenger, E. (1998) *Communities of Practice: Learning, Meaning, and Identity*, Cambridge, Cambridge University Press.

Williams, J. P. (2011) *Subcultural Theory: Traditions and Concepts*, Cambridge, Polity Press.

Willis, P. E. (1977) *Learning to Labour: How Working Class Kids Get Working Class Jobs*, New York, Columbia University Press.

Willis, P. E. (1990) *Common Culture: Symbolic Work at Play in the Everyday Lives of Young People*, Buckingham, Open University Press.

Wyn, J., and Dwyer, P. (2000) 'New patterns of youth transition in education', *International Social Science Journal*, vol. 52, no. 164, pp. 147–159.

5 Reforms and innovations in Nordic vocational education

Improving transitions to employment and to higher education

Christian Helms Jørgensen

The aim of this chapter is to present and examine policy reforms and innovations to manage the two main challenges for VET that are examined in the preceding chapters. The first part focuses on innovations to link the VET system to the labour market. This is a major challenge for the mainly school-based VET systems of Sweden and Finland. However, the apprenticeship systems of Norway and Denmark also face the challenge of connecting students' learning in school-based and work-based training, and of safeguarding the quality of work-based training. The second part focuses on innovations to link VET to higher education, which is a major challenge for the VET systems of Norway and Denmark. In these two countries, hybrid programmes that combine apprenticeships with preparation for higher education are examined. This part also examines new higher education institutions intended for former students from VET in Finland and Denmark. The chapter does not examine specific innovations related to the esteem of VET and social inclusion in VET, because these issues are closely related to the two main concerns of this chapter. Social inclusion is related to the students' access to employment and esteem is related to students' access to higher education.

The chapter's interest in innovations arises from the identification of trade-offs for policy in the field of VET. Trade-offs imply that an advantage gained in one dimension involves a disadvantage in another. However, sometimes a trade-off can be evaded or reduced by changes to the institutions or practices that define the trade-off. In this sense, innovations need not be revolutionising. The innovative institutions and practices examined here are not associated with the displacement of existing institutions or radical shifts in the historical trajectories of the national VET systems. It is more appropriate to regard them as processes of layering, where new initiatives are introduced alongside existing institutions in processes of gradual institutional change (Mahoney and Thelen, 2010).

The Nordic labour markets and education systems are characterised by centralised, egalitarian and standardised regulation, and they have therefore been criticised for being rigid and slow to adapt to changing market conditions. However, this is contradicted by the continuous capacity of these countries to combine strong economic performance with low levels of social inequality in international comparisons (Engelstad and Hagelund, 2015). The innovative

96 *Christian Helms Jørgensen*

capacity of the Nordic countries is supported by the 'beneficial constraints' provided by strong state regulation, which commit employers to pursue a high-quality production strategy and invest heavily in training (Streeck, 1992). In addition, the strong Nordic tradition for collaborative and consensual labour relations promotes trust and knowledge-sharing in organisations with low hierarchies (see Chapter 1). The highly organised and consensual labour markets encourage solutions to the problem of collective action in the field of training. The following section examines innovations to improve the links between VET and the labour market, and new institutions for collaboration on work-based training.

This challenge is a result of the process where school-based training has gradually replaced work-based learning in all the Nordic VET systems, as was analysed in Chapter 2. This process has been most extensive in Sweden and Finland, where work-based learning was marginalised in the statist upper secondary school. Many different drivers can be identified to explain this development (Jørgensen, 2015a). One of these is the political aim of giving all young people access to higher education by increasing the academic subjects in VET. Another is a critical assessment of the workplace as a site of learning due to the priority of profitmaking, and the deficient capacity of training companies in relation to the social demand for training placements. In addition, while employers in general have strong interests in a highly skilled labour force, the individual employers have little interest in investing in transferable skills, if they are not able to gain the benefits of this investment (Busemeyer and Trampusch, 2012). The Nordic VET systems have historically developed different solutions to this problem by relying on either state-organised training in schools or on employer-led institutions to coordinate employers' engagement in training (Michelsen and Stenström, 2018). As it is difficult for training in public vocational schools to relate to the world of work, governments have taken an increasing interest in engaging the employers in vocational training.

Connecting VET to the labour market

Since the early 1990s, reforms in all four countries have sought to strengthen the connection between VET and the world of work, and to strengthen the employers' involvement in training through new corporatist institutions and financial incentives. The apprenticeship systems of Norway and Denmark have expanded into new sectors, and longer periods of work-based learning have been included in the Swedish and Finnish VET systems. However, integrating work-based learning in upper secondary VET has two challenges. One is the problem of connecting school-based and work-based learning for the students in the VET programmes. Work is organised according to the logic of production, the requirement of improving efficiency, the demands of customers, and economic considerations. Teaching in the vocational schools is organised according to the logic of education, the curricular requirements and the organisation of activities for the students' learning. The two learning environments represent two diverging epistemic cultures (Akkerman and Bakker, 2012). In addition, the individual students have diverse learning processes in different training companies that can be difficult to connect to the curricular-based teaching of whole classes in schools.

The other problem is the supply of high-quality training placements, and students' access to work-based training. This is especially a challenge in apprenticeships that require training contracts of two to four years' duration covering a wide range of skills. The training market is non-transparent and employers' hiring practices tend to be selective and discriminate against minorities (Helland and Støren, 2006; Lancee, 2016). The capacity of work-based training systems is vulnerable to the economic fluctuations that periodically reduce the supply of training places. This results in recurrent mismatches between the supply and students' demand for training placements. These conditions are in contrast to the basic aim of creating an upper secondary school for everyone in the Nordic countries. Generally, the opportunities for learning are increasing in modern companies that are constantly changing, innovating and improving their performance. However, the access to work-based learning in VET is subject to structural constraints (Jørgensen, 2015a). While most of these constraints are not new, some are becoming more acute, such as the increasing specialisation of the production process. When the production process becomes increasingly dispersed in global supplier chains, each individual company becomes more specialised, and can offer only a limited part of the broad range of vocational qualifications necessary to learn for an occupation. Another constraint is that technological, economic and organizational changes tend to limit inexperienced students' access to learn in companies. Shorter delivery times, tighter production chains (Lean and Just-in-Time production) and stronger quality management reduce the opportunities for experimentation, trying out and learning from mistakes. In addition, increasingly volatile markets limit the opportunities, especially in smaller firms, for entering into two-year or three-year training contracts. Following the shift from a 'stakeholder' to a 'shareholder' economy, companies tend to adopt a short-term approach to creating financial returns for investors, and they reduce their long-term investments in a skilled workforce (Casey, 2012). These changes exacerbate the collective action problem of employers' investment in training (Busemeyer and Trampusch, 2012). These constraints on work-based learning are challenges for the increasing interest in all the Nordic VET systems of strengthening work-based learning. However, the Nordic countries also offer promising reforms and innovations that address the problems of linking school and workplace in VET and involving employers in training. This chapter examines examples of these innovations in two fields (see Table 5.1 for overview). Firstly, by analysing three new institutions for coordination between vocational schools and training companies; secondly, by analysing four new pedagogical practices to connect students' learning in schools and workplaces in VET. The examples have been selected to cover all four Nordic countries.

98 *Christian Helms Jørgensen*

Table 5.1 Two fields of innovation in VET: institutions and pedagogical practices

New mediating institutions	• Training agencies in Norway
	• Training centres in Denmark
	• Vocational colleges in Sweden
New connective practices	• Skills demonstration in Finland
	• E-logbooks in Norway
	• Tripartite meetings in Sweden
	• Practicum in Denmark

New mediating institutions

The Norwegian training agencies

Following the VET reform in 1994, VET was included in a coherent national system of public upper secondary education under a unified legal framework. The extent of school-based education and of general subjects increased, and the vocational subjects became broader and less specific in the first two years. In the standard 2+2 model, the programmes start with two years of broad school-based preparatory education followed by two years of apprenticeship. Alternatively, the students have the option of shifting into a general programme after two years to gain eligibility for higher education.

The reform was initiated from above, and the employers saw it as an extension of state control over the VET system. In addition, the employers' administrative work increased and the need to coordinate with schools, students and public authorities became more demanding. The response of the employers was to expand Local Training Agencies (LTA) as new institutions to manage their common employer interests in training. The LTAs represent an interesting innovation for collective skill formation in a period where collective institutions in general are under pressure from neo-liberal policies (Thelen, 2014).

Like the other Nordic countries, Norway has a strong tradition of institutionalised cooperation in all fields of labour market regulation. However, the LTAs are initiated and managed by the employers alone. Around one quarter of the LTAs have invited representatives from local trade unions onto their boards. Generally, the local trade unions have not pressed hard to get access to the LTAs, and this does not seem to be any significant issue for the unions (Høst et al., 2014). The role of the LTAs resembles that of the German chambers (*Kammern*), but in contrast to these, the employers' membership of the LTAs is voluntary. The LTAs are private organisations owned by the training companies, whose representatives make up the governing boards of the agencies. The LTAs have strong roots in the local employer communities and have considerable local autonomy in relation to the national employer organisations. They cannot be seen as local representatives of the national employer organisations or as departments of the local employer organisations. The LTAs have also maintained their autonomy in relation to the county authorities for

VET (*fylkeskommune*). Some of the tasks of the LTAs overlap with the county authorities, but generally the two institutions have close cooperative relations and recognise each other as equal partners (Høst et al., 2014).

Since the reform in 1994, the role of the LTAs has expanded, so that in 2014 they are a contractual partner responsible for the training for around 80% of all apprentices in Norway. Around 80% of all training companies are members of a LTA, with the highest density in the traditional private industries (Høst et al., 2014). In the early phase of development, the primary motive of the training companies for joining the LTAs was to be relieved of the legal and administrative responsibilities connected to the training of apprentices. Currently, the reasons given by the companies for participating in the LTAs emphasise the support by the LTA for securing the quality of apprenticeship training and the future supply of skilled labour for local businesses (Høst et al., 2014). This is partly the result of the stronger quality requirements in the VET reform in 2007. In addition, the LTAs have contributed to the remarkable growth in the supply of apprenticeships since the reform in 1994 and to the matching of students and training placements.

The financing of the LTAs derives mainly from the state's financial support for in-company training of apprentices, which is channelled through the LTAs. On average, half of these resources go to the LTAs. The generous state funding has contributed strongly to the LTAs' expansion of coverage, capacity and tasks. The amount of funding for the individual LTA depends on the number of apprentices in the member firms. The average number of apprenticeship contracts of the LTAs has grown from 62 in 1997 to 118 in 2013, and the average number of member firms has increased from 36 firms in 1997 to 77 firms in 2013. The LTAs have on average three full-time employees, which represents a doubling since 1997 (Høst et al., 2014). The growing number of members and resources has raised the LTAs capacity, and their tasks have expanded from working mainly with administrative matters to working to improve the quality of apprenticeship training. The quality work includes assisting member firms to organise apprenticeship training, regularly visiting and interviewing the apprentices, managing the portfolio or training logbook of the apprentices and organising training courses for in-company trainers (Nore and Lahn, 2014). In addition, most LTAs organise supplementary off-the-job training for apprentices, mostly theoretical, but also workshop based. The LTAs also engage in conflict resolution in companies, the organisation of multiple site training of the apprentices and training of workplace trainers. In addition to these internal services, the LTAs play a significant role in representing the interests of the training companies in relation to the public and the local authorities. They are active in mobilising resources and public support for apprenticeship training and the organisation of skills competitions.

In doing this, the LTAs have developed a diversified organisational structure adjusted to the local conditions (concentration of training companies, degrees of specialisation and the resources available). The training agencies have acquired a function as local mediators, who facilitate a flexible exchange of resources,

100   Christian Helms Jørgensen

knowledge and tasks between public institutions and the training companies. In connection with the growth in the size and capacity of the average LTA, they have been 'professionalised' through the standardisation and formalisation of practices. Vehicles for this process are county and national networks of LTAs that organise annual seminars, homepages and mutual support. More than 80% of the LTAs are members of a network of LTAs, and more than 40% of the local LTAs are localised together and share facilities (Høst et al., 2014). These local LTA communities often have more employees than the county authorities responsible for VET. However, the LTAs have not acquired a formal position in the neo-corporatist governance structure for VET at the local level. The reason for this is primarily that the employer organisations still reserve this role for themselves, and that the trade unions oppose this as long as the LTAs are purely employer organisations and not institutions for collaboration between labour and capital.

The Danish training centres

In contrast to the dual systems of VET in countries like Germany and Switzerland, students in Denmark can start in a VET programme without having a contract with a training company (Juul and Jørgensen, 2011). A contract must be obtained during the first full-time, school-based basic course (6–12 months) before switching to the work-based training in the main course, which is typically of three years' duration. However, since the 1970s, the shortage of training placements has been a major reason for students dropping out of the basic course of VET. As all the stakeholders consider the apprenticeship model to be a core quality of the Danish VET system, there is no support for replacing this system with a full-time, school-based system, like the Swedish gymnasiums. However, the substantial number of young people not in education, training or employment (NEETs) in the early 1990s, led to the introduction of a system of 'School-based Training', SKP ('skolepraktik'). The SKP was intended to be a compensatory measure in times of economic recession, not as a permanent institution, and it acquired a tarnished image of being a 'second-rate' option. A reform in 2013 converted the SKP into a new and permanent institution, the training centre ('praktikcenter'), which takes responsibility for realising the 'educational guarantee' declared by the Ministry of Education. This guarantee implies that students who start in a basic VET course are guaranteed the right to complete a VET programme, though not necessarily the specific programme they have chosen. VET students who are unable to obtain a contract with a training company after completion of the basic course can sign a contract with a training centre. When students enrol in a training centre, they must continue to search for an ordinary apprenticeship, which most of them find before completing the programme.

The aim of the training centre is to offer students temporary training placements until they can obtain a permanent training placement in a company. In addition, the purpose is to coordinate the students' multiple, shorter placements in different companies and to supplement this with school-based training to ensure that the students acquire all the qualifications necessary to complete the programme. Responsibility for the apprenticeship training hereby shifts from the individual training companies to the training centres, which acquire a central coordinating function for the training. Work-based training in companies can take place through short contracts, partial contracts or combined training contracts (two or more companies), where the apprentice is employed in the company, or as 'relocated tuition', where the apprentices are not employed and do not work. The curricular requirements and the final test is similar to the ordinary apprenticeships. The functions of the 50 Danish training centres in the institutional architecture can be compared to the Norwegian LTA. However, the LTAs have weak links to the vocational schools. Moreover, the Danish training centres are established at the initiative of the state, in contrast to the situation in Norway, where the LTAs are organised by the employers, although they rely on substantial state funding. The operation of the Danish training centres is financed by the state and the allowance paid to the students is financed by the employers' collective training levy (The Employers' Training Fund, AUB). The centres function under the auspices of the vocational schools but have a separate board consisting of representatives of the local labour market organisations.

Compared to the earlier SKP, the training centres have the advantage of being permanent institutions, where the vocational schools invest in creating attractive institutions with qualified trainers. Otherwise, they face the same weaknesses that gave the SKP a poor reputation (Juul and Jørgensen, 2011). The enrolled students are students who cannot find an apprenticeship and who are more disadvantaged than the average students in VET. Moreover, the centres can only to a limited extent engage in real production of goods and services for customers or citizens, and they thus lack the authenticity of the ordinary workplace. The centres are connected to the vocational schools and the students retain an identity of being students, in contrast to apprentices who are employed in a company, and thus are craftsmen/women 'in the making'. An assessment of the centres indicates that they are working more systematically and are well structured with higher standards (EVA, 2014). They vary significantly in size, as some have only 10 students in 1 programme and others up to 500 students in 18 different programmes. The centres strive to find niches to organise production for customers in order for the students to have the experience that their work is valued by others.

The share of students in the training centres has increased from 3% in 2007 to 16% in 2017. A significant share of the students eligible for school-based training do not enrol, partly because the student grant in the training centres is lower than the apprentices' wages. While the centres struggle to overcome the negative image of the earlier SKP, they have the potential of developing into a new 'third learning space' between school and work. To fulfil the government's target of increasing the share of a youth cohort enrolling in VET, a substantial increase in the supply of apprenticeships is required. Judging by the development since 2008, this is only possible through a continued increase in the capacity of the 50 Danish training centres. Accordingly, the training centres

102 *Christian Helms Jørgensen*

can acquire a more prominent role in the Danish dual VET system as an intermediary institution that bridge the world of work and the world of education, and function as a hub for the coordination of the students' multiple placements in different specialised training companies.

The Swedish Health and Technical Colleges

While the Swedish employers have been ambivalent towards the new apprenticeship programmes initiated in 2011 (see Chapter 2), they have been strongly engaged in establishing a new and promising partnership model for collaboration between school and work-life, the Health and Technical Colleges. The Technical Colleges were established in 2004 in a joint initiative by the key employer organisation (*Teknikföretagen*) and the main union for employees in industry (*IF Metall*). They are now controlled by the Industry Council, which is a partnership between the major labour market organisations in industry. A few years later, a parallel initiative was taken to establish the Health Colleges. The aim of the Vocational Colleges is to raise the quality of VET and increase the enrolment of students in order to secure the future supply of skilled workers on a regional basis. The colleges are not schools, but regional partnerships for vocational training. A group of training companies, together with at least three municipalities and vocational schools, can be certified as a Vocational College by meeting 10 quality requirements. These requirements include high-quality learning environments and up-to-date equipment, systematic quality control and an infrastructure for collaboration between vocational schools and work-life.

The colleges represent a new form of collective skill formation in partnerships between municipalities, the vocational schools and training companies (Persson Thunqvist and Hallqvist, 2014). In 2016, 150 certified providers of vocational education cooperated with 3,000 training companies and 25 counties in Sweden in the Technical Colleges (www.teknikcollege.se, 2016), and the number of certified Health Colleges was at around 90 in 2014. The colleges are strongly engaged in the improvement of the quality of training and the supply of skilled labour. The apprenticeship training in these partnerships is organised in accordance with the curricula defined by the state in collaboration with the labour market organisations. Due to the extensive decentralisation of the Swedish upper secondary schools, the colleges have many opportunities to adapt the VET programmes to the requirements of local companies. The colleges are employer driven, like the Norwegian training agencies, but in contrast to these, the colleges rely on a formalised cooperation with the vocational schools and public authorities.

New connective pedagogical practices

Collaborative skills demonstration

While the Finnish VET system has been mainly school-based, a number of initiatives have strengthened the cooperation between vocational schools and working life since 2000. The skills demonstrations represent an innovative practice, where schools and training companies cooperate in the assessment of the VET students' skills. Vocational skills demonstrations are competence-based tests carried out in a work situation, or as part of a work process organised by an education provider in cooperation with representatives from working life. They were included in all vocational qualifications as a standard practice in 2006, and after a reform in 2018, they can be organised flexibly and more individualised by the local education providers (http://minedu.fi). At different points during their training in initial VET, students must demonstrate their skills in tests that bring together representatives from workplaces and teachers. A local tripartite board with representatives from the local labour market, teachers and students supervise the skills demonstrations. The board also approves assessors and the plans for the skills demonstrations. The competences assessed, and the criteria used, are defined in the national core curriculum. This includes vocational knowledge, mastery of work processes and methods, occupational safety procedures and core qualifications common to all vocational areas, such as problem solving, communication and cooperation. Stenström (2009) emphasises the advantages of this practice-oriented assessment in relation to the students' learning. The assessment encourages the students' explicit reflection and self-assessment, which stimulates the development of higher-order skills and self-regulated learning. Every skill demonstration concludes with an assessment discussion, where the student receives feedback from the teacher and the workplace trainer. This tripartite assessment discussion not only provides a broad perspective on the student's skills, it can also enhance broader reflection and discussion among all the participants. Organising the assessments around authentic work situations increases the motivation of the students and contributes to the integration of theory and practice in VET (Stenström, 2009). The skills demonstrations were introduced in connection with other initiatives that bring VET closer to work-life, and this has made VET in Finland more attractive and increased the enrolment of students, in contrast to what has occurred in the other three countries.

A practicum connecting school and workplace

The practicum concept was originally developed by Donald Schön (1983) in studies of professionals learning in practice across different learning environments. In the Danish VET system, the intention behind the Practicum is to establish a new 'third learning space' between the world of work and the world of education. This is manifested through a shared developmental project defined jointly by the student, the company and the school. The Practicum becomes a partnership that connects the schoolteachers and the company trainers in supporting the students working on the project across the workplace and the school (Jørgensen, 2015b). It combines the authenticity of the workplace with the time and room for reflection in a school setting. It links practical problem-solving in a workplace with theoretical knowledge offered in the school. The model for the practicum was developed in 2000 and is currently only mandatory in two occupations. The reason why it has been slow to spread is that it requires more resources from firms and schools. However, a practicum has been shown to have major learning benefits for the students and contributes to partnerships between schools and companies. One experience gained from the pilot projects is that the state and the trade committees must make the practicum mandatory in all apprenticeships. Due to the risk of 'poaching', some companies are reluctant to invest in high-quality training of apprentices, such as the practicum. A common, binding regulation can ensure that all companies maintain the same high standards of training with regard to coherence in the students' learning process across school and training companies.

E-portfolios and tripartite meetings

Two more innovative pedagogical practices should be highlighted: e-portfolios and tripartite meetings. E-portfolios are used in the Norwegian VET system for communication and exchange between training companies, training agencies and apprentices (Nore and Lahn, 2014). The VET programmes in Norway are regulated by a common national curriculum, and the programmes are divided into two years of school-based and two years of workplace learning. This separation is deeper than in other dual VET systems that have more frequent shifts between school and workplace, in either day-release or block-release for attending vocational school during apprenticeships. However, the problem is similar in all countries: lack of connection and coherence in the students' learning across the two venues (Akkerman and Bakker, 2012). A central objective of the e-portfolios is to raise the quality of work-based learning by documenting that the apprentices attain the learning goals of the national curriculum. The e-portfolios are also used for articulation, communication and reflection on the students' experiences and learning process. In addition, the platform is also used for the students to solve learning tasks, for example for mathematical problem-solving in online cases. Nore and Lahn (2014) demonstrate that the e-logbook can contribute to connecting the apprenticeships to higher education by making the apprentices' reflection and learning explicit and visible.

The tripartite meetings in the new Swedish apprenticeship programme represent another institutionalisation of a connective practice between school and workplace. As the educational authorities in Sweden are traditionally sceptical towards the quality of workplace learning, they have a strong focus on quality procedures. One of these procedures is the regular 'tripartite meetings' in the training companies between the workplace trainer, the apprentice and the vocational school teacher to monitor and support the progress and learning of the apprentice. When these regular meetings become an institutionalised practice, they can be a valuable support for the apprentices' learning across school and workplace. A study shows that it is difficult for the teachers to manage both the teaching and the visits to the training companies, especially when the schools do not devote the time and resources required (Lagström, 2012).

A government report recommends that the schools 'professionalise' this task and appoint a special coordinator for monitoring the apprentices' workplace learning (SOU, 2011).

New mediating institutions and practices

In the Nordic model of education, the state provides equal access to education for all and gives priority to education for democratic citizenship. This contrasts with entrusting training in upper secondary VET to private employers. However, workplaces are increasingly recognised as important sites for learning state-of-the-art technologies, procedural knowledge and social skills. Moreover, including work-based learning in upper secondary VET increases the students' subsequent access to employment. Therefore, all the Nordic countries have introduced measures to extend work-based training in the VET programmes.

In all the Nordic countries, the governments have taken initiatives to improve the quality of work-based training. Responsibility for this regulation lies with either the public school system, collaborative labour market institutions or new mediating institutions between work and education. All these solutions are represented in the Nordic VET systems. The objectives of this regulation are to ensure that the quality of workplace training conforms to the national standards and to support the students' transitions between education and work. In addition, the aim is to link the students' learning in school and workplace, to coordinate the students' training in multiple placements and to match the demand and supply of training placements and match students and training companies.

In the Swedish VET system, the school (teacher/coordinator) is assigned the role of controlling the students' work-based training in relation to the requirements in the national curriculum. This is not very successful, as the teachers or coordinators from the schools have limited authorisation to control or organise training in private companies (Skolverket, 2016). They share this problem with the Danish training centres, which are established and controlled by the vocational schools. In relation to supervising work-based training, the Norwegian LTAs are in a more favourable position, as they are owned and controlled by the training companies.

The Danish training centres represent a renewal of the apprenticeship model. The current model is based on a single two- or three-year relationship between an apprentice and a master (company) that is approved to offer all the skills required for a full occupational qualification. For some apprentices, this is changing towards becoming a relationship between an apprentice and a mediating institution that organises training in multiple companies and workshop schools. In the Danish construction industry, for example, short contracts now make up one third of all apprenticeship contracts, and this requires a coordinating institution, like the training centres.

The local training agency in Norway is an interesting innovation, as it is established and owned by the local training companies. It represents their collective interests in training a highly skilled work force. Even though the companies'

106 *Christian Helms Jørgensen*

membership is voluntary, the training agencies are partners in around 80% of all Norwegian apprenticeship contracts. Their missions have expanded to include quality work, the training of apprentices and workplace trainers, networking across industries and regions and recruitment to VET. The Vocational Colleges in Sweden have a similar mission of securing the quality of VET in a local/ regional area. This concept is initiated and controlled by the employers and is organised in collaboration with vocational schools and municipalities. They appear much more promising than the new apprenticeship programme initiated by government. This initiative has had little success, however, primarily because it targets youths who are 'tired' of school, and it therefore has low status and has failed to gain support from the employers. The Swedish Vocational Colleges demonstrate that building close connections to training companies can raise the esteem of VET, when the initiative is combined with high-quality standards.

Connecting VET to higher education

This section investigates two new types of measures to improve the linkages between VET and higher education. The first is the new hybrid programmes that combine certification for higher education with the apprenticeship model. The second is reforms of higher education that broaden the direct access for VET graduates by recognising vocational qualifications for admission to higher education institutions. These reforms correspond to the two types of measures examined for the German-speaking countries by Nikolai and Ebner (2012). A key aim of the Nordic model of education is to provide permeability from the lowest to the highest level with no dead ends. However, a major challenge identified in the foregoing chapters is to manage the trade-off in VET between providing direct access to higher education and providing direct access to employment. The Swedish and Finnish VET systems include only 15–20 weeks of work-based learning and can offer all students eligibility for higher education. However, the transition from VET to employment is difficult in these two countries. Moreover, a substantial proportion of students in Sweden complete upper secondary education without attaining eligibility for the tertiary level of education. The reform of the Swedish VET system in 2011 increased the connections to the labour market and simultaneously reduced the opportunities for progression to higher education. It demonstrated the trade-off between social inclusion and educational progression. The Danish and Norwegian VET systems are based on the apprenticeship model and do not provide general eligibility for higher education. The lengthy periods of work-based learning make it difficult to offer the general curriculum that provides access to higher education. The challenge in these countries is to simultaneously obtain direct access to skilled employment and to higher education. Two hybrid programmes, the eux in Denmark and the YSK in Norway, offer a journeyman's certificate and eligibility for higher education in the same four-year programme.

Eux, connecting apprenticeships to higher education

The apprenticeship system has become increasingly popular among policy-makers in Europe, but in Denmark the system is losing its attractiveness for young people. A major reason is that it appears to be a dead end in the education system, because it does not offer general eligibility for higher education. Today, when 60% of a youth cohort are expected to complete an education at the tertiary level, it is important for young people to keep open the opportunity for educational progression. This has become an urgent policy problem, because it is believed that it lowers the esteem of and enrolment in apprenticeships and also because labour market forecasts predict a serious shortage of skilled labour in the future (Jørgensen, 2017).

The innovative response to this challenge in 2010 was to launch the eux programme, and a reform five years later implemented the programme as an option for all students in VET. A vocational route to higher education, the vocational gymnasiums, has been available in Denmark since the 1980s. However, similar to the Swedish VET programmes, this programme does not provide a journeyman's certificate. The eux is innovative in a Nordic context because it adds general subjects to the apprenticeship model and integrates the learning of general and vocational qualifications in a hybrid programme. In this way, the eux also differs from the successful Swiss programme for double qualifications, the '*Berufsmatura*', which in most popular versions offers an additional year for study preparation after completion of the vocational programme (Schmid and Gonon, 2011).

A major challenge for the new programme is to integrate subjects from the gymnasiums and the apprenticeship schools that have different origin, traditions and different forms of governance and learning cultures (Jørgensen, 2013). Another challenge in organising the programme is to offer in one four-year programme what was earlier offered in two different programmes with a total duration of seven years. One solution to this challenge is to give credit for the general qualifications acquired in learning the vocational subjects. When electricians learn technical skills, they also learn applied maths, which can give credit in the academic subject of maths. Another solution is to introduce new hybrid subjects that integrate multiple subjects such as physics, maths and language skills. Yet another solution is project-based teaching, where content from different subjects is integrated in the students' work in groups on a common project. Considering the deep historical divisions between the two tracks in Denmark, this has been a conflictual and drawn out process. Another challenge for the eux programme is to acquire training placements, when the length of in-company training is reduced, and the recurrent school-based periods are extended to six months. Compared to the ordinary apprentices, it is more difficult for the eux students to obtain a training contract. The long school periods are especially a problem for smaller firms, where the apprentices count as part of the workforce required to run the daily business. Larger companies that take

108   *Christian Helms Jørgensen*

on apprentices with a long-term perspective of recruitment, do not experience the same problem.

There is a good chance that the introduction of the eux will improve the esteem of the VET system by demonstrating that it offers opportunities for educational progression and is no 'dead end'. However, it is also likely that the eux programmes will contribute to the hierarchisation of upper secondary education, where the ordinary technical vocational programmes rank lowest (Jørgensen, 2013).

Fruitful compromises in Norway: *YSK* and **Y-veien**

The Norwegian VET system is based on the apprenticeship model and does not provide eligibility for higher education. Therefore, it shares with the Danish system the challenge of being a 'dead end' in the education system. However, the Norwegian system offers some unique qualities that appear as fruitful compromises between the Danish apprenticeship model and the unified upper secondary school in Sweden. First, it provides an opportunity for horizontal mobility into a general programme after two years in a vocational programme. It also offers a hybrid programme, *YSK*, which combines preparation for higher education with the journeyman's certificate. In addition, it has developed a new direct route from VET to higher education, called *Y-veien*. These initiatives are described below.

The opportunity for a horizontal shift from a VET programme to a general programme makes it less risky for students to choose a vocational programme, because they can change direction without wasting time. In some programmes, like health, this has become a problem, because students shifting out of the programme represent a significant drain that reduces the supply of skilled labour (see Chapter 6). The so-called 'vocational and study competence programme', YSK, (earlier *TAF*) was initiated by the manufacturing and construction industries in order to recruit engineers with practical experience from the shop floor. Since the programme started in 1992, it has been extended to other sectors like health, childcare and agriculture. The main purpose of the YSK is to offer a four-year programme that provides both a journeyman's certificate and an exam for admission to the universities. During the first two years, the students have the status of school students, and during the last two years, they are employed as apprentices in training companies and attend vocational schools on day release every week. The volume of the programme is small (around 300 every year) and the competition for admission to the programme is intense. After completion, most of the students from YSK progress to higher education, mostly in university colleges, which was also the intention of the programme. The YSK has succeeded in attracting students who are mainly oriented towards general education. It does not drain the other vocational programmes, which was a concern when the programme was established (Olsen et al., 2015). A third interesting initiative in Norway is to link VET directly with higher education through the 'vocational route' ('*Y-veien*'). A number of vocational colleges offer direct access to special bachelor programmes for graduates from VET. During the first year, the programmes have less practical subjects and more intense studies of the general subjects required to complete a bachelor of engineering. Despite initial scepticism towards this initiative in the colleges, it has proven to be a success (Olsen et al., 2015). By providing eligibility for higher education, the new initiatives improve the apprenticeship model.

Reforming higher education to widen the access from VET

Until the comprehensive school reforms in the 1960s, the educational systems in all the Nordic countries remained strongly segregated regarding the students' social background and gender. In particular, universities recruited mostly from narrow, elite, social groups. Since the 1970s, post-secondary and higher education in all the Nordic countries has expanded strongly to become mass education (Börjesson et al., 2014). This has increased enrolment of young people from less privileged families, even at the highest levels of education. However, at this level there is still a strong underrepresentation of children of parents whose highest attainment is upper secondary education (Jæger and Holm, 2007; Berggren, 2013). The institutional architecture of the education system is decisive for the strength of the intergenerational transmission of educational inequality. Some of the key qualities of education in the Nordic countries, the unified lower secondary school, the low degree of stratification and the high permeability throughout the education system are associated with lower inequality (Breen and Johnsson, 2005; Pfeffer, 2008). These qualities of the Nordic systems of education can explain why the students' socio-economic background in these countries is less influential in determining their educational attainment in these countries (Causa and Johansson, 2011). Moreover, Nordic countries deny the assumption of a trade-off between equality and quality, as their education systems score high in both dimensions (Pfeffer, 2015). However, the Nordic systems of upper secondary education differ significantly with respect to the opportunities for progression from upper secondary VET to higher education. These differences are determined not only by the extent of preparation for higher education offered in VET, but also by the admission procedures and the structure of higher education (Aamodt and Kyvik, 2005).

The Nordic countries differ with respect to the organisation of their higher education systems. After 1945, upper secondary and post-secondary education expanded with the dual purpose of delivering professionals to the institutions of the welfare state and for the rationalisation of industry. With different timing from the 1960s, all the Nordic countries developed binary systems of higher education, where students had few opportunities to transfer from the colleges to the universities (Kyvik, 2009). In that period, a sizeable proportion of the programmes in technical, nursing and teacher training colleges were accessible without a formal entrance examination for the universities. A range of post-secondary vocational educations were offered by the local institutions that were

110   *Christian Helms Jørgensen*

also responsible for upper secondary VET. These educations were recognised as progression routes for skilled workers, and they were directly accessible with an upper secondary vocational examination (a journeyman's certificate). The first process of rapid and fragmented growth of local post-secondary institutions outside the universities was followed by a process of contraction and integration of these institutions into larger regional universities of applied sciences (or university colleges). Subsequently, the post-secondary programmes were standardised and upgraded to become part of a rationalised higher education system (Kyvik, 2009). Following this academic drift, the curricula, staff and culture of the college sector went through processes of academisation and the institutions were renamed as university colleges and universities of applied sciences. Many post-secondary programmes were upgraded to bachelor status in accordance with the Bologna process, and the opportunities for direct access to these programmes from VET were reduced (Jørgensen, 2017). In some of the Nordic countries, the university colleges have become vertically integrated with the universities and disconnected from the upper secondary vocational schools. The gap between VET and higher education has widened, and the opportunities for students' progression has been reduced. However, the situation is different in the four Nordic countries. While universities and colleges in Sweden and Norway have developed towards a unified system, Finland has followed a route of strengthening and upgrading the universities of applied sciences (UAS) as a distinct sector with close links to upper secondary vocational education. In the following section, the successful Finnish UAS is contrasted with the less successful Danish introduction of new institutions for post-secondary education aimed at graduates from the VET system.

Universities of applied sciences in Finland

A reform in Finland in the 1990s upgraded and merged a large number of post-secondary educational institutions into a new type of regional universities of applied sciences (UAS), separate from the universities. The aim was to increase the quality, popularity and status of higher vocational studies and redirect some of the students from the universities to the short and practical educational route (Ahola, 1997). This reform created an attractive destination for graduates from upper secondary VET, who have direct access to the UAS. The establishment of the UAS more than doubled the number of higher education institutions overnight, especially institutions that are easily accessible for students from the VET system (Börjesson et al., 2014). This was promoted by the limited admission (numerus clausus) at the universities and the high unemployment in the 1990s. After another reform in the late 1990s, all students completing VET gained formal eligibility for higher education. The establishment of the UASs in the 1990s succeeded in attracting a rapidly growing number of students, while enrolment in the universities stagnated (Börjesson et al., 2014). As early as 2003, 24% of entrants to UAS had upper secondary VET as their previous educational background, and 13% had completed both general upper secondary education and upper secondary VET (Virolainen and Stenström, 2014). The establishment of the UAS as a destination for the VET students has removed the stigma of upper secondary VET being a dead end in the education system. VET provides pathways to higher education and offers a faster route to graduation and employment than going to the universities. This can help explain why enrolment in upper secondary vocational schools in Finland has increased slightly, while it has decreased in the three other Nordic countries. The role of the UAS and the eligibility for higher education provided in upper secondary VET can explain why completion of VET in Finland is much more likely to lead to the tertiary level of education than in Denmark and Norway (Hillmert and Jacob, 2003). The popularity of the UAS helps to explain why the enrolment rate in higher education in Finland is higher than in the other Nordic countries (Virolainen and Stenström, 2014). The high level of enrolment is also explained by the high youth unemployment and the strict activation policy (Kananen, 2016). The high permeability from VET to the UAS in Finland corresponds to the ideals of the Nordic model of education. It helps to reduce social selection and social inequality in the education system. In Finland, as in other countries, youth from disadvantaged families are over-represented in the vocational schools. Even this group of students has good opportunities for progressing to the UAS, which contributes to reducing social inequality in tertiary level educational attainment. However, trade-offs for education policy can also be observed in Finland. While the Finnish VET system offers good opportunities for transfer to higher education, students' transitions from VET to employment are not very smooth. In spite of a number of reforms to improve the links between VET and the labour market, the employment rate for graduates from upper secondary VET is lower in Finland than in the other Nordic countries (see Chapter 1). Moreover, the NEET rates and the youth unemployment rates are significantly higher compared to Norway and Denmark, where the VET system is based on apprenticeships (see Chapter 2). The high rate of participation in higher education in Finland can partly be attributed to the difficult conditions for entering the labour market for students leaving upper secondary education. The difficult transitions to employment for students leaving upper secondary VET is partly due to the competition from the large supply of higher education graduates (Virolainen and Stenström, 2014). In addition, the enrolment in higher education in Finland is still quite selective with regard to the educational background of the students (Kilpi-Jakonen et al., 2016). Admission to the universities and the UAS is selective, because it is based on the principle of restricted entry or numerus clausus (Pinheiro et al., 2014). In addition, the strengthening of the binary system of higher education in Finland is associated with a stratification of higher education institutions (Triventi, 2011). Although all upper secondary students gain eligibility for higher education, the actual progression rates differ strongly between programmes. Of the students who complete with a general exam, 83% enrol in higher education, while only 19% of the students who complete with a vocational exam enrol (Kilpi-Jakonen et al., 2016). Almost all the students from the vocational programmes who

112 *Christian Helms Jørgensen*

enrol in higher education go to the UAS and very few go to the universities. This indicates that the establishment of the UAS provides new opportunities for progression to the tertiary level for VET students, but that they imply a stratification at this level of education that diverts vocational students from the universities.

The vocational route to the Danish vocational academies

Similar to the situation in Finland, policy-makers in Denmark have tried to improve the opportunities for educational progression for students from the VET system by strengthening reformed institutions for post-secondary education. A reform in 1997 standardised and broadened the short-cycle technical programmes of higher education, which were reduced from 75 to 15 programmes. Another reform in 2009 established new Vocational Academies (*'Erhvervsakademier'*), which offer further training courses and higher vocational education up to the Bachelor level. Many of the post-secondary programmes and the Vocational Academies were hosted by the vocational schools that also had responsibility for the school-based periods of training for apprentices. After the reform, the Vocational Academies were separated from the vocational schools and promoted as a strengthened and independent institution of higher education. One of the aims of this reform was to create more visible, attractive opportunities for progression for graduates from upper secondary VET. However, in this respect, the reform has not succeeded.

The reform has been a success measured by the enrolment of students, which nearly doubled in the period from 2007 to 2013 (UFM, 2016). The number of students coming from the VET system has also increased, but still the figures are low. Only 13% of the students in the Vocational Academies come from the VET system and this proportion has not increased. The overall rate of progression from VET to higher education has declined from 1991, especially for the traditional manufacturing and craft occupations. Moreover, the proportion of students with double qualifications (both a journeyman's certificate and entrance examination for higher education) has been declining over the past 20 years (Jørgensen, 2017). Contrary to the intentions of the education policy, the permeability and the progression rate from the VET system to higher education has decreased in recent decades. This has reinforced the image of VET as a 'dead end' in the education system, which is seen as a reason for the declining enrolment in VET. A relevant question is why repeated reforms to improve the links between VET and higher education in Denmark have failed, in contrast to the successful Finnish reform of the UAS? Answers to this question can be found in the history, the structure and the culture of the Danish VET system.

Historically, the vocational gymnasiums were established in the vocational schools in the 1980s to offer an alternative route to higher education compared to the traditional, academic gymnasium (Jørgensen, 2017). The vocational gymnasiums have succeeded in recruiting from wider social groups that are unfamiliar with academic education. Since the 1980s, the programmes have become a remarkable success and they recruit more than 15% of a youth cohort today. Graduates from the vocational gymnasiums have come to constitute a majority of the participants on the short-cycle higher education programmes, which have traditionally been the main destination for students from the VET system. This success indicates that young people planning to take a higher education (including short-cycle higher education programmes) increasingly choose the vocational gymnasiums rather than an apprenticeship, even though apprenticeships provide access to the Vocational Academies. In addition, the labour market partners have historically pursued an enhancement strategy to improve apprenticeships as a separate track and emphasised the distinct vocational qualities of apprenticeships (Lasonen and Manning, 2000). As a result, some of the programmes in the Danish VET system are of five years' duration and at the same level of qualifications as the short cycle tertiary programmes of the vocational academies.

At the structural level, an explanation for the low rate of progression to higher education is the well-known effects of the early tracking that diverts students in the vocational track away from higher education (Shavit and Müller, 2000). Culturally, the VET system is dominated by an 'employment logic' (Raffe, 2008) and two-thirds of the total time is spent in work-based training. Less than half of the technical vocational teachers have a higher education degree, and the teachers' authority is primarily based on their skills as capable craftsmen. In addition, the comprehensive system of continuing training (CVET) for skilled workers in employment provides an attractive alternative to higher education. Moreover, the proportion of low-performing students in VET has increased as a consequence of the active labour market policy (Jørgensen, 2018). The combination of all these conditions has resulted in a declining number of students progressing from VET to higher education, despite the improved formal opportunities for progression.

Conclusion

The preceding chapters have examined how VET is increasingly required to simultaneously prepare students for a future in a skilled occupation and in higher education. These two challenges represent a trade-off for policy. This chapter has examined major reforms and innovations to manage this trade-off. The first part examines the decoupling of the VET system from the labour market, which has resulted from the gradual integration of VET into a state-led upper secondary school. In Sweden and Finland, this has opened the way for students' direct transition to higher education, but it has also made the transition to employment more difficult. To improve the links between VET and the labour market, a number of reforms and initiatives have been implemented. In addition, three types of new local institutions have developed with the aim of improving the quality of work-based training in VET. The Danish training centres are organised by the vocational schools and the state, the Swedish Health and Technical Colleges are organised in collaboration between municipalities, employers

114 *Christian Helms Jørgensen*

and schools, and the Norwegian local training agencies (LTA) are organised exclusively by the employers. The LTA especially represent an important institutional innovation to secure the quality of work-based training in VET. In addition, they relieve the companies of the administration associated with hiring or employing apprentices. It is interesting that this institution for collective skill formation is expanding strongly in a period characterised by neo-liberal deregulation. This can be explained by both the employers' engagement in high quality training of apprentices and the state's interest in expanding the opportunities for training for young people through generous funding. The LTAs have parallels to the Swiss training networks that consist of training companies that collaborate to offer training for all the competences required for an occupation (Imdorf and Leemann, 2012). While the control and organisation of these intermediary institutions differs, they share collective long-term interests in high-quality training of the future, local, skilled workforce. The LTAs are important, not only for the articulation of shared interests, but also for the formation and stabilisation of interest groups for collective skill formation. They emerge in a period of decentralisation and deregulation of the earlier, highly centralised form of neo-corporatism in the labour markets and vocational training systems in the Nordic countries. This has been pursued most strongly in Sweden and has resulted in the fragmentation and weakening of the common quality standards for VET (Lundahl et al., 2013). In this perspective, the new intermediary institutions can be seen as a local neo-corporatist collaboration that emerges in parallel to the weakening of the traditional, centralised corporatism.

The second part of the chapter examines initiatives to bypass the trade-off for VET, between giving access to higher education and to the labour market, by hybridisations that combine academic preparation with the journeyman's certificate. These initiatives are interesting because they can improve the attraction of VET for the students and for employers. The question is whether these programmes are manageable for anyone other than small elite groups of ambitious students who are capable of completing two programmes in the time normally required for one. The small volume of the Norwegian YSK indicates that it is not a relevant option for the large majority of students in VET. Nevertheless, the hybrid programmes can help to break the lamentable divide between vocational and academic programmes, and demonstrate how a mutual enrichment and integration of subjects can be achieved. A high level of theoretical knowledge in VET is important in order to maintain the autonomy of the skilled worker, as Brockmann (2012) has demonstrated in a comparison between the English and the German VET systems. Moreover, the application of academic knowledge in vocational practice can make this knowledge more meaningful and useful for students. While initiatives for hybridisation can improve the esteem of VET, we should be aware that policy making with contradictory aims in the complex field of VET, tends to have unintended consequences. An example of what can happen is the introduction in the 1980s in Denmark of the vocational gymnasiums. Although the vocational gymnasiums were located in the vocational schools, they seem to have reduced the esteem of the ordinary VET programmes

Reforms and innovations   115

(apprenticeships), because they attracted the most ambitious students. It is also likely that the new hybrid programmes contribute to a hierarchisation in VET, where the ordinary technical vocational programmes rank lowest.

References

Aamodt, P. O., and Kyvik, S. (2005) 'Access to higher education in the Nordic countries', in Tapper, T. and Palfreyman, D. (eds.), *Understanding Mass Higher Education: Comparative Perspectives on Access*, London, Routledge Falmer, pp. 121–138.

Ahola, S. (1997) '"Different but equal": Student expectations and the Finnish dual higher education policy', *European Journal of Education*, vol. 32, no. 3, pp. 291–302.

Akkerman, S. F., and Bakker, A. (2012) 'Crossing boundaries between school and work during apprenticeships', *Vocations and Learning*, vol. 5, no. 2, pp. 153–173.

Berggren, C. (2013) 'The influence of gender, social class and national background on education and work career'? *Nordic Journal of Migration Research*, vol. 3, no. 3, pp. 135–144.

Börjesson, M., Ahola, S., Helland, H., and Thomsen, J. P. (2014) *Enrolment Patterns in Nordic Higher Education*, Oslo, NIFU.

Breen, R., and Jonsson, J. O. (2005) 'Inequality of opportunity in comparative perspective: Recent research on educational attainment and social mobility', *Annual Review of Sociology*, vol. 31, pp. 223–243.

Brockmann, M. (2012) *Learner Biographies and Learning Cultures-Identity and Apprenticeship in England and Germany*, London, Tufnell Press.

Busemeyer, M. R., and Trampusch, C. (eds.) (2012) *The Political Economy of Collective Skill Formation*, Oxford, Oxford University Press.

Casey, C. (2012) 'Organizations and learning: A critical appraisal', *Sociology Compass*, vol. 6, no. 5, pp. 389–401.

Causa, O., and Johansson, Å. (2011) 'Intergenerational social mobility in OECD countries', *OECD Journal, Economic Studies*, vol. 2010, OECD Publishing.

Engelstad, F., and Hagelund, A. (eds.) (2015) *Cooperation and Conflict the Nordic Way: Work, Welfare, and Institutional Change in Scandinavia*, Berlin, De Gruyter Open.

EVA. (2014) *Evaluering af praktikcentre del 2*, Copenhagen, Danish Evaluation Centre.

Helland, H., and Støren, L. A. (2006) 'Vocational education and the allocation of apprenticeships: Equal chances for applicants regardless of immigrant background?' *European Sociological Review*, vol. 22, no. 3, pp. 339–351.

Hillmert, S., and Jacob, M. (2003) 'Social inequality in higher education: Is vocational training a pathway leading to or away from university?' *European Sociological Review*, vol. 19, no. 3, pp. 319–334.

Høst, H., Skålholt, A., Reiling, R. B., and Gjerustad, C. (2014) *Opplæringskontorene i fag-og yrkesopplæringen – avgjørende bindeledd eller institusjon utenfor kontroll?* Rapport 51/2014, Oslo, NIFU.

Imdorf, C., and Leemann, R. J. (2012) 'New models of apprenticeship and equal employment opportunity: Do training networks enhance fair hiring practices?' *Journal of Vocational Education & Training*, vol. 64, no. 1, pp. 57–74.

Jæger, M. M., and Holm, A. (2007) 'Does parents' economic, cultural, and social capital explain the social class effect on educational attainment in the Scandinavian mobility regime?' *Social Science Research*, vol. 36, no. 2, pp. 719–744.

Jørgensen, C. H. (2013) 'Linking the dual system with higher education in Denmark: – when strength becomes weakness', in Deissinger, Th., Aff, J., Alison, F., and Jørgensen, C. H.

116   *Christian Helms Jørgensen*

(eds.) *Hybrid Qualifications – structural and Political Issues in the Context of European VET Policy*, Zürich, Peter Lang, pp. 53–78.

Jørgensen, C. H. (2015a) 'Challenges for work-based learning in vocational education and training in the Nordic countries', in Jørgensen, C. H., Wallo, A., Toiviainen, H., Haake, U., and Bohlinger, S. (eds.) *Working and Learning in Times of Uncertainty*, Rotterdam, Sense Publishers.

Jørgensen, C. H. (2015b) *Recent Innovations in VET in Denmark*, Nord-VET report, Roskilde, Roskilde University.

Jørgensen, C. H. (2017) 'From apprenticeships to higher vocational education in Denmark – building bridges while the gap is widening', *Journal of Vocational Education & Training*, vol. 69, no. 1, pp. 64–80.

Jørgensen, C. H. (2018) 'The modernisation of the apprenticeship system in Denmark 1945–2015', in Michelsen, S. and Stenström, M-L. (eds.) *Vocational Education in the Nordic Countries: The Historical Evolution*, Abingdon, Routledge, pp. 171–189.

Juul, I., and Jørgensen, C. H. (2011) 'Challenges for the dual system and occupational self-governance in Denmark', *Journal of Vocational Education & Training*, vol. 63, no. 3, pp. 289–303.

Kananen, J. (2016) *The Nordic Welfare State in Three Eras from Emancipation to Discipline*, Abingdon, Routledge.

Kilpi-Jakonen, E., Erola, J., and Karhula, A. (2016) 'Inequalities in the haven of equality? Upper secondary education and entry into tertiary education in Finland', in Blossfeld, H. P., Buchholz, S., Skopek, J., and Triventi, M. (eds.) *Models of Secondary Education and Social Inequality: An International Comparison*, Aldershot, Edward Elgar Publishing, pp. 181–195.

Kyvik, S. (2009) *The Dynamics of Change in Higher Education: Expansion and Contraction in an Organisational Field*, New York, Springer.

Lagström, A. (2012) *Lärlingsläraren-en studie om hur vård-och yrkeslärares uppdrag formas i samband med införandet av gymnasial lärlingsutbildning*, Ph.D. dissertation, Göteborg University.

Lancee, B. (2016) 'The negative side effects of vocational education: A cross-national analysis of the relative unemployment risk of young non-western immigrants in Europe', *American Behavioral Scientist*, vol. 60, no. 5–6, pp. 659–679.

Lasonen, J., and Manning, S. (2000) 'Improving the standing of vocational as against general education in Europe: A conceptual framework', in Lasonen, J. and Stenström, M-L. (eds.) *Strategies for Reforming Initial Vocational Education and Training in Europe*, Jyväskylä, University of Jyväskylä, pp. 316–325.

Lundahl, L., Arreman, I. E., Holm, A-L., and Lundström, U. (2013) 'Educational marketization the Swedish way', *Education Inquiry*, vol. 4, no. 4, pp. 497–517.

Mahoney, J., and Thelen, K. (2010) 'A theory of gradual institutional change', in Mahoney, J. and Thelen, K. (eds.) *Explaining Institutional Change: Ambiguity, Agency, and Power*, New York, Cambridge University Press, pp. 1–37.

Michelsen, S., and Stenström, M-L. (2018) *Vocational Education in the Nordic Countries: The Historical Evolution*, Abingdon, Routledge.

Nikolai, R., and Ebner, C. (2012) 'The link between vocational training and higher education in Switzerland, Austria, and Germany', in Busemeyer, M. R. and Trampusch, C. (eds.) *The Political Economy of Collective Skill Formation*, Oxford, Oxford University Press, pp. 234–258.

Nore, H., and Lahn, L. C. (2014) 'Bridging the gap between work and education in vocational education and training: A study of Norwegian apprenticeship training offices and e-portfolio systems', *International Journal for Research in Vocational Education and Training*, vol. 1, no. 1, pp. 21–34.

Olsen, O. J., Høst, H., Michelsen, S., and Tønder, A. (2015) *Institutional Innovations in Norwegian VET – responses to Key Challenges*, Nord-VET report, Roskilde, Roskilde University.

Persson Thunqvist, D., and Hallqvist, A. (2014) *The Current State of the Challenges for VET in Sweden*, Roskilde, Roskilde University. Available at www.Nord-VET.dk

Pfeffer, F. T. (2008) 'Persistent inequality in educational attainment and its institutional context', *European Sociological Review*, vol. 24, no. 5, pp. 543–565.

Pfeffer, F. T. (2015) 'Equality and quality in education: A comparative study of 19 countries', *Social Science Research*, vol. 51, pp. 350–368.

Pinheiro, R., Geschwind, L., and Aarrevaara, T. (2014) 'Nested tensions and interwoven dilemmas in higher education: The view from the Nordic countries', *Cambridge Journal of Regions, Economy and Society*, vol. 7, no. 2, pp. 233–250.

Raffe, D. (2008) 'The concept of transition system', *Journal of Education and Work*, vol. 21, no. 4, pp. 277–296.

Schmid, E., and Gonon, P. (2011) 'Übergang in eine Tertiärausbildung nach einer Berufsausbildung in der Schweiz', *bwp@*, Spezial 5, HT 2011, pp. 1–17.

Schön, D. (1983) *Educating the Reflective Practitioner*, San Francisco, Jossey-Bass.

Shavit, Y., and Müller, W. (2000) 'Vocational secondary education: Where diversion and where safety net?' *European Societies*, vol. 2, no. 1, pp. 29–50.

Skolverket. (2016) *Det arbetsplatsförlagda lärandet på gymnasieskolans yrkesprogram*, Rapport 437, Stockholm, Skolverket.

SOU. (2011) *Gymnasial lärlingsutbildning – med fokus på kvalitet! SOU 2011:72*, Stockholm, Fritzes.

Stenström, M-L. (2009) 'Connecting work and learning through demonstrations of vocational skills – experiences from the Finnish VET', in Stenström, M-L. and Tynjälä, P. (eds.) *Towards Integration of Work and Learning: Strategies for Connectivity and Transformation*, Amsterdam, Springer, pp. 221–238.

Streeck, W. (1992) *Social Institutions and Economic Performance: Studies of Industrial Relations in Advanced Capitalist Economies*, London, Sage Publications.

Thelen, K. (2014) *Varieties of Liberalization and the New Politics of Social Solidarity*, Cambridge, Cambridge University Press.

Triventi, M. (2011) 'Stratification in higher education and its relationship with social inequality: A comparative study of 11 European countries', *European Sociological Review*, vol. 29, no. 3, pp. 489–502.

UFM. (2016) *Årsberetning 2015*, Rådet for Erhvervsakademiuddannelser og Professionsbacheloruddannelser, Copenhagen, Styrelsen for Videregående Uddannelser.

Virolainen, M., and Stenström, M. L. (2014) 'Finnish vocational education and training in comparison: Strengths and weaknesses', *International Journal for Research in Vocational Education and Training*, vol. 1, no. 2, pp. 81–106.

6 Vocational education for health care workers in the Nordic countries compared

Håkon Høst and Lene Larsen

Introduction

In the decades following the Second World War, all the Nordic countries established formal education programmes for the subordinate health care workers, who are located in the work organization between professional nurses and unskilled health care assistants. This can be seen both as a result of policies for establishing public health care services and policies for providing education for all, as part of building a welfare state. It represented an important contribution to educational and vocational career options for women entering the workforce in the 1960s and 1970s. From the start, the educations were linked to hospitals and other health care institutions. Reforms from the 1970s introduced more comprehensive education systems at the upper secondary school level in all Nordic countries and these came to include health care education.

The occupational categories that emerged as a result of these education programmes in the Nordic countries have developed many similarities. However, they also exhibit differences in the way they have linked to other parts of the education and training system, in educational models, recruitment patterns, position in the field of work, and collective organization. What they have in common is that, as part of building the Nordic welfare states, they have become one of the largest VET educations and occupational groups in each of the countries. Consequently, they influence these systems significantly.

In this chapter, we trace the historical development of the health care worker educations and occupations in the four countries and look at their positions today. We discuss whether the factors making the health care worker category quite similar in the four countries, while rather different from the traditional parts of VET, make it possible to speak of a Nordic model in health care education.

As this study is part of the Nord-VET project, we have a particular interest in illuminating how the care worker educations have gradually been integrated into and formed by both the comprehensive school and the national VET systems. In line with the four challenges investigated in the Nord-VET project, the chapter discusses the esteem of the educations today, what groups are recruited and included, in what way the educations are connected to and give access to work, and to what extent they give access to higher education.

Vocational education for health care workers 119

In the chapter, we trace the historical development of the health care educations and occupations in Norway, Finland, Sweden and Denmark, and look at their positions today. We want to explore how these welfare educations and categories have gradually been shaped by their integration into the educational systems and the national VET systems, but also how these categories contribute to changes in the same systems.

The chapter is part of a broader Nordic research project. To a significant extent it is based on national reports produced by members of the project team,[1] tracing the historical development in each country through research and public reports, complemented by qualitative case studies on the health care worker education. The production of the national reports was guided by a common design and research questions.

Historical background

During the second half of the 19th century, the increased range of possibilities provided by medical treatment contributed to the development of hospitals (Melby, 1990). During the same period, homes for the elderly, asylums for psychiatric patients and institutions for people with mental disabilities were established in all the Nordic countries. These institutions largely employed unskilled persons, predominantly women. An exception was heavy work in psychiatric hospitals and asylums for people with intellectual disabilities, which was mainly seen as men's work, while also unskilled. However, despite the growth of these institutions, most care work continued to be carried out in the private sphere and within families, again predominantly by women.

In all the Nordic countries, the first nurse education programmes were established at the end of the 19th century and were aimed at recruiting unmarried daughters of the bourgeoisie (Melby, 1990). The emergence of the nurse occupation was part of strong international trends and cooperation.[2] The Red Cross movement and Florence Nightingale's work and school of nursing in London from 1861 onwards had a major influence, including in the Nordic countries. Students from all over the world came to attend Nightingale's nursing school. After completing their studies, they returned to their home countries, mostly as managers and educators (Johansson, 1979). Nurses' primary mission was to establish hegemony over care and nursing work within hospitals by replacing the unskilled labour of the 'lower classes' (Melby, 1990; Meyerson, 1917).

Education for the assistant groups

During the social democratic era after the Second World War, political initiatives in all Nordic countries supported the professionalization of the occupational groups that were vital in forming the welfare services. Among these occupational groups were the nurses. They obtained state authorization and standardization of education. Although the number of registered nurses increased rapidly during the first half of the 20th century, this expansion fell

120   *Håkon Høst and Lene Larsen*

short of covering the demand for care and nursing. The majority of those employed as nurses did not have a recognized nursing qualification.

State support for the new professions was just one part of building the welfare services. Another part of the social democratic project in the different Nordic countries was education for all. Together with the aim for modernization of the health care sectors, which in the Nordic countries were public, this contributed to the state also engaging in the establishment of education for the subordinate care and nursing personnel (Høst, 2006b). By the early 1960s, each country had established countrywide educations in auxiliary nursing,[3] primarily directed towards work in hospitals (Høst, 2006a). From the beginning, the subordinate role of auxiliary nurses relative to fully qualified nurses was clearly specified in both the educational plans and job descriptions. The educations concentrated on training the auxiliary nurses in a range of precisely defined tasks that they were allowed to undertake, combined with short theoretical courses. Auxiliary nurse training soon became very popular, and the number of applicants was enormous in all the four countries. A large share of the students were older youths or adults with practical experience of paid and unpaid care and nursing work.

The registered nurses' organisations did not welcome the auxiliary nurse education. They guarded the boundaries between their own education and the new one. Both in Norway and in Denmark, collective actions were undertaken by the registered nurses in order to obstruct the auxiliary nurse education from encroaching on what they regarded as the nurses' jurisdiction.[4]

The auxiliary nurse educations were established prior to the institutionalization of both a coherent VET system and an upper secondary education system, and instead they were linked to the health care sector, to hospitals and to other health care institutions. Parallel educations were established in the social sector, but only the homecare worker (*hemvårdare*) education in Finland managed to reach a significant size (Simonen, 1995).

Both in Denmark and Norway, efforts were made by the auxiliary nurse group to be accepted as members of the nurses' organization, but such applications were rejected (Poulsen, 2004; Melby, 1990). In Norway, the auxiliary nurses chose instead to establish their own professional organization, very much modelled on the nurses' organization, and independently of the central trade union confederation (LO). In Denmark, the auxiliary nurses became members of the LO from the very beginning, but with their own trade unions based on the occupational principle.[5] In Finland, the auxiliary nurses also formed their own professional organization based on the occupational principle, but as part of the central organization for public servants, where the nurses' organization was also affiliated. The Swedish auxiliary nurses seem to have had the strongest orientation towards traditional trade unionism. They established their own trade union in 1923, and it was accepted as a member of the LO in 1945. The trade unionism of the auxiliary nurses, understood as giving priority to economic and political demands, contributed to strong antipathy from the nurses' organizations, for whom concentrating on occupational matters was seen as the only natural approach for health care sector occupations (Emanuelsson Blanck, 2000).

Vocational education for health care workers 121

In all the Nordic countries, the auxiliary nurse educations became popular during the 1960s and 1970s. In Sweden, this also became a main route to becoming a registered nurse, as the auxiliary nurse education was accepted as the first of three years' education to become a nurse.

Integration into the upper secondary school systems

While the educations had been the responsibility of the social and health care authorities from the beginning, the forming of upper secondary school systems in the 1970s and 1980s changed this both in Norway, Sweden and Finland. Gradually, responsibility for vocational education was moved from the sector authorities to the education authorities, and the auxiliary nurse education became part of a common upper secondary school.

In Denmark, both the state and the social partners at the central level wanted to integrate the educations for social and health care into the national VET system based on apprenticeships, but this was rejected by both the employers' and the employees' organizations in the health care sector. Instead, an initiative was taken by the employers' organizations in the municipalities to organize a separate system for social- and health care education (AKF, 1988). This was a stepwise, school-based system, which also integrated lengthy periods of practical training. Completing the first step gave the title social- and health care helper (*social- og sundhedshjælper*), and completing the second step lead to the title social- and health care assistant (*social- og sundhedsassistent*). This occupational group established its own jurisdiction, partly independent of the registered nurses, which contributed to a slightly different situation than in the other Nordic countries, where the health care educations at this level led to assistant positions clearly subordinate to the registered nurses, with little or no autonomy.

The social- and health care assistant training introduced in Denmark was a broad generalist education, which incorporated the previous educations directed towards hospitals, psychiatric care, home economics, and care and nursing homes. Along with reforms in the upper secondary educations, the introduction of more generalist educations in health care was also to become a common feature in the other Nordic countries in the 1990s, which reflected changes in the organization of the welfare services at the municipal level. In Finland, the new education for practical nurse (*närvårdare*) included several educations that were previously more specialized. In Sweden, a broad programme for social and health care replaced auxiliary nursing and other more specialized vocational educations. In Norway, a new trade as care worker (*omsorgsarbeider*) was introduced into the apprenticeship system in 1994, in competition with the existing auxiliary nurse education. This was a slightly more generalist education in that it included all kinds of care work in the health and social care sector. The auxiliary nurse education retained its school-based education for 10 more years, before the care worker and the auxiliary nurse educations were merged into a new health care worker (*helsefagarbeider*) education based on apprenticeship.

With Denmark as an exception, the new, broad educations for health and social care in the Nordic countries were integrated into the new upper

122 *Håkon Høst and Lene Larsen*

secondary educations, and as such they were age specific, directed mainly towards 16–19-year-olds. Denmark kept an age heterogeneous system until 2015.

Hybrid apprenticeship models

According to national education statistics for the year 2015, education programmes for subordinate positions for health and social care are the largest vocational programmes in both Denmark, Finland and Norway, and of a significant size also in Sweden. Although being part of the comprehensive school and the national VET systems, the health care educations have kept many of their distinctive features. They are female dominated, they educate for positions subordinated to the nurses, and they still recruit a large share of adults. Due to the size of these programmes, they are becoming influential inside the VET systems in the different countries. A high membership rate in trade unions made them influential in the central trade union confederations, and thus also in the national VET boards.

The integration of the health care educations in Finland, Norway and Sweden into the upper secondary education systems contributed initially to a strengthening of their character as broad, school-based educations governed by the state, directed towards positions in the public welfare services. Also, the Danish educations were school-based from the beginning. When Norway introduced an apprenticeship system for all VET in 1994, this represented a move away from the dominance of the school-based education in VET. The apprentice reform in the health care sector, as in other parts of the public sector, lead to a process of layering (Høst et al., 2014). The social and health care educations are still governed by the state, and the employers still play a rather passive and subordinate role in the VET system and with a weak ownership to the apprentices. The result is a kind of hybrid education, where the state decides upon educational matters and the number of school places, while the number of apprenticeships are decided upon – not by the local employers – but by the municipalities, who also pay the salaries. In this way, the municipalities act as part of the welfare state, being responsible for education. The number of apprentices is not connected to the demand for employees, and the apprentices are usually not offered a fixed contract when they have finished their apprenticeship and become skilled workers, something which is a pattern in most other trades. In parallel to this, the municipalities continue to recruit unskilled adults for part-time positions, who are gradually being trained informally at the work place.

In the school-based system in Sweden, the social and health care programme does not give an occupational competence, but is a broad national programme directed towards various kinds of health and social care work. In parallel to this, a new apprenticeship scheme has recently been tested. This can also be described as a hybrid model. It is school-based, with a bias towards social policy (Persson Thunqvist, 2015). As an alternative to the youth education, an adult education for social and health care has been introduced, and after existing for only a few years, it already attracts far more students than the youth programme for social and health care. So-called vocational colleges (*yrkescollege*, see Chapter 5) have also been established. These are institutions based on close cooperation between employer and employee organizations, intended to stimulate VET in social and health care, and other sectors. These institutions also give high priority to adults.

Vocational education in Finland is organized as a school-based system parallel to, but independent of general education. The programme for social and health care has a separate specialization for practical nurses. Although it is school-based, it contains extended periods of practical work in the social and health care sector. The practical training in the field of work is organized in cooperation between the schoolteachers and a tutor at the work place (Virolainen, 2015). The training ends with a so-called skills demonstration, which is performed as a cooperation between the school and the workplace. About half of the students start directly from lower secondary education, while the rest are somewhat older. For adults, an alternative training is offered, based on practical training at the workplace.

In spite of several efforts to integrate them into the ordinary VET system, the social- and health care educations in Denmark remained an autonomous system until 2007. When these educations were introduced in the early 1990s, as combined school- and work-based educations, it was the municipalities and the counties that decided upon the student intake, while the state authorities had the right to intervene only if they anticipated the number of training places to be too low (Høst, 2006a). The students are paid salaries by the municipalities, both while they are in school and in the workplace. Today they are seen as part of the Danish apprentice system. There are, however, tensions between the national education authorities and the municipalities regarding the steering of the system. In 2000, the original model was modified and the schools were given the authority to decide upon the intake of students/apprentices (Larsen, 2015). The employers protested heavily, and in 2007 the municipalities were given back the authority to decide upon who and how many applicants would be accepted. A reform in 2015 integrated the social and health care education closer into the ordinary VET system, and strengthened the links to general education. Another aim is to make the education more age homogeneous – in line with the other Nordic educations. From 2015, the education is integrated more closely into the youth education system, and students above the age of 25 years are offered separate courses. The adult group still represents two thirds of all students in health care education in Denmark (Larsen, 2015).

Access to work

The auxiliary nurse educations were directed towards hospital work in the 1960s and 1970s. The connection between education and work seems to have been strong during this period, and at its highest, the auxiliary nurse groups could be compared quantitatively with the registered nurses in the hospitals. Through the modernization of the hospitals, the registered nurses have come to dominate in care work, while the auxiliary nurses, and later the health care workers, have gradually been marginalized. Technological and medical development, and a larger share of patients with serious diagnoses, have all been important arguments for such a shift. The registered nurses' profession has been a key actor in these processes, although not to the same extent in all countries. In general, their argument was that auxiliary nurses were not qualified to meet new demands in hospital care.

The educational reforms that integrated the auxiliary nurse educations into the upper secondary systems giving them a more generalist profile, took place during the same period as the auxiliary nurses started losing their position in hospitals. Instead the new and broader health care educations that were established are directed primarily towards elderly care in the municipalities. This has probably contributed to the educations' loss of appeal among youth. New patterns are being formed, where the students and apprentices in health care increasingly view the health care worker education as a basis for further and higher education, most frequently the registered nurse education. At the same time, in all four countries, the workplaces continue recruiting adults, many of whom lack a formal vocational education.

In Denmark, the health care workers (the social and health care assistants) still occupy a significant position in the hospitals, although even here it declined by 17 percent between 2012 and 2017 (Fagbladet FOA, 2017). The relatively stronger position of the Danish social- and health care assistants compared to health care workers in the other Nordic countries may to some extent be explained by the tradition for the state intervening in policies of what kind of personnel to hire. The Danish state has negotiated with the registered nurses' organization on the division of labour. In change for a more academic nurse education, the nurses have been forced to accept sharing their position in hospitals with the social and health care assistants (Høst, 2006a).

Even if the health care workers in all the Nordic countries to day work mainly in care for the elderly and for disabled in the municipalities different patterns are evident across the countries. In Norway, the share of health care workers is now decreasing, also in the care and nursing sector in the municipalities (Stølen et al., 2016). Both the share and number of registered nurses, among them also a sizeable number of immigrants from other countries, have been growing steadily for the past 10 years. It is no longer easy for health care workers to obtain a permanent position (Høst et al., 2015). Instead, temporary positions and part-time work in the weekends is the most typical pattern. On average, only one third of the health care workers have obtained full time positions two years after they finish their education (Nyen et al., 2014). Full-time positions are normally reserved for registered nurses or part-time health care workers with long seniority. Recruitment of new health care workers is still dominated by adults being informally trained without an apprenticeship contract (Høst et al., 2014). They are entitled to qualify through the so-called practical skilled worker scheme and sit the craft and journeyman test. Due to their seniority, they are given priority for permanent positions.

In Sweden, as well, young health care workers are struggling to find a position in the field of work, where age and experience from care work seems more important than school merits (Persson Thunqvist, 2015). The speed of transition from school to established positions in the labour market is slow. According to Swedish statistics for 2012, only 39 percent of females and 49 percent of males were established in the labour market three years after graduation from the track for social and health care; 27 percent of females and 22 percent of males had a temporary and unsecure position in the labour market. Given these figures, transitions from school-based education to full-time and permanent positions in the care sector do not seem to be a straightforward linear affair. Register-based studies of this vocational track covering transition patterns in the period 2000–2008 (Ahnlund and Johansson, 2011) reveal that both the horizontal and vertical mobility is rather high in a long-term perspective (eight years) Eighty percent of females, but only 56 percent of males who completed their vocational education in the health care programme in 2000, were established in the target field by 2008; 42 percent of the females, however, had supplemented the VET programme with an exam from higher education and were employed as nurses.

Among the entrants for the practical nurse education in Finland in 2007, 76.5 percent were employed in 2012, which means they succeed fairly well in finding work (Virolainen, 2015). Around 60 percent of the practical nurses in Finland are employed in the social sector, predominantly elderly care, around 20 percent in what is defined as the health sector, and 20 percent in other sectors. The share of practical nurses in full-time employment is around 90 percent, and part-time work is a minor problem compared with Norway and Sweden.

In Denmark, the transition from education to work is described as good. Around 85 percent of the candidates educated in 2013 were employed one year later. Around 10 percent entered further education. The prevalence of part-time work is significant among young people in public services but has actually been decreasing for the past 20 years (FOA, 2012).

In all the countries, one of the most critical tensions between the health care programme and the health care sector seems to be the recruitment system. The logic of educational planning on the national policy level is characterized by attempts to predict future needs for competence enhancement in the health and care sector in relation to available forecasts. Some aspects of this multifaceted tension could be described in terms of a gap between actual poor conditions for proper employment in the care sector for young people, versus long-term forecasts about their future opportunities to obtain fixed positions and good careers. Most predictions suggest a severe shortage of health care workers in 15–20 years, but as it seems increasingly difficult for health care workers to find a full-time job in many places, the forecasts may be questioned.

An occupation between hierarchies

Recruiting young people to the health care education depends among other factors on the esteem of the occupation. As esteem is a relational and multi-dimensional concept, different indicators of esteem must be observed. As health care is the largest vocational programme in three out of four Nordic countries, this can be taken as an indicator that the education has a good level of popularity. Measured in this way, it has good esteem among many young people, even if we don't have data on how many applicants there are for each school place. It may seem like a paradox that the programme, and the occupations it leads to, must nevertheless struggle to strengthen and maintain its position.

As a female-dominated programme, directed towards work in the public sector, health care experiences lower esteem compared with the traditional, male-dominated programmes aimed at positions in the private sector. Despite many years of gender policies in the Nordic welfare states, education still plays the role of reproducing a gender segregated labour market. At the same time, the labour market contributes to shaping the way many educations emerge as strongly gendered (Emerek and Holt, 2008; Larsen and Thingstrup, 2014). The explanations for the gendered division of work, and its reproduction, are diverse and complex. Some of the most important seem to be the gendered division of work within families, the educational choices, the preferences of the employers and the political organization of the labour market (Emerek and Holt, 2008).

The question of esteem could also be understood in a historical context. Previously the auxiliary nurse educations used to be very popular among women in all Nordic countries, in particular among adult women, who saw the education as a vehicle for moving from unpaid household work into the paid labour market (Høst, 2006**a**). During the first period of women entering the education system, in the 1960s and 1970s, an auxiliary nurse education was considered opening a respectable career for a woman. As women in all the Nordic countries are gradually forming the majority at all levels in the education system, the registered nurse education has turned into a realistic option for most girls, not only those from the upper social strata. This, in turn, may be one explanation for the health care worker educations at upper secondary experiencing a fall in popularity. Women, in particular, seem to consider prospects of further education as vital when they choose an education (Brown et al., 2011). For the health care worker students also, further education and mobility in the labour market has become more important.

The seemingly declining esteem of the health care worker education seems as well to be connected to a stronger educational hierarchy, where education itself is considered decisive in the competition for social positions (Beck, 1997; Bourdieu and Wacquant, 1996). Thus, when young people make a choice about their further education upon completion of their compulsory education, they not only see a choice between several horizontal possibilities, they also see a vertical hierarchy of different kinds of education defined by their theoretical and scholastic content and orientation (Andreasen et al., 1998; Larsen, 2003). From an educational sociological perspective, the sorting function of the educational system is reflected in young people's view of the educational opportunities. The discourse about educational society and the importance of cognitive knowledge challenges the esteem of the VET. The health care education defined as a more practical education contributes to placing them in the lower end of the educational hierarchy. However, the educational hierarchy is not necessarily unambiguous: for many young people (and their families), several of the vocational programmes have high value. Many health care students have a mother or other family members who have the same education and job, and they are very proud of it and feel they are doing an important job (Larsen, 2004, 2005, 2006).

In particular, vocational education targeting the eldercare sector seems to have low esteem among young people in all the four countries. Care work has for many years been under pressure from standardization, Taylorization and time control on the one hand, and increasing professionalization on the other, also to increase the esteem of care work (Tidsskrift for Arbejdsliv, 2006). It has also been formulated as a dilemma between two forms of rationality: a rationality of treatment, connected to standardized tasks of the care work expected to be undertaken, and a rationality of care, connected to the care givers' life history competences of care, which is all the time being subjected to professionalization (Eriksen, 2001). Newer research highlights that the struggle for recognition has changed. Previously there was a struggle for recognition of professionalism in a female-dominated field, but now it is also a struggle for recognition between technology and humanity. For the health care workers, it is not technology that makes care possible, but human care (Rehder, 2013). At the same time, welfare technologies represent progress and upgrading.

Finally, it is important to see how esteem is influenced by boundaries and jurisdictions between different professions and occupations, and the hierarchies developing from this. The registered nurse profession in all the Nordic countries is trying to draw a strong line of demarcation between themselves and the health care workers, both in the education system and in the field of work. In recent decades, the registered nurses are increasingly monopolizing work in hospitals, while the health care workers are predominantly left to apply for work in the municipal care and nursing sector. This is a challenge that relates to the low esteem of working inside the elderly care sector. Moreover, the health care workers are subject to some very explicit professional demarcations. They are part of a gender hierarchy, a professional hierarchy and a 'dirt' hierarchy, where the latter refers to the fact that working with tools ranks higher than work related to the body and its maintenance and/or decay, which is more often associated with odours, privacy and taboos. In the hospitals, the nurses perform care work that is associated with growth, results and maintenance, whereas care for the elderly is associated with decline and ultimately results in death (Liveng, 2007).

Access to higher education

In order to secure individual mobility and to strengthen the status of the health care educations, the health care programme has a double challenge: it must simultaneously qualify its graduates for a specific occupation and give access

128   *Håkon Høst and Lene Larsen*

to higher education. This means the health care education no longer merely qualifies graduates for employment within the social and health care sector, it also prepares and motivates the graduates to continue to higher education. To some extent, this involves enhancing the theoretical and general education profile of the programmes.

In Denmark, social and health care assistants have had access to several professional bachelor educations since 1991, including nursing, pharmacology, pedagogy and social working, and through supplementary courses, to occupational therapy, physiotherapy, medical laboratory technician, midwife etc. In total, 40 percent of the social and health care assistants who went on to study in a professional bachelor education in 2013 went into nursing, and 10 percent entered the pre-school teacher programme (UNI-C, 2016). So, it is mainly nursing that is an obvious and relevant opportunity for further education for social and health care assistants. The VET system has also introduced eux, which is an option to combine vocational and general education (see Chapter 5). The first period of practical work is replaced by general subjects, because the students in this model will supposedly need less time to learn the practical skills. In addition to this, so-called talent tracks are offered, in which subjects are taught at a higher level of theory. The aim is to strengthen the education and link it more tightly with the system of higher education. The students start in school and have three periods of practical work in between, before they complete their education with a school exam.

In Sweden, there has been a strong focus on access to higher education from the health care programme. While the broad programme has a weak connection to specific occupations, it has become more academic and has been most successful over time at providing access to further education at the tertiary level. Within three years after graduation from upper secondary school, transition to higher education has been 25–35 percent (Persson Thunqvist, 2015). The rather strong focus on access to higher education conflicts with the prerequisites, particularly for those students who want to find a fast route to skilled work, earn money and become independent.

In Norway, different models of health care worker training have been established to reduce the contrast between young people dominating the education system and adults dominating the workplaces. The supplementary, general programme, which is an alternative to the third year of vocational training, has been more popular among the students in the health care programme than completing an apprenticeship. The supplementary programme does not involve any recognition of the occupational competence that the students have obtained during the first two years of education. Instead, it gives students the possibility of taking general subjects to achieve a general admission to higher education. Along with the supplementary programme, several counties offer other models of health care worker training, among them the YSK (vocational and general skills), which provides access to both the trade certificate and admission to higher education. Most health care students on this track proceed directly to higher education. Some counties also offer school-based health care education, where students graduate with a general university admission certification instead of the trade certificate (Skålholt et al., 2013). From 2017, higher education institutions are for the first time trying out recruiting health care workers with a trade certificate and shorter additional courses, instead of a general certificate. The project, initiated by the state, has neither been welcomed by the nurses' organization, nor the university college given the responsibility to organize it (Høst and Schwach, 2017).

In Finland, all students who complete a three-year, school-based initial vocational education are eligible for polytechnic and university studies. For practical nursing students, the typical route to higher education within the same field is studies in the of social and health care field in the universities of applied sciences. Degree programmes leading to a bachelor's degree in nursing, such as midwifery, nursing, occupational therapy, physiotherapy and social services, are typical choices. The number of students continuing to higher education within two years after VET was 14 percent in 2008, but since then it has decreased to 10 percent.

Health care education as social inclusion

One aim of the VET system is to enhance social integration, which entails challenges of including students from different social backgrounds, gender, age and ethnicity. This has specific implications when we look at the health care sector. As a female-dominated programme, it has difficulties in attracting male students. However, in both Sweden and Denmark, the number of male students in health care has been increasing slightly in recent years. In Sweden, the proportion of males in the programme reached 17.5 percent in 2012 (Skolverket, 2013). In Denmark, the proportion of males increased to 11 percent in 2014 (Statistics Denmark, 2015). The increase may be a result of the financial crises that affected the labour market in the predominantly male private sector harder than the public sector. There have also been several recruitment campaigns aimed at males (Nielsen and Helms, 2011). In Finland, only 8 percent of the students in the education for practical nurses are males. Males applying receive a bonus for representing a gender minority group in the programme. The Norwegian health care programme has for many years had a quite stable share of around 10 percent males. Health care has, generally speaking, not succeeded in increasing the share of males very much. This reflects the fact that the gender segregated labour market and education system reinforce each other, and it is difficult to enter a field of work dominated by the opposite gender (Korp, 2013; Nielsen and Sørensen, 2004). The strong efforts to include males in this female-dominated area can be understood in several ways: as a question of gender equality, as a question of demand for labour, as a question of males' particular contributions, and as a way of legitimizing public institutions' professional performance (Larsen and Thingstrup, 2014; Nielsen, 2008).

In Denmark, the proportion of students with an immigrant background has remained stable at around 20 percent (UNI-C, 2016). The main results from a Swedish analysis reveal that the health care programme provides for equal opportunities in career choices regardless of the students' social background, but people with a Swedish background chose to become registered nurses to a higher degree than those with an immigrant background, regardless of gender (Johansson and Ahnlund, 2014). Norway has experienced a significant increase in the number of students with an immigrant background. This is even stronger in the field of work, which employs a large group of both unskilled immigrants and immigrants educated in their native country. This includes nurses not being accepted as registered nurses in Norway. In Finland, there are fewer immigrants than in the other Nordic countries, which creates cultural barriers to immigrants' participation in the health care programme. The strong increase in the share of immigrants in the health care occupation in three out of four Nordic countries proves that this field of education and work has a capacity to integrate immigrants. It also reflects the strong demand for labour in health care.

Health care education has also succeeded in integrating a significant share of students with special needs. In Finland, these students are offered special education and personal study programmes, which can be organized in smaller specialized groups or with the help of a personal tutor. The Danish VET system has similar initiatives, but cuts in state funding have reduced such possibilities, including support for weak learners and students with other special needs. In Sweden, students with special needs are challenged by its mainly school-based character, and experience calls for new ways of creating more and better opportunities for workplace learning. In Norway, the school-based part of the education is one of the programmes that has been open for students with special needs. The other side of this coin is that this could weaken the esteem of the education. The Danish model of stepwise education, where the lowest step is the health care helper and the next is a skilled health care worker, has contributed to the integration of unskilled women and immigrants into education and work. The model was replaced in 2017 by a model separating the two steps into independent educations, reflecting the hierarchy of work tasks.

Historically, the health and care sector represents what was perhaps the most important labour market for increasing the number of women entering the workforce during the 1960s and 1970s. The recruitment patterns established in that period, dominated by adult women, has survived, even if the educations have been gradually integrated into the youth education system and the comprehensive school. However, despite numerous measures taken to increase the share of young people in the education, including discriminating against older applicants, they never succeeded in attracting a sufficient number of young people in any of the countries (Høst et al., 2014). Even if the programmes have succeeded in attracting an increasing number of young students in Norway and Sweden, many of them tend to choose to continue in further education rather than trying to enter the labour market. Hence, adults still represent a dominant proportion of the health care workers (Table 6.1).

Vocational education for health care workers 131

Table 6.1 Health care workers in four Nordic countries compared

	Denmark	Finland	Norway	Sweden
Adult share of recruitment	High	Significant	High	High
Access to work	Good	Good	Problematic	Problematic
Access to work in hospitals	Problematic	Problematic	Problematic	Problematic
Part-time/full-time work	Full time	Full time	Part time	Part time
Access to higher education	Good	Good	Problematic	Good
Percent females in education	90	92	86	83
School-based/apprenticeship	Apprenticeship	School-based	Apprenticeship	Both

What characterizes health care worker education in the Nordic countries?

In all the Nordic countries, the introduction of education for health care workers was part of building welfare states after Second World War, where central aims were public health care and education for all. From the start, the educations were initiated and governed by the state. They contributed to thousands of women in all the Nordic countries entering the labour market, not as unskilled workers, but with a vocational education. Though subordinate to the registered nurses and low in the hierarchy of healthcare, the auxiliary nurse educations provided access to work in hospitals, and they soon became popular in all the countries. Older youths and adults came to dominate the educations from the beginning.

Were they to be a substitute for a lack of registered nurses, or an occupational group with its own jurisdiction? This has been and remains a long-lasting source of tension in the auxiliary nurse and care worker category. Because of the almost continuous expansion of the health care services, there has generally also been a continuous demand for skilled health care workers in the Nordic countries, but there have been major changes regarding the demand, and hence where auxiliary nurses, and later health care workers, have access to jobs. In this way, the health care worker education could to a certain extent be characterized as a "buffer education" (Larsen, 2015).

During the 1970s, 1980s and 1990s, reforms in all the countries contributed to a gradual integration of the educations for both auxiliary nurse and other care workers into the upper secondary school systems as part of broad programmes for health and social care. Due to the age structuring of upper secondary educations, the care worker educations were to an increasing extent directed at 16–19-year-olds. The philosophy behind the reforms seems to be that the welfare state needed skilled health care workers with a more generalist profile, meeting the expanding, but ever-changing needs of the population.

Although school-based from the beginning, health care educations in recent decades have mutated into apprenticeship models in the Nordic countries (Table 6.1). The apprenticeship models have distinct characteristics that differ from similar models in industry and crafts. They are state-led, they are female-dominated, they have a closer connection to general education and the school, and they represent occupations that are differently structured in the labour market. They are embedded in work organizations that are strongly structured by professions, something which gives them less space for autonomy. While VET students in the craft and industrial occupations traditionally opt for further VET education based on their work experience, the health care workers instead opt for higher education, and different alternative routes connect them to higher education in general, and the nurse education in particular.

The educational reforms integrating the auxiliary nurse educations into the upper secondary systems took place in the same period as the auxiliary nurses' main field of work changed dramatically, from the hospitals which had been their main field of work to the care and nursing sector, mainly elderly care, in the municipalities. With some variations between the countries, there is today difficult for health care workers to get positions in the hospitals, where the registered nurses dominate (Table 6.1). In Norway and Sweden, it is difficult in general for the care workers to get access to permanent positions and full-time work, including in elderly care in the municipalities. In this situation, apprenticeships do not generally seem to establish better transitions to work for health care workers. Apprenticeship in this sector is primarily education, and not recruitment to work. There are reasons to question the forecasts about the future need for health care workers as the conditions for proper employment seem to be problematic, either in all or at least in some parts of the health care sector.

While the transition from education to work seems to function quite well in Denmark and Finland, this is not the case in Norway and Sweden. Combined with changes in the education system, the transition problems have contributed to new patterns, where many students and apprentices in health care, instead of educating themselves for care work, are aiming for further or higher education, most frequently the registered nurse education.

The links between health care education and higher education are strong in the sense that in all the countries, except for Denmark, it is more common for the health care workers than other VET categories to continue to higher education. The models are, however, different. While health care workers in Denmark may take a shorter route to become a registered nurse, the Norwegian skilled health care workers were offered access to the nurse education for the first time in 2017, but only after having gone through additional courses (Table 6.1).

Health care education in the Nordic countries does not represent a periphery of the VET system, as female-dominated VET educations in other European countries have done traditionally (Mayer, 2001). They are the largest vocational programmes and in many ways, they are at the centre of discussions on how to develop the national VET systems. Skilled health care workers today represent one of the largest female-dominated groups in the labour market as a whole.

The changes in the labour market and the education system from the 1960s on has also caused changes in the trade unions, as the new, female-dominated

Vocational education for health care workers 133

service sector has strengthened its position. To illustrate this change, the leader of the LO in Norway is no longer a metal worker, but an auxiliary nurse. Furthermore, the former leader of the central trade union in Sweden was an auxiliary nurse, while the leader in the Danish LO is a woman, representing the private service sector. On both the employer and the employee side, the organizations engage actively in the VET councils, contributing to a diversification and change of policies compared with the previous situation.

Being the largest VET programme, and totally dominated by women, health care also includes a broad range of students. The programmes tend to have large numbers of both young students and of adults, of students opting for work and for students opting for higher education, of students of different national backgrounds, of weak learners and of students with other special needs. Balancing between being inclusive and at the same time keeping its esteem and position in a competitive education system and labour market represents a major challenge for the health care programmes and occupations in all the Nordic countries.

A common characteristic of the Nordic VET systems in health care seems to be that they are all, in different ways, framed by welfare state policy, seeing education and training as a right, including the whole youth cohort. This is also reflected in the vast public investments in VET, whether school-based or apprenticeship-based. In all four countries, the educations are directed towards publicly funded health care systems, characterized by well-regulated labour markets.

Notes

1 Daniel Persson Thunqvist (Sweden), Maarit Virolainen (Finland), Lene Larsen (Denmark) and Håkon Høst (Norway).
2 National nurses' associations in Scandinavia (founded in Finland in 1867; in Denmark in 1899; in Sweden in 1910; and Norway in 1912) also monitored the development of nurses' education in other western countries and international models. Formal cooperation between the Nordic Countries started in 1920 when the Nordic Nurses' Federation (NNF) was founded. The formation of NNF represents an early strategy driven by nurses in developing their own further education (Råholm et al., 2010).
3 The term 'auxiliary nurse' covers very parallel educations and occupational categories in the Nordic countries. In Denmark, it was termed *sygehjælper*; in Norway, *hjelpepleier*; in Sweden, *undersköterska*; and in Finland, *hjälpsköterska*.
4 In Denmark, the actions were directed against '*plejehjemsassistensuddannelsen*' (managers of care and nursing homes), while the case in Norway was further education of auxiliary nurses for assisting in surgery (Høst, 2006a; Wingender 1999).
5 One example is the Copenhagen trade union of auxiliary nurses (Høst, 2006a).

References

Ahnlund, P., and Johansson, S. (2011) *Omvårdnadsprogrammet: genomströmning, etableringsgrad och utbildningens relevans*, Rapport 2011: 19, Uppsala, IFAU – Institutet för Arbetsmarknadspolitisk Utvärdering,

AKF. (1988) *Fremtidens social- og sundhedsuddannelser*, Copenhagen, Amtsrådsforeningen og Kommunernes Landsforening.

134 Håkon Høst and Lene Larsen

Andreasen, L. B. et al. (1998) *Veje til forbedring og fornyelse af ungdomsuddannelserne*, Copenhagen, AKF-Forlaget.

Beck, U. (1997) *Risikosamfundet – på vej mod en ny modernitet*, Copenhagen, Hans Reitzels Forlag.

Bourdieu, P., and Wacquant, L. (1996) *Refleksiv sociologi – mål og midler*, Copenhagen, Hans Reitzels Forlag.

Brown, R., Vestergaard, A. L., and Katznelson, N. (2011) *Ungdom på erhvervsuddannelserne – delrapport om valg, elever, læring og fællesskaber*, Odense, Center for Ungdomsforskning, Erhvervsskolernes Forlag.

Emerek, R., and Holt, H. (2008) *Lige muligheder – frie valg? Om det kønsopdelte arbejdsmarked gennem et årti*, Copenhagen, SFI- Det nationale forskningscenter for velfærd.

Emanuelsson Blanck, A. (2000) 'Profession, genus och makt: Aktuella tendenser i svensk forskning om vårdyrkernas utveckling', in I Roger Qvarsell och Ulrika Torell (red.) *Humanistisk hälsoforskning: en forskningsöversikt*, Linköping, Linköping University.

Eriksen, T. R (2001) 'Omsorgsteori – i et kritisk og videnskabsteoretisk perspektiv', in I: Bjerrum, M. and Christiansen, K. L. (red.) *Filosofi – Etik – Videnskabsteori*, Copenhagen, Akademisk Forlag, pp. 268–303.

Fagbladet FOA. (2017) 'Sosu'er presses ud af sygehusene', *Fagbladet FOA*, June 26, 2017. Available at www.fagbladetfoa.dk (Accessed 15 January 2018).

FOA. (2012) 'Unge FOA-medlemmer er tvunget på deltid', *Fagbladet FOA*, May 2, 2012. Available at www.fagbladetfoa.dk (Accessed 15 January 2018).

Høst, H. (2006a) *Kunnskapsstatus vedrørende rekruttering og utdanning til pleie- og omsorgstjenestene i nordiske land*, Notat 4–2006, Rokkansenteret, University of Bergen.

Høst, H. (2006b) *Utdanningsreformer som moderniseringsoffensiv: En studie av hjelpepleieryrkets rekruttering og dannelseshistorie, 1960–2006*, Bergen, University of Bergen.

Høst, H., and Schwach, V. (2017) *The Institutional Divide Between VET and Higher Education in Norway: Tracing the Historical Background*, Paper presented at the European Conference of Educational Research 2017, Copenhagen.

Høst, H., Seland, I., and Skålholt, A. (2015) 'Gender policies meet VET practices – The case of health and social care in Norway', *Journal of Vocational Education and Training*, vol. 67, no. 1.

Høst, H., Skålholt, A., Reiling, R. B., and Gjerustad, C. (2014) *Hvorfor blir lærlingordningen i kommunal sektor annerledes enn i privat sektor?* Oslo, NIFU.

Johansson, B. (1979) *Kunskapsbehov i omvårdnadsarbete och kunskapskrav i vårdutbildning*, Göteborg, Acta Universitetas Gothoburgensis, Göteborgs universitet.

Johansson, S., and Ahnlund, P. (2014) 'The significance of education for establishment in the care sector: Women and men as care workers with a migrant background', *Educational gerontologi*, vol. 40, no. 6, pp. 442–457.

Korp, H. (2013) 'Hvem regnes for dygtige her? – intelligens og maskulinitet i erhvervsuddannelserne', in Jørgensen, C. H. (ed.) *Drenge og maskuliniteter i erhvervsuddannelserne*, Frederiksberg, Roskilde University Press, pp. 103–124.

Larsen, L. (2003) *Unge, livshistorie og arbejde. Produktionsskolen som rum for liv og læring*, Forskerskolen i livslang læring, Roskilde, Roskilde University.

Larsen, L. (2004) *Det bedste af det vi kan: Fastholdelse af elever i de grundlæggende social- og sundhedsuddannelser i Vejle Amt og Randers*, 1. Delrapport, Roskilde University.

Larsen, L. (2005) *Det bedste af det vi kan: Fastholdelse af elever i de grundlæggende social- og sundhedsuddannelser i Vejle Amt og Randers*, 2. Delrapport, Roskilde University.

Larsen, L. (2006) *Det bedste af det vi kan: Fastholdelse af elever i de grundlæggende social- og sundhedsuddannelser i Vejle Amt og Randers*, 3. Delrapport, Roskilde University.

Larsen, L. (2015) *The Social and Health Care Assistant Education in Denmark: When an Adult Education Programme Becomes an Upper Secondary Level Education*, Roskilde, Roskilde University.

Vocational education for health care workers 135

Larsen, L., and Thingstrup, S. H. (2014) *Rum for mænd? – en vidensopsamling om drenge og mænd i uddannelse*, Center for Velfærd, profession og hverdagsliv, Roskilde, Roskilde University.

Liveng, A. (2007) *Omsorgsarbejde, subjektivitet og læring. Social- og sundhedshjælperelevers orienteringer mod omsorgsarbejdet og deres møde med arbejdets læringsrum*, Forskerskolen i Livslang Læring, Roskilde, Roskilde University.

Mayer, C. (2001) 'Transfer of knowledge and practices in vocational education and training from the centers to the peripheries: The case of Germany', *Journal of Education and Work*, vol. 14, no. 2, pp. 189–208.

Melby, K. (1990) *Kall og kamp – Norsk Sykepleierforbunds historie*, Oslo, Norsk Sykepleierforbund og J.W. Cappelens Forlag A.S.

Meyerson, A. (1917) *En blick på utvecklingen af Sveriges sjukvård och sjuksköterskeväsende*, Stockholm, Svensk Sjuksköterskeridningens Förlag.

Nielsen, S. B. (2008) 'Mænd i kvindefag – om kønnede arbejdsdelinger, kvalifikationer og barrierer for integration af mænd i daginstitutioner', in Emerek, R. and Holt, H. (ed.) *Lige muligheder – frie valg? Om det kønsopdelte arbejdsmarked gennem et årti*, Copenhagen: SFI, pp. 263–289.

Nielsen, S. B., and Helms, S. (2011) 'Finanskrisens arbejdsløshed som udgangspunkt for rekruttering af mænd til kvindefag', in Nielsen, S. B. (ed.) *Nordiske mænd til omsorgsarbejde!* Center for Velfærd, Profession og Hverdagsliv, Roskilde, Roskilde University, pp. 18–39.

Nielsen, S. B., and Sørensen, A. (2004) *Unges valg af uddannelse og job – udfordringer og veje til det kønsopdelte arbejdsmarked*, Center for Ligestillingsforskning, Roskilde, Roskilde University.

Nyen, T., Skålholt, A., and Tønder, A. H. (2014) 'Fagbrevet som grunnlag for videre arbeid og utdanning', I Høst, H. (ed.) *Kvalitet i fag- og yrkesopplæringen. Fokus på bedriftsopplæringen*, Oslo, NIFU.

Persson Thunqvist, D. (2015) *Health and Social Care-Programme in Sweden*, National report Nord-VET, Linköping, University of Linköping.

Poulsen, J. (2004) *Sygehjelper – vær aktiv. Bornholm 1974–2004*, Bornholm, Sygehjælpernes faggruppe.

Råholm, M-B., Larsen Hedegaard, B., Löfmark, A., and Slettebø. (2010) 'Nursing education in Denmark, Finland, Norway and Sweden – from Bachelors', *Journal of Advanced Nursing*, vol. 66, no. 9, pp. 2126–2137.

Rehder, A. (2013) *Teknologiske fix og (post)human omsorg: Konstituering af omsorgspraksisser i et SOSU-felt i forandring*, Speciale, Sociologisk Institut, University of Copenhagens.

Simonen, L. (1995) 'Organisation, yrken och hierarkier 1958–1992', in Johansson, S. (ed.) *Sjukhus och hem som arbetsplats: Omsorgsyrken i Norge, Sverige och Finland*, Stockholm, Bonniers.

Skålholt, A., Høst, H., Nyen, T., and Tønder, A. H. (2013) *Å bli helsefagarbeider: En kvalitativ undersøkelse av overganger mellom skole og læretid, og mellom læretid og arbeidsliv blant ungdom i helsearbeiderfaget*, Oslo, NIFU.

Skolverket. (2013) *Elever i gymnasieskolan*, Stockholm, Skolverket.

Statistics Denmark. (2015) *Kvinder og mænd i 100 år – Fra lige valgret mod ligestilling*, Copenhagen, Hans Reitzels Forlag.

Stølen, N. M., Bråthen, R., Hjemås, G., Otnes, B., Texmon, I., and Vigran, A. (2016) *Helse- og sosialpersonell 2000–2014: Faktisk utvikling mot tidligere framskrivinger*, Oslo, Statistisk sentralbyrå.

Tidsskrift for Arbejdsliv nr. 1, 2006, Indledning, Roskilde, Roskilde University.

UNI-C. (2016) *Undervisningsministeriets Database*, Copenhagen, Undervisningsministeriet.

Virolainen, M. (2015) *IVET for Practical Nurses in Finland*, National report Nord-Vet, FIER, University of Jyväskylä.

7   Building and construction

A critical case for the future of vocational education

Ole Johnny Olsen, Daniel Persson Thunqvist and Anders Hallqvist

Introduction

In this chapter we shall look at all four challenges facing the Nordic systems of vocational education and training (VET) which are addressed in this book: the fit between training and labour market, the question of access to higher education, the problem of esteem and the problem of social inclusion. As with the chapter on health care in the public sector (Chapter 6), we will concentrate on one specific field of VET in the private sector. The chapter aims to explore how these challenges are perceived and managed in the building and construction industry. In line with the book's overall ambition, our aim is also to examine the complex and partly contradictory relations between the goals underlying these challenges.

The first main goal is to attract well-performing VET students and to train high-skilled workers for building occupations. This challenge is analysed in relation to current transformations of work and labour within the construction industry. Technological and organisational changes, together with deregulation and liberalisation of the labour market, constitute a new reality for the industry which profoundly affects the conditions for VET. Another significant question is how the goal of securing equal access to higher education might contradict the first goal by enabling a possible leakage of well-performing students towards academic careers and white-collar labour markets. How will a stronger orientation towards higher education influence the social status and esteem of qualifications and subordinate labour market positions in this field? Furthermore, how can the goals of social inclusion be balanced with the general ambition of high esteem for the VET programmes? Building and construction is well suited for examining these questions. It is one of the core fields of VET in all four countries both when it comes to size – the number of students and training places involved – and when it comes to its historical roots and traditions.

As we have learned throughout the book, there are clear differences between the basic features of the national Nordic VET systems: Denmark has an apprenticeship system regulated within an order of typical collective skill formation, Sweden and Finland have characteristic state-regulated school-based systems, while the Norwegian system can be described as a mixture of the two types.

VET programmes for building and construction are of course also part of these overall systems. However, as this chapter will demonstrate, it is not the well-known differences between these systems that are most striking in the case of building and construction. In fact, the roots of the traditional crafts are still evident, and much of the artisan character of the work and work organisation has remained in this industry. This is due partly to a delayed technological and organisational shift from craft-based work to industrialisation. In addition, the labour force in the Nordic countries has been massively and powerfully organised, constituting a driver for collective skill formation systems.

Today, however, these structures and traditions are strongly challenged by increased industrialisation, market liberalisation and international labour migration. These processes challenge long-lasting systems of skill formation as well as the Nordic countries' organised labour markets, which skill formation is closely related to. It is thus necessary and important to address these questions thoroughly in the first section of this chapter, before we discuss the other challenges.

The empirical basis for our comparative analysis is four internal reports from the Nord-VET project[1] discussing the four challenges in relation to the building sector and the carpenter occupation. The national reports build on analysis of research reports or other secondary literature and national statistics, extended by expert interviews and interviews with a small sample of students and teachers.

Carpenters in transition: education for a changing labour market

Over the last few centuries, many crafts entered the maelstrom of industrialisation and the dynamics of capitalism. New tools and materials were developed, work was reorganised, and specialisation encouraged. Workers became degraded to labourers, masters became employers and artisans employees, and work organisations became machines for the control of labour (see e.g. Braverman, 1974; Edwards, 1979). This process was not without resistance – the struggle against degradation was important in the formation of labour unions – and it was not universal: these changes took place to various degrees and in various ways within different crafts and in different countries. In some countries, work organisation based on autonomous and highly skilled workers survived and even became the leading model for all sectors and industries. The model was supported by the development of VET systems qualifying occupational categories with professional skills and self-reliance. Germany is a well-known case for the success and strength of a production model based on this kind of occupational principle, while France has exemplified a history of work and skill formation adapted to the principles of bureaucratic administration and direct control (cf. Piore and Sabel, 1984; Maurice et al., 1986; Thelen, 2004).

Our point here, however, is that even in countries where work organisations and the national VET systems are less affected by this occupational principle, several craft occupations within the building and construction sector have kept some of their artisan character. This has been done by adjusting the scope of the craft to technological change and development and by defending workers' relative autonomy and professional sovereignty in the workplace. Fundamentally, this defence was made possible through the collective organising of work and through institutions for collective skill formation.

Collective organising in the workplace has included all parts of the work process, such as planning, coordination, execution and quality control as well as negotiating contracts with management and employers. The general concept *trade union (fagforening)* reminds us of the latter aspect. But while trade unions in general deal with collective bargaining on the company or national level, the collective organising of the trades in the building sector also has an important role at the workplace level. By contrast with unions in typical industrial work, which have mostly opposed piecework and contract work, occupations like carpenters have built their relative autonomy on the basis of agreements on particular jobs for particular work teams, negotiated by an elected team foreman (*bas*).

For employers, of course, this has always meant a relative loss of organisational control. But on the other side, in organisations based on this kind of relationship of trust (cf. Fox, 1974), management do not need to use resources on planning, coordination and quality control; these are dealt with by the teams themselves. This is why Arthur L. Stinchcombe, in his seminal study on the "bureaucratic and craft administration of production" from 1959, particularly using the building industry as a case study, could sum up the character of the crafts in this industry as follows:

> Craft institutions in construction are more than craft trade unions; they are also a method of administering work. They include special devices of legitimate communications to workers, special authority relations, and special principles of division of work, the 'jurisdictions' which form areas of work defining labour market statuses.
>
> (Stinchcombe, 1986, p. 178)

Looking at the Nordic countries, these general characteristics are still very relevant. In Sweden the occupational principle is fully intact in the construction sector, by contrast with the manufacturing sector where it has more or less vanished (Fjellström, 2017). The same is true in Denmark and Norway. In Denmark and Sweden, the main rule in the building and construction industry is that the work organisation is built on organising teams led by an elected foreman (*bas*) and their piecework (Ajslev, 2014; Kronlund, 1982; Carlén et al., 2009).

This is also widely practiced in the Norwegian construction industry. Here there are, however, some regional variations. In some regions, for example around Bergen, where we did some of our expert interviews, the work is largely paid by fixed salaries and the team foreman is appointed by management (by the master). The transition to fixed salaries in this region goes back to the

1980s, and was part of a joint struggle of employers and local unions against the growth of 'contractors' (individuals or loosely-knit groups of carpenters with or without craft certificates) who were disrupting the market in construction and housebuilding at the time (Løvseth and Strand, 1992). In this case, abandoning the organising practice of an elected team foreman with piecework was not part of a management strategy to abandon the principle of occupational based work organisation. In fact, many of the medium-sized construction firms around Bergen are core members of the masters' 'guild', whose common political activity has very much been and still remains focussed on securing and fighting for collective responsibility for the apprenticeship system and for training young carpenters. They also represent a strong voice in recent years' sectoral and public political debate on how to fight the 'unserious' firms who sponge off the collective good of occupational skills while undermining its future formation, basing their production too much on subcontracting, migrant labour and temporary work agencies (see Moen et al., 2014).

By addressing this theme of the short-term labour strategies enabled by the liberalisation of international markets, we want to highlight what we see as a devastating challenge – even threat – to collective skill formation. The general liberalisation of the market for temporary work agencies – in Sweden in the early 1990s, in the other Nordic countries around 2000 (Dølvik et al., 2015, p. 68) – also opened the door to new staffing strategies in building and construction. The trend in large parts of the industry was to cut down on permanent staff and hire short-term workers from agencies. With EU enlargement in 2004, including new members from Eastern Europe, this practice increased dramatically, especially in Norway where building and construction activities experienced a boom during these years.

A recent study carried out by local unions in the Oslo region shows that in 2011 a total of 50% of workers on the building sites of the big contractors came from recruitment agencies (Elstad, 2017, p. 13). This dropped to 12% in 2013, most likely, the report comments, as a consequence of the implementation of the 2012 EU directive on temporary work, which laid down that agency workers should be treated equally with workers employed in the companies using them. Moreover, the construction market shrank substantially when the oil crisis hit in 2014. This drop didn't last long: today the proportion of agency workers working for large construction firms in the region has reached 35%. Short-term flexibility was once again given priority over long-term employment. Furthermore, subcontracting has increased. In 2011 the share of workers from subcontractors was 21%. Already in 2013 this number was doubled, and in 2015 it was as high as 47% (Elstad, 2017). Studies from other countries have indicated the same change in practice: the answer to the EU directive on agency work was an increased use of subcontracting (König and Detje, 2016). For the Norwegian building and construction industry, subcontracting predominantly means awarding contracts to foreign companies, mainly Eastern European, which can offer rates that are out of reach for their Norwegian competitors.

140   *Ole Johnny Olsen et al.*

The consequences for VET are clear: recruitment agencies do not train people, they have no apprentices and do nothing more than arrange the hiring and firing of workers (cf. Eldring et al., 2012; Eldring, 2015; Bals, 2017). Foreign subcontractors do not train Norwegian apprentices and have no commitment to Norwegian VET. Moreover, staffing strategies often go hand in hand with changing strategies of work organisation and labour processes on construction sites. The new short-term staffing of these sites enables new differentiations: some workers do the simple jobs, under the close supervision of frontline foremen. Other workers and the traditional teams get the more demanding tasks.

Hence labour strategies and the development of work organisations enter a vicious circle: when the market encourages firms to take shortcuts on staffing and quality in order to win contracts, using recruitment agencies, temporary employment and subcontracting, the need to hire skilled workers is reduced, as is the motivation to invest in training. Over time this leads to demands for further simplification of the work process, increased use of prefabrication and Taylorisation of construction sites (cf. Friberg and Haakestad, 2015), which in turn weakens levels of interest among young people searching for autonomous work and opportunities for self-development. Overall, well-established learning environments crumble and the basic foundations of collective skill formation are threatened.

All the national reports in our project (see endnote 1) address the problems stemming from the pressure of market liberalisation and from technological and organisational change. The potential consequences of weakening the national-level skill formation of building and construction workers are far-reaching. Economically, the lack of highly skilled construction workers endangers national building industries as a whole. Being dependent on importing builders would imply a huge set-back for a differentiated modern economy. Socially and culturally, a degradation of the situation of autonomous carpenters and construction workers and a dissolving of the collective structures of training and work would ruin one of the largest and best-functioning institutions for integrating and socialising young people – young men predominately in these occupations – into social collectives and identities with high societal recognition and thereby for individual development of self-respect and self-esteem, pride and dignity. This capacity for integration and socialisation is a well-recognized quality of VET systems based on the occupational principle of work organisation, well-documented in several studies, including recent ones (see i.e. Olsen et al., 2015; Jørgensen, 2013).

We should also remember that occupational structuration is not only to be found in systems of skill formation and work organisation alone. The collective regulation of labour relations is also very important. Integration and socialisation into working life in building and construction has also implied integration and socialisation into a world of labour regulated – in the Nordic countries – by national collective agreements and labour law that have given individual workers high social security and recognition as employees with a broad spectrum of labour rights. The young apprentice carpenter has become part of the collectives on the building site, learned the rules and norms of how to build houses, and developed the skills needed to make an independent contribution to this work. At the same time, he or she has learned the rules and norms of the working life more generally – about permanent employment contracts, working hours, holiday rights, sick leave, pensions etc. – and he or she has learned about the processes for democratic participation in establishing such rules and norms, through collective bargaining, organisational councils or political elections. The existence of these collective regulations, and the integration and socialisation of young workers into the norms of these regulations, have been important elements of the socio-cultural foundation for democratic capitalism in these countries (Sejersted, 2011; Streeck, 2014; Honneth, 2014; Olsen, 2018).

Meeting change in labour market and work organisation

Modularisation: Finland takes the lead

Of the four national VET systems, the Finnish stands out as exceptional in relation to building and construction. While the other three systems in this sector are still shaped by the occupational principle as discussed above, the Finnish system is directed towards broad and loosely structured qualification profiles. Finnish VET, organised until recently through vocational schools, has been rather weakly connected to the labour market, including VET for construction work (Virolainen, 2015, p. 15).

However, during the new millennium there have been several initiatives in the VET system aimed at improving connections to the labour market. Within the Finnish three-year model, construction profiles are built up of one part of vocational modules (2 ½ years) and another part of general subjects. The programme for the 'builder', one of four construction profiles, has two compulsory modules, called foundation work and carcassing, which amount to about the half of the credits for vocational modules. In addition, students take optional modules within a relatively varied spectrum of trades, e.g. masonry, tiling, interior carpentry work, scaffolding construction, reinforcing and concreting or renovation. The completion of the modules is done by specific skill demonstrations.

Planning course completion is very much up to each student, who can independently decide how many optional skill demonstrations he or she will do. The majority of students complete four to six modules with a demonstration. One-fourth complete only three at most and one-tenth take more than six demonstrations. The training is relatively practical overall, with the production of small cottages etc. in school workshops, and a relatively high amount (20 credits of 90) must be done as on-the-job training at a workplace. The construction industry is also relatively present in actually shaping the training, for example through the demonstrations, which are mainly organised by the school (about 60%) partly in cooperation with workplace supervisors or by workplaces themselves (40%).

142   *Ole Johnny Olsen et al.*

The point we want to make is therefore not that the Finnish training is more general or 'theoretical' than in the other countries. Nor is there a weak relation between school and industry. The significant difference is rather the very individualised and modularised training and certification system. Based on a common one-year training in foundation work and carcassing, students can specialise in many occupational qualifications. By passing the different skill demonstrations, students get formal qualifications in the respective occupations, in masonry, tiling etc. There is no common skill profile of a graduated 'builder' except for the two obligatory modules. In a special system for further education, builders can specialise in specific occupational trades. Within the upper secondary level, however, the 'builder' is an educational umbrella for the short-cut specialisations taken by students.

The development of this kind of multi-skilled qualification profile corresponds with the interests and politics of central actors in the industry itself. The expectation of technological change is a very important dimension of its justification. The Finnish report refers to central actors and documents which argue for the need for a broader and multi-skilled construction worker because of expected technological change.

Similarities and differences in Denmark, Norway and Sweden: occupational goals

The building and construction VET programmes (BC programmes) in Denmark, Norway and Sweden can be described by emphasising their similarities both around structural content and around occupational direction. Becoming a construction worker involves, in most cases, school-based training and specialised training in subsequent apprenticeships. At the same time, the VET programmes for construction work differ regarding regulations and the organisation of school-based VET and apprenticeship.

All programmes in Denmark, Norway and Sweden have the following structure: They start with broad introductions. Subsequently, students choose specialisation in school. Finally, they follow a work-based training, preferably as apprentices, directed towards a craft certificate. The most important differences between the three countries are found in the institutional regulations and particularly in the institutional role of the actors in the craft.

The Swedish case

The Swedish programme for building and construction originates from a two-year school programme launched in 1971. This had a first year, common to all students, composed of five tracks, and then a second year concentrated on one of the five, for example carpentry. The second year was partly workplace-based. After these two years, regulated by a national curriculum, students could apply for final apprenticeships in firms, governed by the social partners in the building and construction branch. With an upper secondary school reform in 1991,

Building and construction   143

all VET programmes were extended by a third year. More general subjects were added, partly to make all students eligible for higher education. Hence, the programme for building and construction got the following structure: a three-year school-based education regulated by the state, followed by a two- or three-year final apprenticeship regulated by the labour market partners. Even though final apprenticeship does not belong to the national VET system, it is vital for students' school-to work transitions (Högberg, 2009; Fjellström, 2017).

If students do not complete the final apprenticeship track after graduating from the school-based programme, it becomes difficult for them to get access to skilled employment (Berglund, 2009; Berglund et al., 2014). The final apprenticeship therefore counts as part of the qualification system. Overall, the Swedish programme for training in construction is a 3+2 model very much like the Norwegian 2+2 model.

However, unlike their Danish and Norwegian counterparts, Swedish employers lack influence over the vocational exams (set by the school). The regulation of the Swedish building and construction programme is distinguished by a far-reaching privatisation and a shift in the governance of VET from the state to the municipalities (Olofsson and Persson Thunqvist, 2018). This partly explains significant local differences in the organisation of, and composition between, school-based VET and work-based training. Unlike in Norway and Denmark, schools and industry are not institutionalised within a single order. Schools direct themselves in training occupations such as carpenters, but the completion of training through the apprenticeship lies outside their field of responsibility, and is governed by the sector itself.

The Norwegian case

In Norway, building and construction is one of nine vocational programmes in upper secondary education. This programme covers 22 different occupations. Of these, carpentry is the largest trade in terms of apprenticeship contracts. Other large trades, with more than 100 new apprenticeship contracts a year, are plumbing, construction vehicle operator, concrete work, bricklaying, and ventilation and tinsmith work. Since 'Reform 94', these trades are organised around a standard 2+2 model, with two years of school-based education followed by two years' apprenticeship. This model was continued as the main model in the 'Knowledge Promotion Reform' (*Kunnskapsløftet*) in 2006.

In Reform 94, the number of introductory courses was reduced from 100 to only 13. The Knowledge Promotion Reform reduced this number even further, from 13 to 9. In addition, the new reform strongly reduced the number of courses in second year. Up till the 1994 reform, all the main trades had had a separate course in second year. In that reform, all the occupational trades lost their trade-specific learning track in the schools. The second year was also restructured into programmes combining different occupations. Today one of these courses, 'construction techniques', covers four different trades: carpentry, concrete work, bricklaying and scaffolding. In principle this means that (for example) students who are planning to be carpenters must also learn concrete work, bricklaying and scaffolding, but they do not learn all trades in the same depth. Both in first and second year, students choose '*in-depth subjects*' where they can concentrate on learning specific occupations. This largely coincides as well with their placements for workplace learning, especially in second year.

Fewer and broader programmes make it easier to provide young people with their statutory right to upper secondary education since 1994. The main training and socialisation for vocational skills does not take place in the classrooms, but in workshops in the vocational schools. However, it is well-documented that what matters most are tasks where students can produce 'real', authentic things under supervision of teachers with a good skilled worker's expertise and authority (Mjelde, 2006; Olsen and Reegård, 2013; Olsen et al., 2014). Training is very much carried out by building small doll houses, garages or other 'real' things. Often the school takes on special orders from neighbouring institutions, either for production in school or on site outside school. Teachers use their networks to get such projects, in the same way as they use these networks to secure adequate placements for work-based learning.

If such placements are heavily emphasised in all the school-based education programmes today, they have a long and strong tradition in the Norwegian system, for example. Bringing in the Finnish experience too, students there reported that their training on the job was strongly motivational and that it was very important in deciding what specialisations they wanted to do their skills demonstrations in. An entirely similar experience was reported by Norwegian students (in this study as in numerous earlier studies: Olsen, 2013). The experience of practical work in firms is decisive, not least for the less school-motivated students. This experience is also important in preparing them for applying for apprenticeships and for acquiring contacts to training companies.

The Danish case

Compared to the other Nordic countries, the role of the trades and their corporate institutions is most significant in Denmark. The Danish system offers two introductory courses, each lasting six months with a gradual specialisation in three steps. The first of the two courses (GF1) is broader than the entry courses in other Nordic VET systems. To become a carpenter, students must first complete the broad basic course (GF1), followed by the second basic course (GF2) for 'woodworking occupations' (carpenter, roofer, floor fitter, etc.) After completion of the GF2 exam, a student can start on the main course for carpenters, in an alternating apprenticeship programme of 3½ years. This programme ends with an exam for the journeyman's certificate, which qualifies students for a trade such as carpenter, with some exceptions and variations (e.g. for students over 25 years old and students with an apprenticeship contract who can take a shorter programme or, in the latter case, can skip the basic course). However, the majority start on a school-based course (GF1), as in Norway and Sweden. Until recently, apprenticeship has been the core institution of the Danish

Building and construction   145

system, not least for the trades in the craft sector. The training has been carried out as classical 'master training', where the apprentice is supervised by his or her master or fellow journeymen at the workplace. It has not only been a tradition to recruit apprentices before they enter any preparatory VET schooling, it has been preferred to train the apprentices with the wanted skills and attitudes.

The regulation of the Danish system, too, is most strongly influenced by the occupational institutions, with the trade committee having the central role. At the general level, the Ministry of Education prepares a legal framework for the programmes, but it is the trade committee, consisting of three representatives from the unions and three representatives from employer organisations, that regulates the national curriculum and the national quality systems of the work-based learning. This committee is also responsible for approving the companies which can offer training placements. At the local level, the committee appoints local education committees, also consisting of equal numbers of representatives from employers' and workers' organisations. The overall task of these local committees is to advise schools and strengthen cooperation with local businesses.

Convergence in meeting the challenges

While the Danish system has kept its characteristic occupational-based institutional architecture and school-based VET systems remain in Finland and Sweden, their Norwegian counterpart has experienced a weakening of its system. In the Reform 94 process the trade-specific committees disappeared and were replaced by broader branch/programme-based committees. The actual consequences of this have not yet been studied in detail, but in general we can expect to see a weakening of general care and responsibility for the occupations, as well as fewer possibilities for direct influence on the formal rules and procedures for trade-based training. The specific character of the curriculum in the Norwegian case, however, with its very general formulations of learning goals, does enable adjustment to trade/sectoral interests at the local level. It seems that such adjustments are made both in school and in work-based training, very much in line with the close cooperation between local schools and firms or local branch interests (training offices). Furthermore, the construction industry actors, both at local and central level, have strongly advocated the need for a clear trade-based education rather than the kind of multi-skilled training seen in Finland. One result of this, for example, is the implementation of a more flexible application of the 2+2 model by normalising a 1+3 model where it serves the interest of students, of schools and firms, or of all three.

As a general conclusion as to the crucial goals of VET in securing a close fit between training and labour market: in all three countries (Sweden, Norway and Denmark), the main actors seem to follow the same general line in their policies for meeting these challenges. Employer organisations as well as unions actively defend trades-based training.

However, we can also point out some significant differences. Generally, Danish actors have been strong defenders of occupational autonomy, both around

146   *Ole Johnny Olsen et al.*

training regulations and in relation to demarcations between different occupations and trades on building sites. There have been strict demarcations between, for example, carpenters and bricklayers when it comes to skill demands and task responsibilities. The borderline between skilled workers (journeymen) and unskilled labour has also been significant in the Danish workplace. Up to 2010, skilled and unskilled workers were organised in separate unions.

The last few years have seen some changes along both dimensions. Several initiatives have been taken, under a programme called 'partnering', to improve interdisciplinary cooperation between trades on the building sites. And at the organisational level, we have seen mergers of craft unions into industrial unions. Such mergers have also been seen among Norwegian unions. Does this tendency signal a stronger focus on general employee/labour interests than on more particular occupational interests? In general, it does not seem to be a case of weakening the politics of trade-based work and training. Even looking at the Swedish construction industry, where industrial-based organisation of interests has been strong, we can see that trades-based politics are entirely possible from such an angle.

A primary challenge to this politics, as discussed above, is the pressure on specialisation and differentiation at the workplace caused by market liberalisation, new employment strategies, labour migration and technological change. In the fierce competition around the increased globalisation of the construction sector, larger as well as medium-sized companies are tempted to take shortcuts on quality of work, labour strategies and staffing of work sites. A decisive condition in meeting this challenge is of course maintaining and securing the general quality of the skilled workers graduating through the established VET system. A continuous good supply of highly competent and autonomous skilled workers is the best defence for the established trade-based system and its fit between VET and labour market.

This is also seen in common concerns regarding a weaker base for recruitment. If in Denmark the school-based route to apprenticeship has become the main route for carpenters, as more than 70% of the enrolled apprentices take this path while 10 years ago it was 45%, this reminds us not only of the vulnerability of the apprenticeship system to economic downturns, since the change is very much due to the downturn after the financial crisis that hit the economy in 2008. The change is also due to more general considerations on the part of companies. They experience a decrease in the general levels of qualification and motivation among students applying for the carpentry programme, to such an extent that they now see, to a higher degree than before, the advantage of recruiting apprentices after introductory courses. Since school authorities have simultaneously extended the intake for school-based practical training and initiated the expansion of training centres, this also gives firms the opportunity of recruiting apprentices with relevant basic skills from preparatory training. In this way the school element is becoming more important in the Danish system. In fact, the Danish 1+3–year model (which is the standard model for young people after compulsory school since 1976) has been developed in a similar direction as the Norwegian 2+2 model, reflecting common ways of dealing with the challenges of finding a good fit between training and labour market.

Overall, as regards the fit between VET and labour market, the Finnish system has moved in the direction of adapting to some extent to the marketisation of labour and specialisation of skills, while in the other Nordic countries there are actors and initiatives trying to keep a broader occupational principle as the basis for training and work. There certainly remain different institutional regulations of these systems. Still, the convergence revolves around the question of a need for introductory/preparatory courses before entering a trade-specific training, whether in school or in apprenticeship. Young people today need some hands-on work experience before deciding on and entering an occupation. Firms see a growing need for basic training and personal maturity before entering an apprenticeship.

Access to higher education: different formal options but similar challenges

While connections between VET and the construction industry have remained strong in the Nordic countries, the links to universities have historically been weak. However, our country comparisons reveal that several formal options have been developed in recent decades across these countries to bring VET closer to universities. Initiatives have been taken in all the Nordic countries to integrate general and vocational education at upper secondary level and thus enable access to higher education. As indicated above, basic eligibility for higher education in building and construction programmes has been prioritised as a goal in Finland and Sweden since the 1990s. In Norway, the reform in 1994 increased general subjects in VET in order to promote transitions from VET to the general university preparatory programme in upper secondary school. In Denmark, a carpentry education formally qualifies for direct access to post-secondary education in professionally relevant areas, such as building technicians in vocational academies, and for qualified craftsmen to get access to a 1–1½ year preparatory course for engineering education. At the same time, the causes and the driving forces behind such endeavours, and the outcomes of consistent policy attempts, to bridge the gaps between VET and higher education remain to be explained.

As discussed in the introduction and earlier chapters, the question of access to higher education for VET students can be put differently from different point of views. In Nordic discourses, one dominant position has been the ideal of equal rights to education for all young people, to the level of their potential capacity. A second position is the idea that more people with higher education are needed to meet the requirements of the post-industrial society and to enable social mobility. Paradoxically, seen as a core element in social democratic educational politics, the first position has also implied the ideal of leaving the working class for a better life in the middle classes. A strong implication of the second position has been that general or theoretical knowledge is more

148   *Ole Johnny Olsen et al.*

valuable than practical knowledge. Furthermore, within the hierarchical order of these educational systems, passing general education subjects at one level is perceived as an absolute precondition for access to the next level. Consequently, the best learners at upper secondary school have been guided to aspire to higher education.

Moreover, a third position or discourse on this question can be identified. Within the building and construction sector, as within manufacturing, one will very often hear the claim that – rather than people with higher education alone – industries need people who combine higher education and practical knowledge and experience from shop floor work. In these sectors, the value of skills collected from below while climbing the ladder up to all levels of management has been strongly appreciated. Many leaders of the construction sector see the danger of widening the gap between theoretical and practical knowledge within firms and on work sites. Part of the popular criticism about too much theory in vocational education has been an inadequate understanding of the qualification of a highly qualified construction worker. An equally important problem is the narrow and purely theoretical competence of engineers and managerial staff. The lack of managerial staff with practical experience is serious: "Soon we will have nobody who can lead a construction site", as a Norwegian branch leader commented.

From a comparative perspective, we can see some important differences in how challenges around this theme have been met. While the two general discourses mentioned above – those on equal rights and knowledge society – have been central in all countries, the relevance of the third discourse – on practical knowledge as a basis for higher education – have varied.

In Norway, even though VET students have had relative easy access to higher education through the opportunity to take an extra school year studying general subjects, relatively few students or graduated journeymen have chosen this path. In one study, only 1 percent of one student cohort could be found in higher education one year after graduation from building and construction. In the middle level tertiary schools, however, 4 percent of the same cohort could be found (Nyen et al., 2013).

This is a good indicator of the relevance of the much-favoured alternative to post-secondary education among graduated students and young journeymen in building and construction. It is also an indicator of an alternative which is highly supported by the industry itself. Employers' associations and educational actors within the industry clearly promote this kind of education, and the idea of giving access from this kind of education to higher education. Today, however, this is not possible, except in some university colleges with special offers for an 'occupational road' to higher education skills (see Chapter 3).

Finland represents an interesting case on this theme. In contrast to Denmark and Norway, where the occupational principle and the emphasis on transition from lower to higher education for broadly-skilled skilled workers have been the ideal, the Finnish solution was to establish a polytechnic education at university level, recruiting students from both vocational and general upper secondary education (Virolainen, 2015). This solution fits well into the trans-formation of vocational education, with a relatively strong emphasis on general subjects and an orientation towards developing a broader spectrum of skills, but with narrower expectations as regards trades. If these changes towards more hybrid and superficial skills learnt in VET and a more applied education of engineers are reflections of, or will lead to, changes of division of labour in the workplace between engineers and workers remains an open question. Thus far it seems that the Finnish students in this sector also do not show strong interest in higher education. Of Finnish students (during the period 2007–2012) with a school-based carpenter's qualification, around 5 percent are found in the poly-technics while less than 1 percent of students continue to traditional science universities (Virolainen, 2015).

The Finnish development of polytechnic education can be interpreted as a response to the second discourse mentioned above – the idea of a general need for competence at a higher educational level. Swedish politics, on the other hand, are much more strongly influenced by the first discourse (until 2011; see below), emphasising equality and life-long learning. In Finland, the focus is on the need for engineers.

In Sweden, while transitions to higher education have particularly grown in female-dominated upper secondary school VET programmes (see Chapters 3 and 6), such transitions have remained low in the construction programme; between 3 and 7 percent during the period 1996–2011 (Persson Thunqvist and Hallqvist, 2014). Since the latest (2011) upper secondary school reform, VET students must attend optional courses to secure access to higher education. In the building and construction programme, only 20–21 percent of students complete these courses, and transitions to higher education have been remark-ably low in recent years (Skolverket, 2017). These patterns are comparable with Denmark, where the rate of progression from VET to higher education in the construction sector is lower than in other sectors (Damvad, 2013). Carpenters, who enrol in programmes at the tertiary level, are concentrated in a few pro-grammes at the bachelor (3½-year) and sub-bachelor (2-year) level, which are directly accessible for some students after completing a VET programme.

All in all, despite formal options supporting transitions from VET to higher education, such transitions have been low in VET for construction work in all four Nordic countries. As we discuss further in the next section, the popu-larity of carpentry education among young people is not so much related to the opportunities afforded for higher education, as it is to the opportunity to work practically and to develop occupational skills and vocational identities in a respectable field of work (Damvad, 2013).

Esteem and social inclusion

While education for construction work might have quite a low prestige in the context of the general educational hierarchy (see Chapter 4), as indicated above, these programmes have high esteem in terms of their strong labour market

150 *Ole Johnny Olsen et al.*

value. It is important to foreground such qualities, connected to the occupational principle and vocational identities, in current discussions about the esteem of VET, since the focus nowadays is largely on the disparity of esteem between vocational education and general education (e.g. Billett, 2014).

Measured in numbers of students, building and construction is one of the most popular VET programmes among men in all four countries. And within this programme the carpentry track is the most popular in Denmark, Norway and Sweden. In the Danish report, carpentry is characterized as a 'trendy trade', which is also shown in a high level of competition between students for training placements. In Sweden, the interest in carpentry education is so strong that school organisers and teachers must redirect students to other trades within the construction sector. The numbers of applicants fell relatively clearly in Norway after the recession hit the country in 2014; but the numbers increased again only three years after, in 2017.

Number of applicants can give an indication of esteem, but only in to some extent. A training programme may generally be acknowledged as a good and respectable education without being ascribed a high position on the scale of occupational status. A programme that is easily accessible, for example, may be seen as belonging to a lower level of esteem. Looking at the accessibility of the building and construction programmes in the Nordic countries, we can see some differences. In Norway, applicants do not need high grades to enter the BC programme because the number of applicants is lower than the available places (the programme is the most 'undersubscribed' among VET programmes). In Finland, on the other hand, there seems to be competition among applicants. Whether this is caused by too few places or too many good students is unclear. According to the Danish report, carpentry students have higher grade averages from primary school than students in the bricklaying and painters' programmes – or in the health programmes – but lower than those in the electricians' programme. In Sweden the grade average among people who enter the BC programme has remained slightly lower than among VET students generally (Högberg, 2009) and significantly lower than among students on HE preparatory programmes since the latest (2011) upper secondary school reform (Skolverket, 2017). With these differences in mind, the overall picture is that the building and construction programmes are popular but also relatively easily accessed.

This picture corresponds to the picture established through other projects (see i.e. Olsen and Reegård, 2013) and through general information about this field of VET. Very often when this picture is presented it comes with an implicit or explicit assessment of the programmes as a whole, how demanding they are and what kind of students they suit. Through such assessments we often find ideas of esteem for the programmes or for the occupations within the programmes.

This was, for example, clearly conveyed in the narratives of some of the students in the Swedish case study. From their own experience and in their own understanding, the BC programme is popular because one does not need high grades to access the programme and it is generally undemanding. Similar ideas and understandings can be found among teachers and school councillors in lower secondary schools. According to the report from the Norwegian case study, based on much secondary research on this point (see i.e. Olsen and Reegård, 2013), weak and less-motivated students are often advised to apply for building and construction. This kind of ideas and practice can even give rise to a general view, as conveyed by some Danish actors worrying about the future of VET, who hold that very often young people with social problems are 'forced into vocational schools'.

If we sharpen the focus of the picture, however, we find that these programmes contain students with a wide range of educational capabilities, motivations and general learning strengths. There are students with high grade averages, and there are those with very low. There are highly motivated students and there are many less motivated. This is not new, and both teachers and employers in traditional VET programmes like building and construction have long experience in handling the differences. A common motivation and perspective on their own education among the different student groups has been found, in an interest in leaving classroom learning to experience practical work and learning. Above all, there has been a strong motivation for 'coming out into working life'. On this basis teachers and trainers have been able to build their work and adapt teaching to different students.

Some students can quickly engage independently in school workshops. Others need more help and attention. Some develop quickly into budding young craftsmen and women. Others need more time. But teachers as well as trainers have also seen many times, as the Norwegian case study indicates, how young students who start with no specific interest or knowledge of a specific occupation, with little motivation for learning and perhaps with a lot of social problems acquired as 'baggage' from life outside school, can develop an occupational interest, practical skills and enough confidence to apply for apprenticeships in specific trades during the first year of vocational school. Firms certainly want the best and most motivated candidates. Still there are well-known observations of how firms may employ apprentices with a general weak school record, but with sufficient evidence of skills or attitudes that fruitful apprenticeship training can be built on. And there are observations of how students – also those with such weak records – have developed during their apprenticeships to become proud and capable young craftsmen (see Olsen et al., 2014).

These experiences tell us about the strength of vocational education based on occupational skills and identities when it comes to socialisation and social integration. It particularly emphasises the role of training and inclusion in the world of work, based on the occupational principle and collective regulations. In a way, they also enable an alternative understanding of the question of esteem. High esteem in occupational trades need not necessarily be decided by recruitment to VET programmes. VET programmes and learning trajectories may well enable those who are considered to be weak learners to become good craftsmen and women. Esteem is therefore very much decided by the strength

152　*Ole Johnny Olsen et al.*

of the craft and the character of the training programme. This brings us back to the challenges – not to say to the threats – to the programmes of VET within building and construction from the changes of labour market and work organisation that we have seen in the last few decades.

Conclusion

Building and construction constitutes a critical case for the future of VET in several respects. First, this chapter indicates the drama between continuity and changes. In all four Nordic countries, several craft occupations in the building and construction industry have kept some of their artisan character, reproduced by forms of collective skill formation systems and tightly embedded in Nordic labour market relations. As we have shown, however, a major question today is how collective skill formation systems in the Nordic construction sectors will be able to cope with the profound contemporary transformations in the labour market towards increased industrialisation, liberalisation, and labour migration, as well as technological changes. As VET systems in the Nordic countries are quite different, as shown throughout the book, we might perhaps have expected to find greater differences in the VET programmes for building and construction work across the four countries too. It is interesting to note, however, that Denmark, Norway and even Sweden's school-based VET system have converged on partly similar responses to the current challenges in contemporary working life. While the chapter has highlighted many specific significant differences regarding VET regulations and the composition of school-based education and apprenticeship, overall it is the similarities which are most striking within this picture.

Second, the integration of initial VET within national educational systems also means that VET targeting building and construction work must balance several, partly competing, institutionalised goals. In addition to providing occupational socialisation and access to skilled employment, educational programmes directed towards construction work are also expected to support progression within national education systems, including access to higher education, and to promote goals of social inclusion and diversity. In all four countries, strong relationships between VET and the labour market in construction work tend to support smooth transitions to the labour market, but transition to universities remain rather modest in all four countries. Weak connections in practice to academic traditions and to higher education risk decreasing the status of VET.

At the same time, as have been shown, VET programmes have given large groups of young people a good and relevant training for relative well esteemed occupations, introduced them to well-paid jobs and integrated them into well recognised craft/labour communities. True, the social group in these programmes have predominantly been young working-class males. And in this sense, these programmes have not been very successful in the task of increasing equality and in including women and broader social groups. Today one may also look for the ability to include young people across ethnic divides. Indeed, building and construction is less heterogeneous in terms of ethnicity and gender

Building and construction   153

by comparison with, for example, health care (see Chapter 6). Acknowledging these challenges, we will conclude by underlining the traditional significance of these programmes in their role of preparing broad groups – well and not so well performing (male) students – for esteemed occupations and skilled jobs in what we should not forget are well-regulated labour markets. Overall, this has proved the relevance of choosing building and construction for a closer look at today's challenges for Nordic VET.

Note

1 These are the following: Andersen and Jørgensen (2015), Case Study of Carpenter Education in Denmark; Olsen and Hagen Tønder (2015), Case Study – Building and Construction in Norwegian VET with Focus on its Largest Trade, Carpenters; Persson Thunqvist and Hallqvist (2015), Case Study, the Building and Construction Programme in Sweden; Virolainen (2015), IVET for Construction Workers (Carpenters) in Finland.

References

Ajslev, J. Z. N. (2014) *Fordelingen af arbejdet i sjakket og muskel-og skeletbesvaer*, Roskilde, Roskilde Universitet, Center for Arbejdslivsforskning.

Bals, J. (2017) *Hvem skal bygge landet?* Oslo, Cappelen Damm.

Berglund, I. (2009) *Byggarbetsplatsen som skola – eller skolan som byggarbetsplats? En studie av byggnadsarbetarnas yrkesutbildning*, Stockholm, Stockholms universitet.

Berglund, I., Höjlund, G., Kristmansson, P., and Paul, E. (2014) *Arbetsgivarnas användning av statsbidraget för gymnasial lärlingsutbildning och deras erfarenheter av att ta emot gymnasiala lärlingselever*, Stockholm, Institutionen för pedagogik och didaktik.

Billett, S. (2014) 'The standing of vocational education: Sources of its societal esteem and implications for its enactment', *Journal of Vocational Education and Training*, vol. 66, no. 1, pp. 1–21.

Braverman, H. (1974) *Labor and Monopoly Capital: The Degradation of Work in the Twentieth Century*, New York, Monthly Review Press.

Carlén, M., Beach, D., and Johansson, K. (2009) 'Nya former av samverkan – i vems intresse? En studie av utbildning, strategier och viljan att förändra i byggbranschen', *Rapport nr. 2:2009*, Borås, Högskolan i Borås.

Damvad. (2013) *Fra erhvervsuddannelse inden for bygge og anlæg til videregående uddannelse*, Copenhagen, Byggeriets Uddannelser og DAMVAD.

Dølvik, J. D., Fløtten, T., Hippe, J. M., and Jordfald, B. (2015) *The Nordic Model Towards 2030: A New Chapter? NordMod2030: Final Report*, Oslo, Fafo-report 2015:07.

Edwards, R. (1979) *Contested Terrain: The Transformation of The Workplace in the Twentieth Century*, New York, Basic Books.

Eldring, L. (2015) 'Tåler den norske modellen arbeidsinnvandring?' in Bungum, B., Forseth, U., and Kvande, E. (eds.) *Den norske modellen: Internasjonalisering som utfordring og vitalisering*, Bergen, Fagbokforlaget.

Eldring, L., Fitzgerald, I., and Arnholtz, J. (2012) 'Post-accession migration in construction and trade union responses in Denmark, Norway and UK', *European Journal of Industrial Relations*, vol. 18, no. 1, pp. 21–36.

Elstad, L. (2017) *Ulovlig innleie i byggebransjen i hovedstadsområdet våren 2017*, Oslo, Elektromontørenes Forening Oslo and Akershus, Oslo Bygningsarbeiderforening avdeling 603, Fellesforbundet Rørleggerenes Fagforening avdeling 605.

154   *Ole Johnny Olsen et al.*

Fjellström, M. (2017) *Becoming a Construction Worker: A Study of Vocational Learning in School and Work Life*, Umeå, Umeå Universitet.

Fox, A. (1974) *Beyond Contract: Work, Power and Trust Relations*, London, Faber and Faber.

Friberg, J. H., and Haakestad, H. (2015) 'Arbeidsmigrasjon, makt og styringsideologier: Norsk byggnæring i en brytningstid', *Søkelys på arbeidslivet*, vol. 32, no. 3, pp. 182–205.

Högberg, R. (2009) *Motstånd och konformitet: om manliga yrkeselevers liv och identitetsskapande i relation till kärnämnena*, Linköping, Linköpings universitet.

Honneth, A. (2014) *Freedom's Right: The Social foundations for Democratic Life*, New York, Columbia University Press.

Jørgensen, C. H. (2013) 'The role and meaning of vocations in the transition from education to work', *International Journal of Training Research*, vol. 11, no. 2, pp. 166–183.

König, O., and Detje, R. (2016) 'Geschäftsmodell Werkvertrag', *Sozialismus*, no. 1–2016, pp. 56–59.

Kronlund, J. (1982) *Mannen i mitten: Om lagbassystemet i byggnadsindustrin*, Stockholm, Arbetslivscentrum.

Løvseth, T., and Strand, O. (1992). *Bergen Byggmesterlaug 100 år. 1892–1992*, Bergen, Garnes Trykkeri.

Maurice, M., Sellier, F., and Silvestre, J-J. (1986) *The Social Foundations of Industrial Power: A Comparison of France and Germany*, Cambridge, MIT Press.

Mjelde, L. (2006) *The Magical Properties of Workshop Learning*, Bern, Peter Lang.

Moen, S. E., Olsen, O. J., Skålholt, A., and Tønder, A. H. (2014) *Bruk av lærlingklausuler ved offentlige anskaffelser*, Fafo-rapport 2014:36, Oslo, Fafo.

Nyen, T., Skålholt, A., and Tønder, A. H. (2013) 'Overgangen frå fagopplæring til arbeidsmarkedet og videre utdanning', in Høst, H. (ed.) *Kvalitet i fag- og yrkesopplæringen: Fokus på skoleopplæringen. Rapport 2 Forsking på kvalitet i fag- og yrkesopplæringen*, Oslo, NIFU.

Olofsson, J., and Persson Thunqvist, D. (2018) 'The formation of the Swedish VET-system (1845–1945)', in Michelsen, S. and Stenström, M-J. (eds.) *The Historical Evolution of Vocational Education in the Nordic Countries*, Abingdon, Routledge, pp. 124–145.

Olsen, O. J. (2013) 'Challenges to the broadening and specialization of Norwegian vocational education', in Kattein, M. and Vonken, M. (eds.) *Zeitbetrachtungen: Bildung – Arbeit – Biographie: Festschrift für Rudolf Husemann*, Bern, Peter Lang Publishing Group.

Olsen, O. J. (2018) 'Socio-cultural foundations of democratic capitalism. Experiences from the Norwegian case', in Trapscott, C., Halvorsen, T., and Cruz-Del Rosario, T. (eds.) *The Democratic Development State: North-South Perspectives*, Stuttgart, ibidem-Verlag, pp. 177-205.

Olsen, O. J., and Reegård, K. (2013) 'Læringsmiljø og gjennomføring i lærer- og elevperspektiv i tre yrkesfaglige opplæringsløp', in Høst, H. (ed.) *Kvalitet i fag- og yrkesopplæringen. Fokus på skoleopplæringen*, NIFU Rapport 21/2013, Oslo, NIFU, pp. 17–72.

Olsen, O. J., Reegård, K., Seland, I., and Skålholt, A. (2014) 'På sporet av kvaliteter i lærlingenes læringsmiljø og overgang mellom skole og læretid', in Høst, H. (ed.) *Kvalitet i fag- og yrkesopplæringen Fokus på opplæringen i bedrift Rapport 3 Forskning på kvalitet i fag- og yrkesopplæringen*, NIFU Rapport 12/2014, Oslo, NIFU, pp. 17–84.

Olsen, O.J., Reegård, K., Seland, I., and Skålholt, A. (2015) 'Læringsmiljø og gjennomføring', in Høst, H. (ed.) *Kvalitet i fag- og yrkesopplæring. Sluttrapport*. Rapport 14/2015, Oslo, NIFU.

Persson Thunqvist, D., and Hallqvist, A. (2014) *The Current State of the Challenges for VET in Sweden*, Nord-VET report, Linköping, Linköping University.

Piore, M., and Sabel, C. (1984) *The Second Industrial Divide: Possibilities for Prosperity*, New York, Basic Books.

Sejersted, F. (2011) *The Age of Social Democracy: Norway and Sweden in the Twentieth Century*, Princeton, Princeton University Press.

Skolverket. (2017) *Uppföljning av gymnasieskolan.* Rapport 2017, Stockholm, Skolverket.

Stinchcombe, A. L. (1986) 'Bureaucratic and craft administration of production: A comparative study', in Stinchcombe, A. L. (ed.) *Stratification and Organization: Selected Papers,* Cambridge and Oslo, Cambridge University Press and Norwegian University Press. (Originally in *Administrative Science Quarterly,* vol 4, 1959).

Streeck, W. (2014) *Buying Time: The Delayed Crisis of Democratic Capitalism,* London, Verso.

Thelen, K. (2004) *How Institutions Evolve. The Political Economy of Skills in Germany, Britain, the United States, and Japan,* Cambridge, Cambridge University Press.

Virolainen, M. (2015) 'IVET for construction workers (carpenter) in Finland. Case study', Unpublished paper, Roskilde, Roskilde University.

8 Learning from vocational education and training in the Nordic countries

Christian Helms Jørgensen

Introduction

There is an increasing diversity of demands on VET from policy-makers, the labour market, young people and other stakeholders. This is demonstrated in the examinations in the preceding chapters of the key challenges for the Nordic VET systems. The demands include the requirement to deliver specific vocational skills at a high level in order to support the competitiveness of business, to prepare students for higher education and life-long learning and to simultaneously include disadvantaged young people and have them complete upper secondary education. In addition, increasing pressure on VET arises from the profound changes in the social, political and economic order in which VET is embedded. These include the Europeanisation of the labour markets and of education policy, the shrinking of the youth labour markets, the increasingly diverse background of the students in VET, the shift towards a knowledge economy, and the shift from welfare states towards workfare states (Kananen, 2014). Because of this multiplicity of political demands and external changes, VET is encountering an increasing number of diverse and even contradictory challenges. The general focus of this chapter is to examine what can be learned from reforms in order to manage these challenges in the Nordic countries. A specific interest is to explore the interdependence of the challenges for VET and the reform initiatives to manage them.

The preceding chapters have shown that there seems to be a policy trade-off between the two main aims for VET, i.e. providing access to skilled employment and providing access to higher education. Previously, VET had the more unambiguous purpose of preparing young people for work. Following the transition from mass higher education to universal access (Marginson, 2017), it has become urgent for VET to offer eligibility for higher education to avoid VET appearing as a 'dead end' in the education system. The growing academic drift of young people in recent decades has been followed by a declining enrolment of young people in initial VET in Sweden and Denmark. Also in Norway since 2006, a declining share of the 16-year-olds choose VET, though the number of has apprenticeships remained stable. This is often explained by the low permeability from VET to higher education, especially from the apprenticeship system in Denmark, and since the reform in 2011, also from the Swedish VET system. However, in the Danish and Norwegian VET systems, where work-based training placements make up a large part of the programmes, it is difficult to prepare for higher education and at the same time provide direct access to skilled employment. In the mainly full-time school-based VET systems of Finland and Sweden, which have given priority to preparing for higher education, it is difficult to give direct access to the skilled labour market. An indicator of this is the post-secondary system of apprenticeships that is controlled by the labour market partners in Sweden, separate from the state-led gymnasium, as described in Chapter 6.

These are key examples of contradictory aims for VET that represent dilemmas for policy-makers and the professionals in VET. Chapters 2, 3 and 4 in this volume demonstrate how the four Nordic VET systems have managed these challenges in different ways. This chapter explores how these key challenges for VET are interrelated and the consequences this entanglement has for policy. First, this is analysed in relation to the egalitarian aims of the Nordic model of education based on examination of major reforms of VET in Sweden and Denmark, the two Nordic VET systems that come closest to a state-led model and an apprenticeship model. Next, the chapter explores the wider configuration of trade-offs for policy, which constitutes the general policy architecture for VET in the Nordic countries. In contrast to the purer Swedish and Danish systems of statist and collective skills formation, the 'mixed' VET system of Norway and Finland are examined in relation to managing the common challenges. This leads to considerations of what can be learned from the Nordic VET systems. Lastly, the chapter sketches some likely future scenarios for the Nordic VET systems.

VET in the Nordic model of education

The first volume of the two books in this series (Michelsen and Steenström, 2018) examines the historical background to the current configuration of challenges for VET. In the first decades after 1945, a primary aim of VET was to provide young people with the skills required for skilled employment. This included socialisation, disciplining and enculturation of young people into the occupational community and culture through work-based training. VET was mainly an institution in the labour market for the coordination and certification of the employers' training of the upcoming generations of skilled workers. In addition to this, the aims of social integration, inclusion and socialisation were given priority by the state during periods of economic downturn. The municipalities initiated school-based systems of VET to accommodate vulnerable groups of unemployed youths. However, these programmes often had weak connections to the labour market and low involvement of the employers.

The 'social question' and the inclusion of young people in society has been a central aim for Nordic VET policy from the early years, from the foundation of the modern VET systems until today (Telhaug et al., 2006; Stolz and

158   *Christian Helms Jørgensen*

Gonon, 2012). When youth unemployment has been high, the issue of social inclusion has been given priority. However, this aim has had to compete with other aims, not least the aim of meeting skills requirements in the labour market. Moreover, the meaning of social inclusion has changed. In the 1950s, the political interest was on including the large youth cohorts in the labour market and on meeting the skills requirements of the expanding production system (Michelsen and Stenström, 2018). In the 1960s, VET was criticised for including young people in society only as manpower, not as active democratic citizens. The specialised VET programmes were seen as serving narrow business interests, and tying the students to a specific occupation (Lundahl, 1997).

The reforms of the 1970s widened the aims of VET and increased the extent of the general subjects in the curricula of the Nordic VET systems. VET was required to provide broader forms of inclusion in the political and cultural life of society, similar to the upper secondary programmes preparing for higher education. The early division of young people into separate general and vocational tracks was criticised for maintaining and reproducing class-based social inequalities (Arnesen and Lundahl, 2006). The policy emphasis shifted from skills provision and social inclusion to citizenship and social equality in education. Students from VET should no longer be excluded from gaining access to higher education. All the Nordic countries took steps to include the diverse and specialised VET programmes in a unified upper secondary school, although the outcomes of these initiatives differed. The aims were realised most consistently by the Social Democratic governments in Sweden, while upper secondary education in Denmark preserved a system of early selection and strong tracking.

The timing of the shifts in policy differed between the Nordic countries (Blossing et al., 2014; Antikainen, 2010). However, in all countries the purpose of VET in the political discourse shifted once again after the economic crises in the decades after the 1970s. As the youth unemployment rates increased strongly, VET was seen as a solution to the threat of marginalisation of a large group of young people who had difficulties gaining access to the labour market. As a consequence, the demand for social equality in access to higher education gave way to the demand for social inclusion of early school leavers and disadvantaged youth. Reforms focused on having all VET students complete their education and on supporting their transition to employment. In Sweden and Finland, this was done by extending periods of internships or apprenticeship programmes.

The current political definition of the key challenge for VET has shifted once again. Today, the attention of policy-makers is on the growing shortage of skilled labour and the declining enrolment of VET in Norway, Sweden and Denmark. The decreasing number of young people choosing VET today is not sufficient to meet future demands, when large cohorts of skilled workers leave the labour market in the years ahead. Consequently, a key concern among the stakeholders in VET is how to increase the attractiveness of VET in order to encourage more students to enrol. This has been pursued in Denmark, for example, by a reform in 2014 that excludes low performing students from access to VET and extends the opportunities for progression to higher education.

All the Nordic countries have combined the aims of including disadvantaged youth in VET and of reducing social inequalities in education. However, the brief outline above indicates shifts over time between giving priority to the integration of young people in the labour market, and giving priority to reducing social inequalities by widening the access to higher education. In addition to the shifts in political priorities over time, reforms in the four countries have given different priority to these aims. The following section examines two critical experiences of policies for achieving social equality and inclusion in VET in Sweden and Denmark, which represent the most diverse VET systems. The examination of how these two challenges are connected, demonstrates the limits to the egalitarian education policy resulting from the unintended consequences of these policies. The cases also demonstrate the interrelations and trade-offs between different policy goals related to the Nordic model of education. In both cases, the reform experiences have subsequently resulted in significant shifts in policy.

Equivalence of general and vocational education in Sweden

Swedish VET is an interesting case, as it has been the most consistent and successful in pursuing the Nordic idea of the comprehensive upper secondary school, with equivalence of the general and vocational programmes. Since the 1960s, reforms of VET in Sweden, like in the other Nordic countries, was driven by two closely connected objectives. One aim was to provide highly skilled manpower to meet the requirements in the labour market. The other was to promote social justice and equality of opportunities for all, with a redistributive aim. This can be seen as a core feature of the Social Democratic strategy to use the state to develop a competitive form of 'egalitarian capitalism' (Thelen, 2014; Brandal et al., 2013). The rapid growth of general and higher education in the 1960s was followed by demands for social equality and for a widening of access to higher education. In this period, the question of social inclusion was not urgent, as industrial growth and the expansion of public sector employment offered many opportunities for women and young people and other newcomers to the labour market.

In the educational reforms in the 1970s that integrated the vocational and the general programmes of upper secondary education, the two political objectives of social inclusion and social equality, appeared fully compatible. Both aims were pursued by the reforms that made the VET programmes broader and increased the share of general subjects. This strengthened the connection of VET to higher education, and it simultaneously provided the broad skills and the flexibility that were considered essential for the continuous adaptation of labour to the shifting requirements in the labour market. Especially in Sweden, little significance was attributed to specific vocational qualifications, as they were considered to be short-lived and of little relevance to the export oriented

160   *Christian Helms Jørgensen*

businesses. Apprenticeships were abandoned in the 1960s, as they were associated with social selection, exploitation and low quality of training. The reformers of education, including the labour unions, had little trust in the value of work-based learning. In addition, the expansion of the general subjects in VET was meant to increase the attractiveness of VET and support the development of the students as democratic citizens (Lundahl, 1997).

The reform of VET in Sweden in 1970 established a unified upper secondary school (gymnasium) that included the formerly separate vocational institutions and programmes. The reform represented a major step towards extending the comprehensive school to the upper secondary level. The vocational programmes became full-time school-based and were brought closer to the general programmes. New programmes were established in sectors dominated by women (health, social work, administration). Following the reform, the share of young people enrolling in upper secondary education increased significantly (Murray and Sundin, 2008). The reform succeeded in raising the esteem of VET, measured by the enrolment levels in the vocational programmes. However, significant differences persisted between the academic and the vocational programmes. The vocational programmes were primarily designed to prepare youths for the labour market and did not provide access to higher education. The vocational programmes were shorter and had lower esteem than the general programmes that prepared students for further study. Moreover, the two types of programmes had different school cultures and recruited from different social groups (Nylund, 2013).

With a reform in 1991, the Swedish government took a major step further to realise the comprehensive upper secondary school. The reform prolonged the vocational programmes from two to three years and expanded the theoretical and academic content in the programmes. As a consequence, all students in upper secondary education were expected to obtain eligibility for higher education. Based on earlier experiences of integrating lower secondary education, this was meant to reduce the social selection in higher education enrolment. However, after implementing the reform, the non-completion rate in the vocational programmes rose dramatically from 10% to over 30% (Table 8.1) (Pettersson, 2006; Hall, 2012). The explanation for this dramatic increase is debated, as a number of policy measures were implemented simultaneously (Nylund, 2013; Svensson, 2007). One of the main reasons was that a number of core academic subjects and the volume of these subjects were extended in all the vocational programmes. In particular, some of the disadvantaged and academically weak students failed in these subjects (Murray and Sundin, 2008).

Table 8.1 Increase in non-completion rate in the VET programmes after the reform in 1991

Year	1990	1991	1992	1993	1994	1995	1996	1997	1998
Non-completion rate, pct.	8.8	11	13.7	19.9	27.1	30.6	33.2	31.2	34.4

Source of data: Pettersson, 2006, p. 189.

Moreover, as the vocational programmes were broad and only preparatory for employment, it became more difficult to gain access to employment for students who entered the labour market after upper secondary school. This was aggravated by the serious economic crisis that hit Sweden in the early 1990s. At the same time, a principle of individual choice was introduced for upper secondary schools and the schools were decentralised, so that responsibility was devolved to the municipalities. This decentralisation and liberalisation tended to increase the social differences between the schools and inside the schools (Lundahl, et al., 2013; Englund and Quennerstedt, 2008).

The consequences of the reform in 1991 has been debated. The reform succeeded in raising the academic level of education of the students who started the vocational programmes. However, contrary to what was expected, the share of students progressing to higher education did not increase after the reform. Nor did it raise the measured levels of democratic citizenship of the students (Persson and Oscarsson, 2009). Svensson (2001) emphasises the effects of a change of the grading system that took place concurrently with the 1991 reform. This change helps to explain the strong increase in the share of students who did not complete their programme after the reform of VET (Nylund, 2013). In a study of the consequence of the 1991 reform, Hall (2012) concludes that especially male VET students with low grades from compulsory school had an increased risk of unemployment after dropping out. Murray and Sundin (2008) finds that this is especially the case for those who dropped out in the first two years of the extended programmes. Olofsson (2005) emphasises the negative consequences of the academisation of upper secondary education for youths from non-academic families. Due to the increasing emphasis on preparation for higher education, the direct link between the VET programmes and the labour market in Sweden was weakened. Half of the students in the vocational programmes did not gain eligibility for higher education, and for them the gap from upper secondary school to the labour market had widened. The 1991 reform demonstrates that the aim of social equality regarding enrolment in higher education had endangered another vital ideal of the Nordic model, social inclusion and full employment, especially for young people. The reform had negative consequences for the most disadvantaged students with low socio-economic background.

The reform in 1991 demonstrated that realisation of the Swedish comprehensive upper secondary school failed to fulfil the meritocratic promise of a society, where access to elite positions should depend on talent and effort in education, not on the students' social background. The upper secondary school is still quite segregated with regard to the social and gender composition of its students in the two types of programmes, general and vocational (Svensson, 2001). Various explanations for the persistent inequalities have been proposed. The Social Democratic governments ruled through a state that was dominated by the traditional academic elite, which successfully resisted the implementation of the egalitarian policies (Rothstein, 1996). More important is it that the social and cultural resources that children bring into

162 *Christian Helms Jørgensen*

the education system from their social backgrounds differ significantly, which continues to influence their educational attainment and careers. Although the Swedish school system is a non-selective system and based on the principle of mixed ability classes, informal tracking with a substantial social gradient is nevertheless common (Ramberg, 2014; Rudolphi and Erikson, 2016). The curriculum of the vocational programmes does not offer the same opportunities for critical thinking and citizenship as the general programmes (Nylund, 2013). The differentiated teaching practices and peer group effects in these programmes tend to maintain or increase the inequalities that students bring into the school form their social background (Gamoran, 2010). The unintended outcomes of the reform of VET in 1991 was one of the reasons for a shift in policy in Sweden with the reform in 2011, which gave priority to social inclusion and employability.

The Danish reforms to improve social inclusion in VET

The Nordic Social Democratic Parties have opposed the division of students and favoured a comprehensive upper secondary school because of the negative effects for social equality of early selection in education. In Denmark however, even the left-wing political parties in Denmark have supported an apprenticeship system organised separately from the gymnasiums. A key argument is that the apprenticeship model is very efficient at facilitating young peoples' transition from school to work, and at including a large group of young people who failed in elementary school (see Chapter 2). The vocational schools are inclusive because they offer an alternative learning environment to the 'bookish' upper secondary schools. They recognise young people, not as students, but as craftspersons-to-be, and through apprenticeship they become participants in a community of adult skilled workers (Jørgensen, 2013b). The vocational students who gain access to a training contract, become well-integrated into the labour market during the programme, because two thirds of the time is organised as work-based training. After the completion of an apprenticeship, the students have high employment rates, as the majority continue as ordinary employees in the training company, similar to the situation in Norway.

The Danish apprenticeship model of VET is in stark contrast to the ideals of the Nordic model of education and the comprehensive school. The early tracking associated with this model, diverts young people from higher education, as apprenticeships do not provide eligibility for higher education. However, apprenticeships are socially inclusive, especially for young people who do not thrive in the academically oriented school system. They are offered not just an upper secondary education, but also access to skilled employment, if they complete an apprenticeship. Observing that globalisation has a particularly adverse effect on employees with low skill levels, the Nordic governments have been increasingly concerned about the share of young people not in education, employment or training (the NEET group) since the 1980s. As a response, they have set targets that all young people must complete an upper secondary education.

In 1993, the Danish government set the target that by 2015, 95% of a youth cohort should complete an upper secondary education. The political initiatives to reach that goal have mainly focused on the VET system, which historically has been very effective at making non-privileged youth and early school leavers complete an upper secondary education and get access to occupational employment and career opportunities (see Chapter 2). The political initiatives to include young people from the NEET-group in VET have shifted from the early 1990s until today. In the 1990s, the emphasis was on measures to make the VET system more inclusive and motivating for disadvantaged youth. From the mid-1990s, the active labour market policy (ALMP) has focused specifically on young people. Since then, a range of policy initiatives have been implemented to make more young people start and complete a VET programme. VET policy has increasingly become integrated with employment policy and social policy. In addition, these policies have shifted from offering supportive and 'soft' measures for disadvantaged students, to 'tough' requirements and coercive measures to direct young people into education and training (Juul and Jørgensen, 2011).

This can be seen as a consequence of the shift from the universal, Nordic type of welfare state towards a social investment state, emphasising workfare over passive welfare provisions (Kananen, 2014). The emphasis is no longer on social security for youths that are unable to support themselves, but on measures to make them employable (Christiansen and Petersen, 2001). In Denmark, this policy includes the reduction of the level of financial support, the tightening of the requirements for being entitled to benefits and the introduction of tougher sanctions (Kananen, 2014). Since 2009, a series of 'youth packages' have imposed stricter requirements on young people to be in education, training or employment. The Youth Counselling Centres (UU) have the obligation to track 'dropouts', and they can punish parents financially if their children, under the age of 18, do not follow their education plan. The latest reform of social security in 2013 extended the requirements to complete an upper secondary education to all unemployed youth below the age of 30 years. Compared to Finland and Sweden, youth activation in Denmark relies much more on training (Tosun et al., 2017). The activation policy (ALMP) has contributed to making almost all young people enrol in upper secondary education, especially in VET. However, at the same time, the dropout rate in vocational education has increased. Due to the ALMP, a growing number of disadvantaged students have enrolled in vocational schools. Many of the students activated into VET are early school leavers, have low grades from basic school, parents with low levels of education, broken families, psycho-social problems and drug problems, etc. (Jørgensen, 2016). This recruitment pattern has contributed to increasing the dropout rate in VET since the mid-1990s (Table 8.2).

Consequently, since 2007, policy-makers have required that the vocational schools make yearly 'retention plans' and set goals for increasing the retention

164   *Christian Helms Jørgensen*

Table 8.2 Drop-out rate from VET basic course in Denmark

Year	1995	1996	1997	1998	1999	2000	2001	2002	2003	2004	2005	2006	2007	2008
Drop-out rate, percent	4.0	5.3	6.0	9.6	16.6	20.5	19.8	23.0	24.3	26.1	27.0	27.1	27.9	25.9

Source of data: Munk, 2011.

rates. To support these goals, the schools offer individual guidance, psychological counselling, mentoring, coaching, contact-teachers, free school meals etc. The effect of these measures has been very limited, and the total non-completion rate in VET has remained at a high level of around 50% (total of basic and main courses) (Jørgensen, 2016).

This policy to improve social inclusion in VET resulted in a crisis for the VET system. The high drop-out rates from VET and the biased social composition of the students seriously reduced the esteem of the VET system. For that reason, the enrolment in VET from the basic school decreased significantly, which caused political concern, because of a predicted future shortage of skilled workers. The employer organisations strongly opposed the government's use of VET for social policy purposes. They have repeatedly criticised the weak motivation and the low standards of the students in VET. The employers' supply of training placements has decreased, and the share of students in compensatory school-based training centres has continued to grow (Chapter 5). These unintended consequences of the policy for social inclusion in VET resulted in a reform in 2014, which ended 20 years of policies for social inclusion in VET.

The reform shifted the political priority from social inclusion to the provision of highly skilled labour to the labour market. The reform introduced admission requirements based on the students' grades in basic school. The aim was to redirect students from the gymnasiums and from higher education to VET. While the targets for enrolment in higher education had been raised a few years earlier, now the number of study places in higher education was reduced, and graduate unemployment was seen as a major problem. In order to raise the esteem of VET, the VET reform introduced new talent streams and high-level courses with the aim of attracting more high-performing students. In addition, all programmes were required to offer a new hybrid programme (eux) that offers eligibility for higher education, as well as a journeyman's certificate in order to neutralise the image of VET as a 'dead end' in the education system (see Chapter 5).

The apprenticeship model of VET in Denmark has been very efficient at including disadvantaged youth and at bringing them into employment. However, when the governments made social inclusion a major purpose for VET from the mid-1990s, the VET system became less attractive for young people and for training companies. The resulting high drop-out rates and the decreasing enrolment rates of students was seen as imminent threats for the future of the Danish VET system, which brought about the reform in 2014.

A trade-off between social inequality and social inclusion

The two Nordic cases examined above demonstrate the tension in VET policies between the aims of social inclusion and equality in education. Both aims are key elements of the egalitarian Nordic model of education and were seen as highly compatible in the comprehensive upper secondary school. It was a key assumption in the reforms of VET in the 1970–90s and onwards in all four countries, that the value of specific vocational skills was declining, and that general and generic qualifications were essential for flexibility and adaptability to the changing requirements of the labour market. Consequently, merging VET into a unified upper secondary school would simultaneously improve its relevance for the labour market and improve the links to higher education. The learning of specific vocational skills was seen as the responsibility of the training companies under the supervision of the labour market organisations after completion of upper secondary education (Olofsson, 2005).

The Nordic model of education, as it was realised in Sweden, is governed by the state and has weak links to the labour market. It offers all students the opportunity to gain eligibility to higher education, if they manage to complete it. However, less than half of those who completed a vocational programme in 2016 gained eligibility for higher education (Skolverket, 2017, p. 31). Many of them only achieve broad and preparatory qualifications for employment. Therefore, the Swedish VET system has become associated with difficult transitions to employment and high rates of youth unemployment (Olofsson, 2005). Following the unification of the upper secondary comprehensive school in Sweden, VET lost some of its qualities as a distinct alternative to the general programmes. VET became more academic and the school-based programmes mainly offered a student identity, rather than a vocational identity. The reform in 1991 gave priority to preparing all students for higher education, but made VET less attractive and less supportive for students who were not aiming for higher education, but for skilled employment. This trade-off for VET, between providing access to higher education and to skilled employment, was demonstrated again by the reform in 2011. This reform shifted the priority to focus on providing employability and it reduced the priority of academic qualifications. Because of the reform, VET came to appear as an option for the less ambitious students and both the esteem of VET and the enrolment of young people dropped significantly.

The Danish situation during the same period also demonstrates the trade-off between social inclusion in VET and high esteem of VET. In Denmark, the apprenticeship model was preserved and modernised. While this model is highly socially selective and diverts students away from higher education, it also offers direct access to skilled employment for large groups of young people who do not thrive in a bookish school environment. Because of this quality,

166   *Christian Helms Jørgensen*

Danish governments made extensive use of VET for social policy purposes to include early school leavers and youth from the NEET group. This policy had serious negative effects for the esteem of VET. Employers' commitment to train the VET students diminished, as did the enrolment of ambitious and high performing students. As a result, the vocational schools appeared increasingly as institutions for social policy, rather than as an attractive route to highly skilled employment.

The Danish and Norwegian VET systems demonstrate that a significant group of young people in upper secondary schools, who do not thrive in a 'bookish' learning environment, can be engaged in vocational and work-related activities, and can be recognised as a coming-to-be craftsperson in a workplace community (Jørgensen, 2013b). Organising work-based learning in a separate vocational track with its own quality has a positive effect on these students' transition to employment. However, international research shows that tracking and streaming of students tends to reduce intergenerational mobility and social equality (Pfeffer, 2008; Brunello and Checchi, 2007). A variety of explanations for this negative effect has been demonstrated, among them the differentiation-polarisation effect (Hillyard, 2010). This effect entails that the division of students into different classes, programmes and schools tends to increase the initial differences in students' performance. The increasing differences between the students are the result of the differences in teachers' expectations, teaching styles and curriculum in different tracks (Gamoran, 2010). Another reason for the polarising effect of tracking is the negative peer effects and the development of polarised attitudes among the students (van Houtte et al., 2012; Niemi and Rosvall, 2013). Students in the high-ranking streams become motivated, because they gain recognition and status, whereas students in the low-ranking streams can develop an anti-school culture, when they do not feel recognised and are even stigmatised by the schools (Oakes, 1985; Johansen and Aarseth, 2012). Consequently, a separate vocational track can improve the inclusion of non-academic students, but reduce their opportunities for educational progression, because VET diverts them from higher education. Indications of these trade-offs have been demonstrated in several comparative studies of VET (Holm et al., 2013; Bol and Werfhorst, 2013).

In the formulation of Shavit and Müller (2000), VET offers a 'safety net' for disadvantaged youth by reducing their risk of unemployment, but simultaneously diverts them from enrolling in higher education. This research demonstrates, in line with the two Nordic cases examined above, that the egalitarian aim of the Nordic model of education has two dimensions (Table 8.3). One stresses social equality in admission to the highest level of education, in order to reduce the selective recruitment to the professional elite. In addition, this dimension emphasises citizenship and the democratic ideals of education, which have priority in the general programmes (Nylund, 2013). The other dimension gives priority to the inclusion of all young people in education and emphasises the capacity of work-based VET to help disadvantaged youth complete upper secondary education and support their successful transition to employment. In

Learning from vocational education 167

Table 8.3 Trade-offs in the policy architecture for VET

Social inclusion of disadvantaged youth	Social equality in access to higher education
Prepare for skilled employment	Prepare for higher education
Mainly based on work-based learning	Mainly based on school-based learning
Employability: integration in work-life and an occupational community	Citizenship: integration in democratic society
Responsive to labour market requirements	Responsive to students demands
Vocational values: priority of vocational skills	Meritocratic values: priority of general qualifications
Standardised programmes, transparent pathways	Flexible programmes, individualised pathways
High stratification – tracking and streaming	Low stratification – mixed ability classes
Occupational standardisation	Individualisation and modularisation
Centralised regulation of VET	Decentralised regulation of VET
Early choice of specific occupation	Postponed choice of specific occupation

other words, the egalitarian aims can be pursued in different ways by giving priority to either the educational equality at the top, by widening the access to higher education, or to social equality at the bottom, by including disadvantaged young people who are excluded due to high academic requirements.

Upper secondary VET plays a key role in attaining these egalitarian aims, because VET can include disadvantaged youth and offer an alternative progression route to higher education for youths from families with low levels of education. However, these two aims are difficult to combine. This is indicated firstly by the reforms to achieve the aims of equality in Sweden and inclusion in Denmark, and secondly by the counter-reforms that gave priority to one aim at the cost of the other. The Swedish reform of 2011 shifted the priority to employability at the cost of eligibility for higher education, and the Danish reform in 2014 gave priority to high esteem at the cost of social inclusion. These trade-offs are central elements in the common policy architecture for VET that we have examined in this book (Table 8.3). Chapters 2 and 3 of this book contain a more in-depth examination of why these aims are conflicting and difficult to combine. The next section further examines how these tensions are connected to some additional trade-offs for VET policy.

Configurations of trade-offs for VET

Our studies and comparisons of the Nordic VET systems have revealed a variety of common policy measures that have contradictory effects for social inclusion and equality. Measures that attract and include some students tend to exclude others. As indicated in Table 8.3, key measures constitute trade-offs for policy, because the pursuit of one aim conflicts with other political aims for VET. This does not imply that they are entirely incompatible, but that there are inherent tensions between the pursuit of these aims. The trade-offs in the table are interrelated, as indicated by their position in the two columns. The

168   *Christian Helms Jørgensen*

way one trade-off is managed has implications for other trade-offs. The various conceptual models of VET in the literature (Greinert, 1999; Gonon, 2016) represent characteristic configurations of these trade-offs. In our studies of the Nordic VET systems, the qualities in the left-hand column are often combined, as are the qualities in the right-hand column. However, we have also found that qualities from the left and right side can be combined.

In addition to the trade-offs between social inclusion and social equality examined above, a number of additional trade-offs from our study are examined in the following. They concern the trade-offs between standardisation and individualisation, between centralisation and decentralisation, and between early and postponed organisation of educational choice and specialisation.

The trade-off between standardisation and individualisation of the VET programmes has become important, as policy measures in all four countries have extended the students' opportunities for choice and the tailoring of the VET programmes to individual requirements. This policy is based on the belief that the high dropout rates from VET are a result of the strong standardisation and the lack of flexibility in the organisation of the VET programmes. Consequently, reforms of VET have aimed to increase the flexibility and the scope for individual choice in the programmes. This view resonates with the neo-liberal ideas that encourage marketisation in order to increase the quality and efficiency of education (Imsen et al., 2016; Wiborg, 2013). In this view, education should be more responsive to the demands of the labour market, on the one hand, and on the other hand to the students, who in the neo-liberal discourse are positioned as 'customers'. This policy was promoted in opposition to earlier Social Democratic policies to standardise and equalise the educational provisions in order to reduce social and regional inequalities (Blossing et al., 2014; Arnesen and Lundahl, 2006). The adaptation of education to individual interests and requirements was believed to both improve the provision of high-level programmes for ambitious students and to improve the retention of disadvantaged students, who do not fit into the standard programmes. Experience, however, indicates that individualisation, like other forms of differentiation of education, has multiple and contradictory consequences. Negative effects of individualisation are seen in relation to the weakening of the vocational identity and occupational profile of VET and the weakening of the social community in VET. As described in Chapter 2, the role of the vocation is crucial for the students' engagement and development of a vocational identity (Jørgensen, 2013b)

This is illustrated by the major reform of VET in Denmark in 2000, which introduced 'the individual programme' that was intended to tailor the teaching to the requirements of the individual student. All VET programmes start with the validation of the students' prior learning, which forms the basis for the design of a personalised programme for the first year of school-based courses. This was expected to increase the retention of the students, but the drop-out rates in VET continued to increase after the reform in 2000. The individual tailoring of the courses increased the retention of the most ambitious students, but simultaneously weakened the social community around the individual student in the vocational schools. The vulnerable and unmotivated students found it difficult to manage the fragmented course structure. Because of this, a new reform in 2007 rolled back part of the individualisation and introduced more structured courses (Jørgensen, 2016).

The decentralisation of educational governance is another political initiative to increase the flexibility of VET in connection with the neo-liberal shift in policy. Decentralisation forms part of the political objective of creating an educational market, where schools compete to deliver services to students and companies. This is intended to increase the efficiency and quality of the schools, and to adjust the VET programmes to the requirements of the students and the local labour markets. Increasing the opportunities for local and industry-specific adaptation of the VET programmes can help VET meet the diversified demands and conditions among students and communities. This flexibility has been an advantage for the Norwegian VET programmes that can be organised, not only according to the 2+2 model, but also according to a 1+3 model to make VET more attractive for youths who have grown tired of school. However, increasing the diversity of the VET programmes weakens the national standardisation, which is crucial for the value of the certification of VET. Another unintended consequence of decentralisation is that the differences between the quality of the schools have increased. This is most evident in Sweden, where the decentralisation of education has been most radical (Lundahl et al., 2013). The students' free choice of schools and the marketisation have resulted in an increasing local and regional segmentation of schools, because resourceful families benefit most from free school choice (Lundahl and Olofsson, 2014).

Another policy issue with ambiguous consequences for inclusion and equality is the organisation of educational choice and specialisation in VET, as examined in Chapter 2. A central quality of the Nordic model of education is to postpone the division and tracking of students in order to reduce the intergenerational transmission of inequality in education (Causa and Johansson, 2010). However, many of the most disadvantaged students have a strong orientation towards work and become demotivated in broad, school-based programmes. That was the reason why the Danish reform in 2006 emphasised that the students should meet the specific occupation right from the start. However, most students are not able to make a qualified choice between over 100 different VET programmes when they start in a vocational school. This is one explanation for the policy oscillation in Denmark between broad and specific entrances to VET (Jørgensen, 2016). The Danish and the Norwegian VET system represent different solutions to this trade-off between offering the students hands-on experiences with work in a specific occupation, and simultaneously introducing the students to a broader variety of occupations in the field. The 'in-depth study project' in Norway (Chapter 2) is an example of a solution that postpones tracking but offers early access to work-based training. This is leading us to the last trade-off between school-based and work-based learning in VET, which is connected to the tensions between general qualifications and specific vocational skills in VET.

170 *Christian Helms Jørgensen*

In the Social Democratic ideal of the comprehensive upper secondary school, especially in Sweden, no significance was attached to specific vocational skills and in-company training. Work-based learning and apprenticeships were associated with businesses' interests in training for specific work functions. Giving priority to general subjects, personal growth and social competencies had the triple aim of developing citizenship, preparing for lifelong learning and long-term employability and preparing for progression to higher levels of education. This priority in policy resonates with a meritocratic ideal of social equality through education, which has failed to deliver the promised equality (Littler, 2018; Rothstein, 1996). During the last decade, reforms of VET have turned around and given priority to work-based learning and vocational skills, even in Sweden, for three reasons. First, internships and apprenticeships are seen as decisive for students' access to employment. Secondly, the workplace is recognised as an important site for learning social skills, new technologies and achieving a vocational identity. Thirdly, it is acknowledged that learning in a workplace is an attractive alternative for many young people who are tired of traditional school-based learning. However, as pointed to earlier, work-based learning is associate with a variety of risks and weaknesses. These include the risk of subordinating students' learning to the demands of production and the exploitation of the students' cheap labour; the volatile supply of training placements and the employers' selective hiring practices; the achievement of short-term employability at the cost of long-term employment opportunities (Hampf and Woessmann, 2017); and the improvement of employability at the cost of eligibility for higher education.

The architecture for policy-making in VET

Above we have identified a variety of common challenges and trade-offs for VET through studies of the key issues in political discourses and reforms across the four countries. The trade-offs can be explained by the ambiguous position of VET in a field of tensions between the state, the overall education system, the labour market and the students in VET. This position involves pressures from competing and contradictory interests of diverse stakeholders and interest coalitions. Therefore, the organisation and the governing of the Nordic VET systems is facing an increasing variety of challenges for policy. This condition for policy-making has become critical because of the multiplication of political aims for VET, and the competing objectives for VET in education policy, social policy and employment policy. Reforms to manage one challenge and achieve one objective influence the opportunities for achieving other objectives. They represent trade-offs for policy. The total configuration of trade-offs in Table 8.3 constitutes the architecture for policy-making in the field of VET. We have found that these basic trade-offs are common for the four Nordic VET systems, like the trade-off between educational equality and social inclusion in VET. These basic trade-offs provide a common framework for the comparison of the VET systems in this book. The common trade-offs also provide an opportunity for policy learning. However, while the Nordic countries share the basic trade-offs, the policies to manage them and the priorities of policy-makers have differed considerably. Due to historical differences in policies and outcomes, we also find significant differences in the institutional structures of the national VET systems. Because of these differences, attempts to borrow or transfer specific policy measures or institutions across VET systems are not likely to succeed, because measures have different effects in different institutional contexts. The opportunities for policy learning are most obvious from the case-based comparisons that provide a holistic understanding of the interrelatedness of the different qualities of VET systems. This approach can improve policy-makers' recognition of the internal tensions between different policy aims and between the strengths and weaknesses of these systems. Because of these internal tensions, political interventions tend to have multiple and contradictory effects, which tend not to be recognised by policy-makers.

Our studies of the four countries indicate that policy-makers are generally occupied with managing the acute and current challenges for VET, as these are defined by the main stakeholders in accordance with their interests and political convictions. By focusing strongly on one challenge, policy-makers tend to ignore the implications of their initiatives for other challenges that appear as less acute. By doing so, they unintentionally jeopardise the capacity of VET to manage other objectives. The interventions contribute to solving one political problem, while simultaneously creating or aggravating other problems for VET. The unintended consequences of political initiatives can even overshadow the intended aims, so that the overall consequences of the initiative turn out to be negative.

In the examination of recent reforms of the Nordic VET systems in this book, we have drawn attention to some of the unintended effects of political measures that emerge due to the interconnectedness of the challenges for VET and the trade-offs for policy. Unawareness of the trade-offs can result in policy oscillations, when the unintended negative consequences of policy reforms result in new reforms to manage the harm inflicted by earlier reforms. This was the case, for example, after the reform in 2000 in Denmark that radically individualised the programmes and contributed to increasing the drop-out rates, contrary to the aim of the reform (Jørgensen, 2016). Moreover, because of the entanglement of the trade-offs for VET policy, there is a risk that reforms can contribute to a chain of negative, self-reinforcing dynamics. This was demonstrated in Chapter 4, where we found these dynamics in the effects of policies for social inclusion that make VET appear as a measure for social policy. While VET plays an important role as an alternative to academic education, it is likely to reduce the esteem and attractiveness of VET among young people, when VET is extensively used for activation of young people from the NEET group. This tends to reduce the enrolment of ambitious students and thus increases the concentration of academically weak and disadvantaged students in VET. A high proportion of disadvantaged students in VET results in high drop-out rates, which weakens the social community in

172 *Christian Helms Jørgensen*

vocational schools and further reduces the esteem of VET. This process also tends to reduce the employers' engagement and willingness to supply training placements, which might further increase the drop-out rate. Such a chain of self-reinforcing effects and multi-causal events has been identified in the Danish VET system (Jørgensen, 2016).

What can policy-makers learn from this? The first point is that VET policies often include trade-offs that constitute dilemmas for policy due to multiple and competing policy aims. Secondly, unobserved dilemmas tend to have unintended consequences, and these unintended consequences might undermine the original intentions of the political initiative, or even aggravate the problem addressed in the first place. Thirdly, the complexities and trade-offs require reflexive policy-making. The policy-making process should include considerations and deliberations on the various potential unintended consequences of policies, due to the way policies are interpreted and transformed by those who are subjected to these policies. The dominant form of policy-making, which addresses acute challenges one by one, involves the risk of being counter-productive because of this complexity. Moreover, reforms that ignore the trade-offs and potential contradictory effects, tend to have unintended consequences. Therefore, instead of pursuing long-term aims, policy-makers become preoccupied with managing the unintended consequences of earlier initiatives, as a recent study of reforms intended to reduce students' dropout from the Danish VET system has demonstrated (Jørgensen, 2016).

This kind of policy-making is often inspired by international rankings and ratings of the performance of education systems. This was also the case when the Swedish government strengthened work-based learning in VET and implemented a new apprenticeship programme in the state-led upper secondary school in 2011, inspired by the low youth unemployment associated with the apprenticeship model. Because of the disappointing results of this reform, a new government partly rolled back the reform and strengthened the links between VET and higher education. This example demonstrates the problems of direct policy transfer and borrowing. When policies from abroad are brought into a national configuration of trade-offs for VET, then multiple and unintended consequences are likely to occur (Phillips, 2015). Consequently, the opportunities for policy learning from this comparison of the Nordic VET systems are not found through the identification of 'best practices' or the transfer of specific measures or institutions. It is in learning to identify the contradictory relations between basic objectives for VET, related to the current configuration of trade-offs for policy. As these basic trade-offs are similar across the four Nordic countries, comparisons can contribute to the awareness of the potential unintended consequences of political interventions in VET. In a simple form, this can encourage considerations of not only the benefits, but also the potential costs of reforms, although these can be difficult to assess. Awareness of the trade-offs can also be an invitation to consider innovative solutions that try to circumvent or go beyond the trade-offs. One way to do this is to look for hybridisations that combine positive features from different VET systems, in order to get at least some of the best from all of them.

Hybridisations of VET: a way to manage the trade-offs?

The comparison of the VET systems of Sweden and Denmark demonstrated the weaknesses of these in relation to equality and inclusion, respectively. An obvious opportunity to manage the trade-off between equality and inclusion is to diversify the programmes in upper secondary education. To get the best from different worlds by combining the qualities of apprenticeships with the qualities of the unified upper secondary school. The Norwegian and Finnish VET systems represent mixed models that combine qualities from the two other VET systems. A relevant question is what can be learned from the way the trade-offs for VET are managed in these two countries.

Norway's VET system is the only Nordic system included in a book that claims to examine the six best VET systems in the world (Hoffman, 2011). Among the advantages of the Norwegian VET system, Hoffman emphasises the combination of opportunities for career exploration in the first year, with the apprenticeship programme in the last two years. In addition, she highlights the strong support for early school leavers and young people dropping out of upper secondary education. The question is how the Norwegian VET system manages to combine social inclusion with social equality and the other policy trade-offs. Compared to the Danish VET system, VET in Norway postpones the separation and specialisation until the end of the second year. After the first two years, students in the vocational programmes have the opportunity to gain eligibility for higher education by switching to a general programme. This option for vertical transfer reduces the negative 'dead end' effect of early tracking found in the Danish system. This quality is combined with apprenticeships that provide direct and smooth transition to employment for students after completing a VET programme. The 'in-depth project' in the first two years provides experiences with working life, which creates varied forms of learning. Similar to the hybrid Danish programme, it offers the YSK programme that combines apprenticeship with preparation for higher education. The system also allows for flexible organisation of the programmes, such as 1+3 years, work-based and individualised programmes. These options make it more inclusive. Students who are unable to obtain an apprenticeship contract can complete VET in a school-based course. While the system gives priority to young people, it also offers dropouts and adults a second chance to gain a certificate ('praksisbrev') based on their informal work-based learning. Although the system has become more state-led after the reform in 1994, it demonstrates strong employer involvement at all levels. In particular, the local training agencies (LTA) are a unique institution, where employers coordinate their interests locally in collective skill formation by monitoring the quality of training in companies. Compared to the other countries, the Norwegian VET system

174   *Christian Helms Jørgensen*

places a stronger emphasis on combining preparation for higher education with preparation for skilled employment. This is because of stronger employer involvement compared to the Swedish and Finnish systems. However, the Norwegian system is marked by some of the weaknesses of the Danish apprenticeship system, namely high drop-out rates, mismatch problems between supply and demand for apprenticeships, weak coordination between students' learning in schools and workplaces, and signs of declining esteem and enrolment levels (see Chapters 2 and 3). This is especially evident in occupations where the labour market conditions have deteriorated, such as in the construction sector due to the influx of migrant labour (see Chapter 7).

Finland also has a hybrid VET system, which has features of the comprehensive school, but has separate institutions for the general and vocational programmes. The two tracks have quite equal esteem (Cedefop, 2017), students in VET can select subjects from the general programme, and the permeability between the two tracks appears to be high. The Finnish VET system is interesting, because it has maintained high levels of enrolment and high esteem. One explanation for this success is that all vocational students gain eligibility for higher education. The reform of the universities of applied science (UAS) has transformed them into a recognised and popular destination for VET students. The connection between VET and higher education is stronger in Finland than in Sweden, where only a minority of the students in the vocational programmes acquire eligibility for higher education. The Finnish case demonstrates that the creation of clear pathways to higher vocational educations with high quality can be a means to increase the esteem of VET. However, a similar measure in Denmark in 2009, namely the establishment of the Vocational Academies, did not succeed in attracting graduates from the VET system. This can be explained by differences in the links between VET and the employment system in the two countries. In Denmark, the VET students are well-integrated into the labour market when they complete their apprenticeship, and they have few incentives to continue studying. In addition, a strong system of non-tertiary further education (CVET) in Denmark provides an alternative to higher education (Jørgensen, 2013b). In Finland, the VET students have difficulties gaining access to employment after completion, and this is one reason why many VET students progress to the UASs. In Finland, all the VET programmes have introduced at least six months of work-based training in order to improve the links to the labour market, which has raised the attractiveness of VET. However, there are clear indications that the well-known weakness of the mainly school-based Finnish VET system prevails. When they complete a VET programme in Finland, it is more difficult for students to gain access to employment than in the apprenticeship systems of Norway and Denmark (Virolainen and Stenström, 2014). Besides the reform of the UASs, some additional explanations for the increasing enrolment rates in VET in Finland have been suggested. The system for admission to the general programmes of upper secondary education leading to the matriculation exam is restrictive. In addition, admission to the science universities is highly competitive and includes entrance exams, and therefore the VET route to the UAS appears to be more promising. Finland demonstrates the limitations of the successful policies for achieving parity of esteem between general and vocational upper secondary education. While this reduces the social selection in the upper secondary school, it postpones selection to a later stage in the students' educational career. When all students are expected to acquire eligibility for higher education, the competition for admission tends to become more intense. Lastly, the workfare requirements and the reduction in social benefits have been tougher in Finland compared to the other Nordic countries (Kananen, 2014). The Finnish VET system has succeeded in maintaining high enrolment levels and direct progression routes to higher education, but it has not succeeded in creating smooth transitions to employment. This confirms that these two qualities of VET constitute a general trade-off for policy.

In addition to the hybridisation of VET systems, Chapter 5 examines the development of hybrid programmes that provide a journeyman's certificate as well as eligibility for higher education. These programmes represent an important step towards abolishing the divide between general and vocational education. The programmes demonstrate that some of the trade-offs that appear at the central level of policy-making can be managed at the local level of teaching and learning. The apparent antagonism between giving priority to academic or to vocational subjects can be resolved through cross-disciplinary teaching that integrates vocational and academic knowledge in projects (Jørgensen, 2013a). However, the effects of the hybrid programmes on social equality remains ambiguous. They offer a more 'practical' route to higher education, but they can also contribute to stronger stratification of VET, where the ordinary programmes are positioned at the bottom, as was the result in the Danish VET system after the introduction of the vocational gymnasiums (Holm et al., 2013). Another type of innovative institution is the new mediating institutions between education and work in Norway and Sweden, which organise collective employer interests in training at local level. Although the role of these institutions in the VET systems are limited, they demonstrate that new institutions for collective skill formation can develop in a period dominated by neo-liberal policies. They can be seen as examples of decentralised corporatism taking over some of the functions of the centralised form of corporatism, which has become weakened (Campbell and Pedersen, 2007).

The future of VET in the Nordic countries

The examination of the Nordic VET systems in this chapter has demonstrated the strengths and weaknesses of these systems in relation to key challenges and trade-offs for policy. It has demonstrated the continued divergence of these VET systems, but also examples of convergence of policies, as well as of VET systems. A relevant question is: how VET in the Nordic countries will develop in the future and what options exist for managing the challenges and trade-offs examined earlier? In each of the countries, the neo-liberal ideas of educational

176   *Christian Helms Jørgensen*

governance have affected the VET systems with initiatives towards decentralisation, deregulation and increased individual choices. It is remarkable that initiatives for marketisation are most radically pursued in Sweden, which previously figured as a model of the Nordic statist, comprehensive school. A common long-term trend in every country is the increasing role of the state in VET, with the aim of having all young people complete upper secondary education. Over the last decade, policies in the four countries have placed increasing emphasis on employability, retention and completion. This has included a change in political priorities, from enhancing equality in access to higher education, to the inclusion in education of all young people.

Our studies indicate that VET is required to simultaneously provide direct access to higher education, as well as direct access to the skilled labour market, and to also respond to a variety of other contradictory requirements. This involves managing trade-offs and dilemmas, which represents a challenge to the established way of using comparisons in policy-making. The dominant approach to comparisons is driven by the search for 'best practices' through rankings and ratings based on the statistical measurement of the performance and outcomes of different VET systems, such as drop-out rates, completion rates or employment rates. In this way, developing VET for the future becomes concerned with technical measurements of performance indicators in order to identify the best models and practices to emulate. However, managing the complex configuration of trade-offs analysed above requires a more holistic approach to the development of the national VET systems. The studies in this book are mainly explorative and do not allow us to analyse in detail the consequences of the different options for VET policy. However, we find it useful to sketch some alternative future scenarios for the Nordic VET systems based on the development of these systems and the recent trends in policy.

Convergence and hybridisation

In recent decades, a number of political initiatives have made the Nordic VET systems converge in some areas. They have all differentiated their programmes and adopted features that make them all appear as a more hybrid system. Finland has introduced work-based learning in all the VET programmes and taken other initiatives to strengthen the links between VET and the employment system. After years of pilot projects, a Swedish apprenticeship programme was launched in 2011, inspired by the Danish VET system and other dual systems in Europe. Initially, the success was limited, but it is expanding steadily to include 9% of the VET students in 2015/16 (Skolverket, 2016). In addition, the significance of work-based learning and internships are emphasised in all VET programmes. The Danish VET system, based on apprenticeships, introduced a hybrid programme in 2011 that simultaneously provides admission to higher education and a journeyman's certificate. This model is the standard for all students in the business programmes, where the first two years are full-time school-based, not unlike the Swedish and Norwegian VET systems. Since 1994, the Norwegian VET system has been a hybrid system that combines the comprehensive school system with apprenticeships. It also offers eligibility for higher education in the YSK-programmes and in a supplementary year. These initiatives can be seen as a recognition in all countries that VET must forge close links to the labour market and provide access to higher education at the same time. Generally, however, these two qualities are rarely provided in an integrated form, but in different programmes. This development can be interpreted as a convergence towards a common model, not unlike the current Norwegian system. The success of the Norwegian reform in 1994 was facilitated by generous state funding and the spread of local institutions (LTA) to coordinate employer interests in training. If the Swedish and Finnish VET system should follow this example, the employers in these countries must be engaged in some form of apprenticeships on a broader scale.

Expansion of work-based learning in VET

The long-term trend of extending school-based learning in VET has been replaced by reforms in all four countries to expand work-based learning and to increase employers' engagement in VET. Our two case studies in Chapters 6 and 7 demonstrate the significance of work-based learning. The post-secondary apprenticeship programme in the construction sector in Sweden is a strong indication of the importance of specific vocational skills for employment. In the health sector in Norway, employers prefer adults with many years of practical work experience, rather than newly educated young people from the VET system (see Chapter 6). This turn in policy towards work-based learning requires a revision of two earlier beliefs. One is that broad and general qualifications acquired through school-based learning are the best way to prepare young people for the future labour market. The other is that work-based learning in VET only offers specific and narrow skills. Although it is a major problem to provide high-quality instruction and training in the workplace, learning at work has significant potentials. In the modern workplace, students can learn problem-solving in practice, situated professional judgement and social norms for interacting with colleagues and customers (Billett, 2011). Moreover, they can develop a vocational identity, a sense of belonging to an occupation and a personal network. However, it is a major challenge to gain access to the required number of high-quality training placements. This requires strong institutions to promote employers' engagement in collective skill formation (Busemeyer and Trampusch, 2012). The successful Norwegian expansion of apprenticeships since the reform in 1994 indicates that this is a long-term process that is difficult to extend beyond the traditional craft and industries sectors. The local training agencies in Norway and the Swedish Vocational Colleges are encouraging examples of new institutions to manage employers' collective action problems in training and to expand VET based on work-based learning.

178   *Christian Helms Jørgensen*

Continued academic drift

The enrolment numbers in VET in Finland have increased slightly, but in the three other countries, VET has lost ground to general education among young people. This follows a general international pattern of 'academic drift' of the students' educational choices. The patterns in Norway and Denmark are more complex, however, as the enrolment of young adults partly compensates for the decline in the number of youths enrolling. In Sweden, enrolment levels decreased significantly after the reform in 2011, which limited access to higher education (Skolverket, 2016). The academic drift is caused by many different factors and might be reversed by rising unemployment among graduates of higher education. When enrolment in VET falls below a certain threshold, it can generate self-reinforcing effects, as described earlier for the Danish VET system. In the construction sector (Chapter 7), this process is driven by the substitution of native skilled labour and apprentices with migrant labour from Eastern European countries, which leads to lower wages, deteriorating working conditions and a lower status for skilled work – and lower attractiveness of VET. There is a risk that VET will develop into a low-status reservoir for low-attaining students and as a social policy measure. However, in industries where occupational work can be shielded by social closure and employment protection, VET can maintain a privileged status in a dualised labour market.

Tertiarisation of VET

Another possible consequence of continued academic drift is an increased tertiarisation of VET. Drivers for tertiarisation are that employers prefer students who have attained eligibility for higher education when hiring for apprenticeships. A growing number of students completing general upper secondary education take up apprenticeships in Denmark. In Sweden, apprenticeships are already a post-secondary education, though it is not recognised as part of the formal education system. A driver for the tertiarisation of VET is the rising skill requirements of increasingly knowledge-intensive production. An expansion of post-secondary VET recruiting graduates from the academic track of the gymnasium can compensate for the decline of upper secondary VET. In the Nordic countries, we have found no parallels to the dual study programmes that combine upper secondary VET with higher education degrees in countries with dual systems of VET (Graf, 2013). But in Norway and Denmark, special VET programmes link VET directly with post-secondary and higher education. In all four countries, the institutions for post-secondary VET are increasingly attracting political interests, because they help to link VET with further and higher education, and they provide favourable opportunities for employment. While tertiarisation is generally associated with academisation of VET, an alternative development path that raises the prestige of VET is the revival of craftsmanship based on an expansion and refinement of craft-based skills found in some occupations, like chefs, food processing, tailors, cabinetmakers and house builders. However, this option for upgrading VET depends on the opportunities for high-quality, diversified production strategies, which might only be viable in selected industries.

Diversification and disintegration

The multiplication of contradictory aims for VET points in the direction of a continued diversification of VET, so that different programmes focus on different target groups and outcomes. This diversification represents a reversal of the strategy for standardisation and system formation that took place from the 1960s to the 1990s. The diversification emerged as the result of the initiatives for deregulation, flexibilisation, decentralisation and the extension of individual choice observable in all four Nordic VET systems. This is probably most manifest in Sweden, where the decentralisation and marketisation of VET has augmented the differences between the vocational schools. In addition, the Swedish VET system now comprises an apprenticeship programme and an expanding introduction programme aiming at refugee youth. The Norwegian and the Danish VET systems have established short VET programmes aimed at weak learners, and hybrid programmes aimed at ambitious learners. In the Finnish system, the module structure offers considerable scope for individual choice and tailoring of the programmes. This diversification and individualisation of the VET programmes weakens the occupational standards, which has potential consequences for the opportunities for developing strong vocational identities and communities. If the sectoral and local diversity increases and the common standards for VET are diluted, the very notion of a 'VET system' can be misleading. Under conditions of strong competition in the educational marketplace, this is likely to imply increased stratification of VET and rising inequality (Busemeyer, 2015). A likely additional consequence of continued deregulation is the growth of internal training schemes for firm-specific skills in large firms and an expansion of their internal labour markets.

References

Antikainen, A. (2010) 'The capitalist state and education: The case of restructuring the Nordic model', *Current Sociology*, vol. 58, no. 4, pp. 530–550.

Arnesen, A. L., and Lundahl, L. (2006). 'Still social and democratic? Inclusive education policies in the Nordic welfare states', *Scandinavian Journal of Educational Research*, vol. 50, no. 3, pp. 285–300.

Billett, S. (2011) *Vocational Education: Purposes, Traditions and Prospects*, Dordrecht, Springer.

Blossing, U., Imsen, G., and Moos, L. (2014). *The Nordic Education Model*, The Netherlands, Springer.

Bol, T., and Van de Werfhorst, H. G. (2013).'Educational systems and the trade-off between labor market allocation and equality of educational opportunity', *Comparative Education Review*, vol. 57, no. 2, pp. 285–308.

Brandal, N., Bratberg, Ø., and Thorsen, D. E. (2013) *The Nordic Model of Social Democracy*, Basingstoke, Palgrave Macmillan.

180 *Christian Helms Jørgensen*

Brunello, G., and Checchi, D. (2007) 'Does school tracking affect equality of opportunity? New international evidence', *Economic Policy*, vol. 22, no. 52, pp. 781–861.

Busemeyer, M. R. (2015) *Skills and Inequality: Partisan Politics and the Political Economy of Education Reforms in Western Welfare States*, Cambridge, Cambridge University Press.

Busemeyer, M. R., and Trampusch, C. (eds.) (2012) *The Political Economy of Skill Formation*, Oxford, Oxford University Press.

Campbell, J. L., and Pedersen, O. K. (2007). 'The varieties of capitalism and hybrid success: Denmark in the global economy', *Comparative Political Studies*, vol. 40, no. 3, pp. 307–332.

Causa, O., and Johansson, Å. (2010) 'Intergenerational social mobility in OECD countries', *OECD Journal: Economic Studies*, 2010, no. 1, pp. 1–44.

Cedefop. (2017) *Cedefop European Public Opinion Survey on Vocational Education and Training*, Luxembourg, Publications Office.

Christiansen, N. F., and Petersen, K. (2001) 'The dynamics of social solidarity: The Danish welfare state, 1900–2000', *Scandinavian Journal of History*, vol. 26, no. 3, pp. 177–196.

Englund, T., and Quennerstedt, A. (eds.) (2008). *Vadå likvärdighet? Studier i utbildningspolitisk språkanvändning*, Göteborg, Daidalos.

Gamoran, A. (2010) 'Tracking and inequality: New directions for research and practice', in Apple, M. W., Ball, S. J., and Gandin, L. A. (eds.) *The Routledge International Handbook of the Sociology of Education*, London, Routledge, pp. 213–228.

Gonon, Ph. (2016) 'Zur Dynamik und Typologie von Berufsbildungssystemen – eine internationale Perspektive', *Zeitschrift für Pädagogik*, vol. 62, no. 3, pp. 307–322.

Graf, L. (2013) *The Hybridization of Vocational Training and Higher Education in Austria, Germany, and Switzerland*, Opladen, Budrich University Press.

Greinert, W. D. (1999) *Berufsqualifizierung und dritte industrielle Revolution: eine historisch-vergleichende Studie zur Entwicklung der klassischen Ausbildungssysteme*, Baden-Baden, Nomos-Verlags-Gesellschaft.

Hall, C. (2012) 'The effects of reducing tracking in upper secondary school: Evidence from a large-scale pilot scheme', *Journal of Human Resources*, vol. 47, no. 1, pp. 237–269.

Hampf, F., and Woessmann, L. (2017) 'Vocational vs. General Education and Employment Over the Life Cycle: New Evidence from PIAAC', *CESifo Economic Studies*, vol. 63, no. 3, pp. 255–269.

Hillyard, S. (2010) 'Ethnography's capacity to contribute to the accumulation of theory: A case study of differentiation-polarisation theory', *Oxford Review of Education*, vol. 36, no. 6, pp. 767–784.

Hoffman, N. (2011) *Schooling in the Workplace: How Six of the World's Best Vocational Education Systems Prepare Young People for Jobs and Life*, Cambridge, MA, Harvard Education Press.

Holm, A., Jæger, M. M., Karlson, K. B., and Reimer, D. (2013) 'Incomplete equalization: The effect of tracking in secondary education on educational inequality', *Social Science Research*, vol. 42, no. 6, pp. 1431–1442.

Imsen, G., Blossing, U., and Moos, L. (2016) 'Reshaping the Nordic education model in an era of efficiency: Changes in the comprehensive school project in Denmark, Norway, and Sweden since the millennium', *Scandinavian Journal of Educational Research*, vol. 61, no. 5, pp. 568–583.

Johansen, L. M., and Aarseth, H. (2012) 'Lads i senmoderne felle? Skolemotstand i individualiseringens tid', *Tidsskrift for ungdomsforskning*, vol. 12, no. 1, pp. 3–23.

Jørgensen, C. H. (2013a) 'Linking the dual system with higher education in Denmark: – when strength becomes weakness', in Deissinger, Th., Aff, J., Alison, F., and Jørgensen, C. H. (eds.) *Hybrid Qualifications – Structural and Political Issues in the Context of European VET Policy*, Zürich, Peter Lang, pp. 53–78.

Jørgensen, C. H. (2013b) 'The role and meaning of vocations in the transition from education to work', *International Journal of Training Research*, vol. 11, no. 2, pp. 166–183.

Jørgensen, C. H. (2016) 'Shifting problems and shifting policies to reduce students' dropout: – the case of vocational education policy in Denmark', in S. Bohlinger, K., Dang, A., and Klatt, G. (eds.) *Education Policy: Mapping the Landscape and scope*, Bern, Peter Lang, pp. 325–353.

Juul, I., and Jørgensen, C. H. (2011) 'Challenges for the dual system and occupational self-governance in Denmark', *Journal of Vocational Education & Training*, vol. 63, no. 3, pp. 289–303.

Kananen, J. (2014) *The Nordic Welfare State in Three Eras: From Emancipation to Discipline*, Abingdon, Routledge.

Littler, J. (2018) *Against Meritocracy: Culture, Power and Myths of Mobility*, Abingdon, Routledge.

Lundahl, L. (1997) *Efter svensk modell. LO, SAF och utbildningspolitiken 1944–90*, Umeå, Boréa Bokförlag.

Lundahl, L., Arreman, I. E., Holm, A. S., and Lundström, U. (2013) 'Educational marketization the Swedish way', *Education Inquiry*, vol. 4, no. 3, pp. 497–517.

Lundahl, L., and Olofsson, J. (2014) 'Guarded transitions? Youth trajectories and school-to-work transition policies in Sweden', *International Journal of Adolescence and Youth*, vol. 19, sup1, pp. 19–34.

Marginson, S. (2017) 'Elite, Mass, and High-Participation Higher Education', in Shin, J. C. and Teixeira, P. (eds.) *Encyclopedia of International Higher Education Systems and Institutions*, Dordrecht, Springer, pp. 1–9.

Michelsen, S., and Stenström, M-L. (2018). *Vocational Education in the Nordic Countries: The Historical Evolution*, London, Routledge.

Munk, M. (2011) 'Social sortering, frafald og manglende kvalifikationer blandt unge', in Jørgensen, C. H. (ed.) *Frafald i erhvervsuddannelserne*, Frederiksberg, Roskilde University Press.

Murray, Å., and Sundin, S. (2008) 'Student flows and employment opportunities before and after implementation of a third year in vocational programmes at upper secondary school', *European Journal of Vocational Training*, vol. 44, no. 2, pp. 110–130.

Niemi, A-M., and Rosvall, P-Å. (2013) 'Framing and classifying the theoretical and practical divide: How young men's positions in vocational education are produced and reproduced', *Journal of Vocational Education & Training*, vol. 65, no. 4, pp. 445–460,

Nylund, M. (2013) *Yrkesutbildning, klass och kunskap*, doctoral dissertation, Örebro universitet.

Oakes, J. (1985) *Keeping Track: How Schools Structure Inequality*, New Haven, CT, Yale University Press.

Olofsson, J. (2005) *Svensk yrkesutbildning, vägval i internationell belysning*, Stockholm, SNS Förlag.

Persson, M., and Oscarsson, H. (2009). 'Did the egalitarian reforms of the Swedish educational system equalise levels of democratic citizenship?' *Scandinavian Political Studies*, vol. 33, no. 2, pp. 135–163.

Pettersson, L. (2006) *Är Danmark bättre än Sverige?* Malmö, ØI Förlag.

Pfeffer, F. T. (2008) 'Persistent inequality in educational attainment and its institutional context', *European Sociological Review*, vol. 24, no. 5, pp. 543–565.

Phillips, D. (2015) 'Policy borrowing in education. Frameworks for analysis', in J. Zajda (ed.) *International Handbook on Globalisation, Education and Policy Research*, The Netherlands, Springer, pp. 23–34.

Ramberg, J. (2014) 'The extent of ability grouping in Swedish upper secondary schools: A national survey', *International Journal of Inclusive Education*, vol. 20, no. 7, pp. 685–710.

Rothstein, B. (1996) *The Social Democratic State: The Swedish Model and the Bureaucratic Problem of Social Reforms*, Pittsburgh, University of Pittsburgh Press.

182   Christian Helms Jørgensen

Rudolphi, F., and Erikson, R. (2016). 'Social selection in formal and informal tracking in Sweden', in Blossfeld, H. P., Buchholz, S., Skopek, J., and Triventi, M. (eds.) *Models of Secondary Education and Social Inequality: An International Comparison*, Cheltenham, Edward Elgar.

Shavit, Y., and Müller, W. (2000) 'Vocational secondary education: Where diversion and where safety net?' *European Societies*, vol. 2, no. 1, pp. 29–50.

Skolverket. (2016) *Samlad redovisning och analys inom yrkesutbildningsområdet*, Rapport 442, Stockholm, Skolverket.

Skolverket. (2017) *Skolverkets lägesbedömning 2017*, Rapport 455, Stockholm, Skolverket.

Stolz, S., and Gonon, P. (2012) 'Inclusion and Exclusion', in Stolz, S. and Gonon, P (eds.) *Challenges and Reforms in Vocational Education: Aspects of Inclusion and Exclusion*, Bern, Peter Lang, pp. 9–30.

Svensson, A. (2001) 'Består den sociala snedrekryteringen? Elevernas val av gymnasieprogram hösten 1998', *Pedagogisk forskning i Sverige*, vol. 6, no. 3, pp. 161–72.

Svensson, A. (2007) 'Dagens gymnasieskola-bättre än sitt rykte?' *Pedagogisk forskning i Sverige*, vol. 12, no. 4, pp. 301–323.

Telhaug, A. O., Mediås, O. A., and Aasen, P. (2006) 'The Nordic model in education: Education as part of the political system in the last 50 years', *Scandinavian Journal of Educational Research*, vol. 50, no. 3, pp. 245–283.

Thelen, K. (2014) *Varieties of Liberalization and the New Politics of Social Solidarity*, New York, Cambridge University Press.

Tosun, J., Unt, M., and Wadensjö, E. (2017) 'Youth-oriented active labour market policies: Explaining policy effort in the Nordic and the Baltic states', *Social Policy & Administration*, vol. 51, no. 4, pp. 598–616.

van Houtte, M., Demanet, J., and Stevens, P. A. (2012) 'Self-esteem of academic and vocational students: Does within-school tracking sharpen the difference?' *Acta Sociologica*, vol. 55, no. 1, pp. 73–89.

Virolainen, M., and Stenström, M-L. (2014) 'Finnish vocational education and training in comparison: Strengths and weaknesses', *International Journal for Research in Vocational Education and Training*, vol. 1, no. 2, pp. 81–106.

Wiborg, S. (2013). 'Neo-liberalism and universal state education: The cases of Denmark, Norway and Sweden 1980–2011', *Comparative Education*, vol. 49, no. 4, pp. 407–423.

Index

Note: Page numbers in **bold** indicate a table on the corresponding page.

1+3 model 145, 146, 169, 173
2+2 model 57, 61, 78, 143, 145–147
3+2 model 143

active labour market policy measures (ALMPs) 81, 163
Apprenticeship Act 12, 15
apprenticeships: capacity of systems 21; for carpenters 140–141, 146; in Denmark 15–16, 32–34, 55, 164; eux programme connecting, to higher education 107–108; in Finland 16–18; health care education 131–132; hybrid models for health care workers 122–123; in Norway 13–15; reviving in Nordic countries 39–43; in Sweden 12–13, 34–35, 61; work-based learning 44–45
auxiliary nurses: access to work 123–125; education for 119–121; integration into upper secondary education 121–122; term 133n3; *see also* health care workers

Bologna model, Nordic higher education 54, 67, 110
building and construction 136–137, 152–153; access to higher education 147–149; carpenters in transition 137–141; changing labour market and work organisation 141–147; contractors in 139, 140; craft institutions 138; esteem and social inclusion 149–152; meeting occupational challenges 145–147; modularisation in Finland 141–142; occupational goals in Denmark 144–145; occupational goals in Norway 143–144; occupational goals in Sweden 142–143; polytechnic education in Finland 148–149
business gymnasium (HHX), Denmark 55, 56

carcassing 141, 142
carpenters: access to higher education 147–149; education in changing market 137–141; Norwegian construction industry 138–140; trade unions 138; *see also* building and construction
central state planning, labour market 31, 32, 43
collaborative skills demonstration, in Finland 102–103
college institutions, in Finland 59; *see also* universities of applied sciences (UAS), Finland
Committee on Vocational Education, Sweden 58
connective pedagogical practices **98**; e-portfolios in Norway 104; practicum connecting school and workplace in Denmark 103–104; skills demonstration in Finland 102–103; tripartite meetings in Sweden 104–105
construction *see* building and construction
coordination regimes labour market 31–32

Denmark 1; active labour market policy measures (ALMPs) 81; adults in higher education (HE) by age and programme type **65**; apprenticeships in 15–16, 32–34, 55, 164; building and construction goals 144–145; business gymnasium (HHX) 55, 56; connecting apprenticeships to HE 107–108; drop-out rate from VET course in **164**; early school leavers (18–24 years) **90**; educational choice in 37–38; esteem of VET in 79–80; eux programme in 56, 61–62, 107–108, 128, 164; flexicurity regime 33, 39; health care education 121, 122–123, 130; health care workers' access to HE 128; health care workers in 124,

184　*Index*

125, **131**; higher education system 54; indicators of social inclusion of youth **90**; Initial Vocational Education (EFG programme) in 55; practicum connecting school and workplace in 103–104; reform of VET in 168–169; reforms for improving social inclusion in VET 162–165; route to vocational academies 112–113; School-based Training (SKP) 100–101; school-to-work transitions of youth **30**; social inclusion in 82–83, 130; technical gymnasium (HTX) 55, 56; training centres in 100–102; transition from VET to HE 55–56, 61, **64**; VET system in 3, 5; youth employment below 25 years **90**

disparity of esteem 76, 150

drop-out rate: Nordic VET programmes 30, 83, 168, 171, 176; problem of 88; for school-based programs 44; social inclusion and 80–82; Swedish students with non-academic backgrounds 78; VET in Denmark 55, 82, **164**, 174

education for all 75, 80, 105, 118, 120, 131

education system: dead ends in 7, 106–108, 111, 112, 156; equivalence of general and vocational, in Sweden 159–162; long-term commitment of Nordic countries 74; Nordic labour markets and 95–96; trade-off between social inequality and social inclusion 165–167; VET and Nordic model of 10–18; *see also* higher education (HE); Nordic model of education

eldercare sector 5, 6; health care workers 10, 127

employment protection 19–20, 31, 178; students' transitions to work 38–39; in Sweden 84

employment system, linking VET and 11, 31–35, 43, 174, 176

e-portfolios, Norwegian 104

equal access to education 75, 105

esteem 74; building and construction programme 149–152; combining social inclusion and high 87–89; concept of parity of esteem 76; Denmark and Sweden as opposites 79–80; disparity of 76; improving, of VET 77–79; as political challenge 75; problem of low, of VET systems 7–8; student participation in VET 86–87; of VET as policy challenge 76–80; of vocational education 74–76

ethnic minorities in Nordic labour market 35–36, 46

eux programme, Denmark 56, 61–62, 107–108, 128, 164

financial crises 129; in 1990s 84; in 2008 8, 22, 32, 146

Finland 1; active labour market policy measures (ALMPs) 81; adults in higher education (HE) by age and programme type **65**; apprenticeships for adults 42; apprenticeships in 16–18; early school leavers (18–24 years) **90**; forecast industry 32; health care education as social inclusion 130; health care workers' access to HE 129; health care workers in 125, **131**; higher education system 52, 54; hybrid VET system in 174–175; indicators of social inclusion of youth **90**; labour movement 9; modularisation in construction in 141–142; polytechnic education development 148–149; polytechnics experiment 60; qualification structure in 62; school-to-work transitions of youth **30**; skills demonstration in 102–103; transition from VET to HE 59–60, 61, **64**; universities of applied sciences (UAS) 54, 60, 63, 65, 67, 110–112, 174–175; VET system in 3; vocational education in 122, 123; youth education experiment 60; youth employment below 25 years **90**

gender: health care worker education 126–127; labour market and education 85–86; segregation in Nordic labour market 35, 46

Germany: adults in HE by age and programme type **65**; production model 137; VET system 20

Green Party, Sweden 79

health care workers: access to higher education 127–129; access to work 123–125; auxiliary nurses 119–121; characterizing education of in Nordic countries 131–133; comparing Nordic countries **131**; education and occupations 118–119; education as social inclusion 129–130; education for assistant groups 119–121; historical background of education 119–122; hybrid apprenticeship models 122–123;

Index   185

integration into upper secondary school systems 121–122; occupation between hierarchies 125–127

Health Colleges, Sweden 102, 113

HHX (business gymnasium), Denmark 55, 56

higher education (HE): access of building and construction to 147–149; Bologna model for Nordic 54, 67, 110; comparing adults attending by country **65**; comparing transitions to 60–66; connecting VET to 106–109; differences between Nordic HE systems 63, 65–66; educational policy for transitions of VET to 53–60; eux connecting apprenticeships to 107–108; health care workers' access to 127–129; massification of 52; Nordic systems of 1–2, 51, 54, 66–68; reforming for wider access to VET 109–113; relation of VET to 51–53; universities of applied sciences (UAS) 52; VET in process to 51–53; VET to, in Denmark 55–56; VET to, in Finland 59–60; VET to, in Norway 56–57; VET to, in Sweden 58–59

HTX (technical gymnasium), Denmark 55, 56

immigrant segregation, Nordic model of education 35–36

Initial Vocational Education (EFG), Denmark 55

institutionalised negotiation, labour market 31–32

intelligence reserve 6, 11

Knowledge Promotion Reform, Norway 143

labour market: access of health care workers to 123–125; carpenters and education in changing 137–141; changes in building and construction 141–147; connecting VET to 96–97; education system and 95–96; hybridisation of job profiles in 68; market-based regulation 31; protection in Social Democratic policy 38–39; shortage of skilled labour challenging VET 158–159; social demands and requirements of 20–21; VET and Nordic model 19–20; work-based learning 97

local training agencies (LTAs), Norwegian 98–100, 105–106, 114, 173, 177

mediating institutions **98**; Danish training centres 100–102; Norwegian training agencies 98–100, 105–106; and practices 105–106; Swedish health and technical colleges 102

mutual enrichment 18, 78, 114

NEET (not in education training or employment) group 84, 85, 171; Denmark 100, 111, 162–163; Norway 111

Nightingale, Florence 119

Nordic countries: academic drift continuing in 178; building and construction in 136–137, 152–153; characterizing health care worker education in 131–133; comparing transitions to higher education 60–66, **64**; connections between VET system and work in 43–46; diversification and disintegration of VET 179; expansion of work-based learning in VET 177; future of VET in 175–179; post-1990 education reforms in 77–79; reforming HE for wider access from VET 109–113; reviving apprenticeships in 39–43; tertiarisation of VET 178–179; transitions to educational hierarchies 83–86

Nordic model, concept of 10

Nordic model of education: choice and selection in transition 35–38; in Denmark 15–16; in Finland 16–18; inclusion and equality in 169; in Norway 13–15; shortage of skilled labour challenging 158–159; in Sweden 12–13; VET in the 157–165

Nordic Nurses' Federation (NNF) 133n2

Nord-VET project 3, 29, 67, 76, 118, 137

Norway 1; 2+2 model 57, 61, 78, 143, 145, 147; adults in higher education (HE) by age and programme type **65**; apprenticeships in 13–15; building and construction goals 143–144; compromises in 108–109; construction industry 138–140; early school leavers (18–24 years) **90**; educational choice 36–37; e-portfolios in 104; health care education 122; health care education as social inclusion 129; health care workers' access to HE 128–129; health care workers in 124, **131**; higher education system 54; indicators of social inclusion of youth **90**; local

186 *Index*

training agencies (LTAs) 98–100, 105–106, 114, 173, 177; partnering programme 146; post-secondary vocational colleges (ISCED 4) 57; promoting apprenticeships in 42–43; Reform 94 process 143, 145, 147; reviving apprenticeships in 40–41; school-to-work transitions of youth **30**; social inclusion 82; state regulation in 33–34; Steen Committee in 56; trade unions 139; training agencies 98–100, 105–106, 114; transition from VET to HE 56–57, 61, **64**; VET system 3, 173–174; vocational route ('*Y-veien*') 108–109; youth employment below 25 years **90**; YSK (vocational and study competence programme) 106, 108, 114, 128, 173, 177

nurses *see* health care workers

occupational labour market 20, 33, 38, 40, 43
occupational principle 36, 120, 137, 138, 140, 141, 147, 148, 150, 151

parity of esteem, concept of 76
participation notion of 75
policy-making/policy-makers: architecture for in VET 170–173; attention on shortage of skilled labour 158; in Denmark's VET system 112–113; hybridisation of VET 173–175; image of apprenticeships 40; labour market protection 38–39; managing trade-offs 46; Nordic VET system 156–157; school-to-work transition for 29; Social Democratic Party 38, 168; VET as option for early school leavers and disadvantaged 45
polytechnics experiment in Finland 60
practicum, connecting school and work in Denmark 103–104

Reform 94 process, Norway 143, 145, 147

safety net, VET as 67, 166–167
school-based training (SKP) in Denmark 100–101
Second World War 14, 53, 54, 59, 118, 119, 131
skills demonstration collaborative, in Finland 102–103
Social Democratic governments 3, 12–13, 31; in Denmark 15; education policies 51–52; in Finland 17; labour market

protection in 38–39; in Norway 14; reform in 1991 in Sweden 161–162; rise of 6; standardisation of education policies 168; in Sweden 13, 158
Social Democratic Party 9; in Denmark 15–16; esteem of VET 77, 79; Nordic model of education 10–11; in Norway 14; social inclusion in VET 162–165; in Sweden 13, 18; universal social security 9–10; in VET systems 18; work-based training 11–12
social inclusion: building and construction programme 149–152; combining high esteem and 87–89; Danish reforms for improving 162–165; dropout issue 80–82; health care education as 129–130; indicators for youth **90**; measures for 81–82; as political challenge 75; student participation in VET 86–87; trade-off between social inequality and 165–167; transitions to educational hierarchies 83–86; VET programmes 8; of vocational education 74–76
social inequality 8–9, 12; in Denmark 43, 55; in Nordic education 95, 111; trade-off between social inclusion and 165–167
social security: building and construction 140; reform of 163; universal 9–10
standardisation, concept of 23
Steen Committee, Norway 56
stratification, concept of 23, 24
Sweden 1; 3+2 model 143; active labour market policy measures (ALMPs) 81; adults in HE by age and programme type **65**; apprenticeships in 12–13, 61; building and construction goals 142–143; central state regulation of labour 34–35; early school leavers (18–24 years) **90**; educational choice 37; equivalence of general and vocational education in 159–162; esteem of VET in 79–80; health care education as social inclusion 129, 130; health care workers' access to higher education 128; health care workers in 124–125, **131**; Health Colleges 102, 113; higher education system 54; indicators of social inclusion of youth **90**; irregular programmes 82; non-completion rate in VET programmes after 1991 reform **160**; qualification structure in 62; reform in 1991 159–162; reforms of VET in

170; reintroduction of apprenticeships in 41–42; school-to-work transitions of youth **30**; Technical Colleges 102, 113; transition from VET to HE 58–59, 61, 62, **64**; tripartite meetings in 104–105; upper secondary education system 58–59; VET system in 3, 5; Vocational Colleges 102; youth employment below 25 years **90**

Technical Colleges, in Sweden 102, 113
technical gymnasium (HTX), Denmark 55, 56
trade union: changes in 132–133; concept of 138; in Denmark 16, 79, 120; membership rates of 122; in Norway 98, 100, 120; supporting apprenticeships 88; in Sweden 79, 120
transition systems: architectures of Nordic 45–46; choice and selection in 35–38; concept of school-to-work 23; concepts of 22; educational choice of 36–38; employment protection in 38–39; school-to-work transitions of youth **30**; social inclusion for young people 83–86; transition to employment 29–31; VET and Nordic 22–24; VET to higher education 53–60, 66–68

United Kingdom (UK) 51, 76; adults in HE by age and programme type **65**
universal welfare states 3, 8–10
universities of applied sciences (UAS), Finland 54, 60, 63, 65, 67, 110–112, 174–175
upper secondary education system: health care workers' integration in 121–122; in Sweden 58–59

VET *see* vocational education and training (VET) system
vocational academies route, Danish 112–113
vocational colleges: in Norway 54, 62; in Sweden 102, 177
vocational education and training (VET) system: architecture for policy-making in 170–173; building and construction in 136–137, 152–153; challenges for managing 3–6; combining high esteem and social inclusion in 87–89; common challenges for 6–8; common for four Nordic countries 8–10; concept of

4–6; configurations of trade-offs for 167–170; connecting to higher education 106–109; connecting to the labour market 96–97; connections to world of work 43–46; connective pedagogical practices 102–105; convergence and hybridisation of 176–177; decentralisation of educational governance 169; employment system and 11, 31–35, 43, 174, 176; esteem and inclusion with participation in 86–87; esteem and social inclusion 74–76; expansion of work-based learning in 177; fields of innovation in **98**; future in Nordic countries 175–179; hybridisations of 173–175; improving esteem of 77–79; individualisation of 168–169; mediating institutions 98–102; Nordic 1–3; Nordic labour market model and 19–20; Nordic model of education and 10–18, 157–165; Nordic transition systems and 22–24; political aims for 2–3; reforming higher education for wider access to 109–113; safety net for disadvantaged youth 166–167; skilled labour shortage challenging 158–159; social demands and labour market requirements 20–21; standardisation of 168; tertiarisation of 178–179; trade-off between social inequality and social inclusion 165–167; trade-offs in policy architecture for **167**; transition to employment 29–31; *see also* higher education (HE)
vocational gymnasiums, Denmark 55–56
vocational pathway, Norway 54
vocational specificity, concept of 23–24

welfare state model, Nordic 9–10
women: as auxiliary nurses 126; in construction work 151, 152; in Danish training centres 101; entering labour market 10, 118, 131; esteem and social inclusion of 75; health care education 126–127, 130, 132–133; as health care workers 119; opportunities for 159–160; participation in transition system 22; strengthening VET with 17

young people: combining esteem and social inclusion for 87–89; early school leavers (18–24 years) **90**; education participation for esteem and inclusion

86–87; indicators for social inclusion of **90**; recruiting to health care education 125–127

Youth Counselling Centres (UU) 163

Youth Education Adapted for Young People with Special Needs 82

youth education experiment, Finland 60

youth unemployment 2, 6–7, **30**, 172; in Denmark 15; in Finland 17, 111; Nordic countries 40, **90**; in Nordic VET systems 22–23, 57, 59, 76, 158; in Norway 14; public statistics of 84; in Sweden 12, 165

YSK (vocational and study competence programme) 106, 108, 114, 128, 173, 177